Praise for Donald Spoto and *Possessed*

"A worthy . . . consideration of one of Hollywood's most distinctive performers."   —*Kirkus Reviews*

"An illuminating look at a bygone era, and [an] entertaining read, that movie fans will enjoy."   —*Booklist*

"A balanced and readable account of a possibly misunderstood and maligned star."   —*Library Journal*

"Spoto does an excellent job of presenting why Joan Crawford deserves to be admired and respected. . . . She came to Hollywood with no knowledge of acting or the movie-making process, but she came in more than willing to learn and, in the end, became one of the most knowledgeable people in the industry."   —*Hollywood Revue*

"'I wouldn't trust the love of any man, after the things I've seen!' That's Joan Crawford in 1950's *Harriet Craig*. . . . It is a spectacular scene, and as Donald Spoto points out in his fascinating new book, *Possessed: The Life of Joan Crawford*, it was basically written by Joan herself (Joan's childhood makes Marilyn Monroe's look like a Sunday picnic). . . . *Possessed* is more than anything a revisionist look at her magnificent career, one of the longest in cinema history. The book also points out, time and again, errors and absurdities in Christina Crawford's savage, get-even screed, *Mommie Dearest*. . . . The book is in essence a wonderful treatise on Crawford's talent, so underrated in her own lifetime because of her beauty and glamour, so derided after her death because of a dissatisfied child. . . . Thank you, Mr. Spoto."   —Liz Smith, wowowow.com

Possessed

The Life of Joan Crawford

DONALD SPOTO

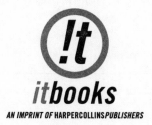

itbooks

AN IMPRINT OF HARPERCOLLINS*PUBLISHERS*

*it*books

A hardcover edition of this book was published in 2010 by William Morrow, an imprint of HarperCollins Publishers.

FIRST IT BOOKS PAPERBACK PUBLISHED 2011.

Designed by Lisa Stokes

The Library of Congress has catalogued the hardcover edition of this book as follows:
Spoto, Donald, 1941–
    Possessed : the life of Joan Crawford / Donald Spoto.—1st ed.
        p. cm.
    Includes bibliographical references.
    ISBN 978-0-06-185600-6
    1. Crawford, Joan, 1908–1977.   2. Motion picture actors and actresses—United States—Biography. I. Title.
PN2287.C67S66 2010
791.430'28092—dc22
[B]
                                                                    2010013095

ISBN 978-0-06-185601-3 (pbk.)

11 12 13 14 15   OV/BVG   10 9 8 7 6 5 4 3 2 1

for Ole—
again, and always

. . . right next to the right one . . .
—Tim Christensen, Danish composer and lyricist

I'll do my own thinking, thank you—and my own existing.

—Joan Crawford, as the title character in *Daisy Kenyon* (1947)

CONTENTS

Possessed

INTRODUCTION

November 18, 1952

ALMOST SIXTY YEARS later, the envelope's California postmark and Thomas Jefferson's profile on the purple stamp remain unfaded. The content is still clear, too—perfectly typewritten and signed with a bold flourish:

Dear Don,

Thank you for writing such a sweet letter.

I am so happy that you liked my new picture, "Sudden Fear." It was a challenge for me, and there were some very hard scenes. But I enjoyed working in San Francisco, and I was very lucky to work with fine actors like Mr. Jack Palance and Miss Gloria Grahame.

I am so impressed that you read Miss Edna Sherry's book that our movie was based on. I don't think there are many eleven-year-old movie fans who do that!

Thank you again for writing to me. I hope you will stay in touch, and that we will meet some day. Good luck in school!

Your friend,

Joan Crawford

I WAS TAKEN TO the movies for the first time on my fourth birthday, in June 1945; the program was an afternoon of Disney cartoons at the Pickwick Theater in Greenwich, Connecticut. When my family moved briefly to White Plains, New York, at the end of that year, I was frequently treated to a matinee at the Pix Playhouse. Then, from 1947 (when I entered first grade) to 1959 (when I left home for college), I went almost every Saturday afternoon either to the RKO Proctor's or to the Loew's in New Rochelle—or to the nearby Larchmont Playhouse, where I saw the thriller *Sudden Fear* in late August 1952. I pestered my mother until she somehow obtained the Hollywood address of the movie's distributor, RKO Radio Pictures. She cautioned me that if I wrote a fan letter telling Miss Crawford how much I liked her movie, I should not expect a reply: "Movie stars don't have time to answer letters from strangers, so try not to be disappointed."

As it happened, my youthful enthusiasm for *Sudden Fear* was not misdirected. A few months after I had pasted Joan Crawford's reply into my scrapbook, the picture was nominated for four Academy Awards, including one for Joan Crawford as best actress of the year. She had already won the Oscar six years earlier, for *Mildred Pierce,* but it took me a long time to catch up with that movie—and much longer to have any clear idea about the actress, her life and her long list of achievements.

By the time of *Sudden Fear,* Joan was in her midforties, well past the age (according to Hollywood's strange standards) for leading ladies to play women in love unless the characters were doomed or pathetic. (That year, the estimable Shirley Booth, fifty-five, was anointed best actress for her role as the grandmotherly wife Lola in *Come Back, Little Sheba.*) But Crawford was having none of the conventional wisdom that nice middle-aged women are or should be indifferent to passion. The role of Myra Hudson in *Sudden Fear* was her own choice; she was the movie's *de facto* executive producer; she supervised the development of the character and collaborated on the screenplay; and she tackled with enormous gusto the part of a wealthy, successful playwright longing for love. Myra does not retreat quietly to life's upper balcony just because she happens to be forty-something.

By 1952, Norma Shearer and Greta Garbo—Joan's two rivals during her years at Metro-Goldwyn-Mayer—had long since retired, and Marlene Dietrich was performing in nightclubs. But Joan Crawford kept fighting for new roles for older women, and she succeeded. For half a century, she assessed what the public wanted in each era: the jazz baby during the 1920s; the independent thinker of the 1930s; the troubled postwar woman of the 1940s; the romantically starved woman of the 1950s; the horror queen of the 1960s and 1970s. But those broad categories never exhausted the range of her roles.

———

MY PARENTS HAD BEEN in high school in the early 1930s, when Joan was already a major star, and when I returned home from the Larchmont Playhouse that Saturday afternoon in 1952, I was astonished to learn that she was very well known to the older generation. By then, 80 percent of Joan Crawford's total motion picture output was behind her: of her eighty-seven feature films, there were only eighteen after 1950. But like Molly Brown, she was unsinkable, unpredictable, indomitable. "I remember that she was a champion Charleston dancer before she was a movie star," my mother said when I received Miss Crawford's reply, "and she had the trophies to prove it." Crawford spanned generations, movie styles—in fact, movie history itself.

Never content with her past achievements, Joan sought only to extend the frontiers of her talent and experience; indeed, one of the major themes of this book is that few are her equal in terms of the sheer volume, variety and quality of her performances. In addition to her movies, she was heard on dozens of radio dramas from the 1930s through the 1950s, and then she eagerly turned to acting on television, appearing on many of the most popular programs of the time—*The Jack Benny Program, I Love Lucy, Route 66, The Man from U.N.C.L.E.* and *The Virginian.* Steven Spielberg's first job in the industry was directing Joan in a terse, tense half-hour thriller. Only work in the theatre eluded her: as she admitted, she suffered from paralyzing stage fright that was exacerbated by a poignant shyness in the presence of strangers.

Joan's accomplishments in television are remarkable: twenty dramas; forty appearances on talk shows; thirteen variety and comedy shows; a dozen award programs and game shows; a half-dozen tribute specials; commercials; and public service announcements for charities. Until grave illness forced her to withdraw from the world toward the end of her life, she considered *retirement* a dirty word.

But a mere catalogue of achievements does not justify a full-scale biography. After surveying the shelf of chronicles published about Joan since her death in 1977, the question must be addressed: Why another life story? Quite simply, because perhaps no other movie star—with the possible exception of Marilyn Monroe—has been so underappreciated, misrepresented by rumor, innuendo, fabrication, unfounded allegation and rank distortion.

Joan Crawford was neither Joan of Arc nor the arch she-devil of popular misconception. She was a recognizably human and passionate woman who entertained millions; she made egregious mistakes and learned from them; and she always had a legion of friends and countless admirers. One's fame or power or influence was never the criterion for friendship with Joan, and she was on warm terms with people from every walk of life. The shift in public opinion from respect to contempt only began a year after her death, with the publication of a book called *Mommie Dearest,* which alleged that Joan was a sadistic alcoholic who took special pleasure in torturing her adopted children.

———

THE BOOK YOU ARE holding is an attempt to set the record straight on a number of critical matters concerning Joan Crawford's complex character. Not the least of these issues is, in fact, *Mommie Dearest,* which ought to be judged in light of certain matters often ignored. In many ways, Joan was a jumble of contradictions, but the contradictions provide clues to what has been mostly discounted or denied—specifically, that she was much more than just a movie star: she was demonstrably one of the screen's most talented actresses. I have attempted to support this large claim by examining all her extant feature film performances (seventy of her eighty-seven motion pictures).

The list of collaborators testifying to her professionalism comprises a virtual Who's Who of memorable names in film history: Clark Gable (with whom Joan appeared in eight pictures), John Gilbert, Robert Montgomery, Gary Cooper, Melvyn Douglas, James Stewart, Spencer Tracy, the brothers John and Lionel Barrymore, John Wayne, John Garfield, Dana Andrews, Henry Fonda and Cliff Robertson. Her directors included some of the most inventive and stylish filmmakers of her era—among them, Edmund Goulding, Clarence Brown, Robert Z. Leonard, Dorothy Arzner, Frank Borzage, George Cukor, Otto Preminger, Michael Curtiz, Robert Aldrich and Lewis Milestone.

Joan's critics claim that she had no gift for comedy, and that the so-called weeping woman's movie was the extent of her range. But that assertion can be made only by those who have not seen comedies like *Chained, Forsaking All Others, Love on the Run, The Women, Susan and God, When Ladies Meet* and *Above Suspicion*. Those movies prove that she was certainly a gifted exponent of high comedy—a fact that comes as a surprise to those who identify Joan Crawford only with *Mildred Pierce, Humoresque* or *What Ever Happened to Baby Jane?*

——

BORN LUCILLE FAY LE SUEUR, she was renamed in a studio-sponsored publicity contest. As Joan Crawford, she never took an acting lesson, nor did she ever study with a drama coach. Working by instinct, intensely focused and observant, she was completely self-educated; as her first husband, Douglas Fairbanks Jr., told me, "She never ceased in her efforts at self-improvement and was dedicated to her art—to a point of almost religious devotion."

Joan moved through several phases in her fifty-year career—from Broadway chorus girl to flaming flapper, from silent movie vamp to comic mannequin, from dramatic actress to businesswoman and corporate executive. Through it all, she was tenacious, tough and tender. When people met her, they were often surprised to see that the woman who seemed so much larger than life on-screen was just slightly over five feet tall.

Perhaps because she had come from a crude, poor background and was mistreated in her childhood, Joan always insisted—sometimes even to her own amusement—that people demonstrate exquisite manners and courtesies, toward both herself and others. "People were in awe of her, but she was never in awe of herself," recalled her friend, the director Herbert Kenwith. "She could speak with all kinds of people on their own levels."

That quality was evident one day not long before Joan died. She was leaving a Manhattan restaurant when a team of construction workers recognized her and whistled loudly. "Hey, Joanie!" shouted one of them.

Smiling, she went over to shake their hands. "I'm surprised you fellas know who I am!"

"You're one in a million," said a workman. "They sure don't make them like you anymore, baby!"

She loved it.

CHAPTER ONE

A Prairie Bernhardt
| 1906–1924 |

S HE WAS OVERDRESSED, overweight and overanxious. Standing outside La Grande railway station in downtown Los Angeles, she felt a momentary desire to hurry back into the terminal and board the next Gulf, Colorado and Santa Fe train that would take her back home.

But she had no home now, and except for a few dollar bills and some coins, she had no financial resources. Her most recent income—for working during the Christmas shopping season in Kansas City—had paid for some new clothes. The train ticket to Chicago, and from there to Southern California aboard the Los Angeles Express, had been subsidized by her new employer.

She was about five feet three inches tall, red-haired and freckled. Her dark coat camouflaged a few of her 140 pounds—too much weight, she knew, for her small frame. But soon she would be dancing again (day and night, if she had her way), and dancing was her preferred method of weight loss. She clutched her purse and put down the rattan valise that contained her few outfits and—her only extravagance—two pairs of dancing shoes that were just right for the shimmy, the Charleston and the Black Bottom.

It was January 1925, the wild era of the so-called flappers and bright young things who emerged after the Great War, and she was a charter member of the new age. She smoked, she drank—even during those Prohibition years, alcohol was not hard to obtain—and she danced until dawn; she flirted, she wore makeup, she was giddy and took risks. She replaced stiff corsets with loose undergarments and raised her hemline to the knee. She conformed to no conventional standard of behavior; so far, she had lived fast, clinging to life as if she might lose it at any moment. She refused to wear long hair piled on top of her head, as her mother's generation did; instead, she cut and bobbed her hair short. She was a new, modern woman—and frankly sexual, without inhibitions. She never talked about her freewheeling love life; she simply got on with it.

———

THREE DAYS EARLIER, ON a wintry afternoon, she had said good-bye to her mother in Kansas City. Now, bundled in a woolen coat and wrapped in a patchwork scarf, her hair tucked beneath a dark cloche, she awaited the man assigned to greet her. The perspiration trickled down her back, for the cold-weather outfit was unnecessary: the sun shone brightly at midmorning, and the temperature was climbing toward seventy.

The railway station and surrounding sidewalks of downtown Los Angeles were thronged with motley travelers. There were poor families from the Indian Territories; East Coast businessmen in striped suits, their watch fobs glittering across tightly buttoned vests; society women, draped in chiffon and pearls; and, it seemed to her, a veritable congress of begrimed and bewhiskered cowboys wearing broad-brimmed hats, leather chaps and colorful bandanas. This cross section of humanity might have been mistaken for a group of players dressed for various productions at a Hollywood movie studio.

Some moments later, a young man, sprucely attired in a summer suit, approached her. As if he had meticulously rehearsed his brief introduction, he removed his rakish straw boater, picked up her suitcase, said that his name was Larry Barbier and asked if she was Miss Lucille Le Sueur. She smiled nervously, said yes and they were spirited away in a waiting taxi.[1]

Larry, as she was told to call him, was an assistant to the assistant to the associate publicity director of the company for which she was about to begin working. He said that he was going to show her an interesting neighborhood near the hotel where a room had been booked for her, and he instructed the driver to head for an area south of the city of Santa Monica known as Venice, on the shore of the bay, twelve miles from downtown Los Angeles. Larry said that he lived in Venice, right near the beach, and that she was welcome to visit any time.

Planned by a man named Abbot Kinney, who made his fortune manufacturing Sweet Caporal cigarettes, Venice was designed to resemble its Italian namesake: it was a fanciful enclave of Los Angeles, the movie capital of the world and a kind of ultimate fantasy land. Kinney had envisioned romantic canals connecting the streets, with beaches and shops linked by bridges to residential areas on flower-banked shores. Construction of lagoons and cottages was begun in 1904, and in 1905 the canals were filled with water. Kinney persuaded merchants, hoteliers and restaurant owners to build in the style of the Venetian Renaissance, and to complete the effect, he imported two dozen gondoliers from Italy, who arrived with a repertory of their native melodies. Venice, California, soon became known as the Playland of the Pacific, and a few months after Miss Le Sueur's arrival, it was sucked into the booming metropolis of Los Angeles.

In those days before freeways and wide boulevards, the journey from the railway station to the hotel required almost four hours as the taxi negotiated heavy traffic along dusty local streets. By midafternoon, they had finally arrived at the Hotel Washington on Van Buren Place, in the separate inland municipality known as Culver City.

Residents of the Washington routinely complained that the rate of four

---

1. Depending on which public and family records are consulted, the surname is variously spelled Le Sueur or LeSueur (or even Le Seur). Lucille and her family used the first form, with the space.

dollars a week was cutthroat extortion; indeed, the word *modest* was too glamorous a description for the rude accommodations. There was only one bathroom for every thirty guests; a sink with cold water stood in the corner of each tiny room; the electrical system worked erratically; and a single telephone near the front desk had to do for all the residents. But Miss Le Sueur may not have been dejected: after all, her residences in Texas, Oklahoma, Kansas and New York had not been more luxurious.

The advantage to living on Van Buren Place was its proximity to Lucille's new employer. A few blocks distant was the company to which she would soon report for work; within its gates and behind its walls were lakes, orchards, jungles, railway stations, parks, streets and neighborhoods of many eras—everything required by a modern motion picture studio.

———

WHEN LUCILLE LE SUEUR arrived in California, a relatively new form of public entertainment was swiftly becoming a vast corporate industry—and the company that had engaged her was at its epicenter. Nine months earlier, in April 1924, New York theater owner Marcus Loew, who already owned Metro Pictures and Goldwyn Pictures, added Mayer Pictures to his holdings. This he did in order to appoint forty-year-old Louis B. Mayer—ruthless, patriotic and paternalistic—as chief of Los Angeles studio operations for the new conglomerate. At the same time, Loew appointed as head of film production Mayer's assistant, the clever, physically frail twenty-five-year-old Irving G. Thalberg, known as the boy wonder of Hollywood. For decades afterward, the business headquarters of the new studio were in New York, the home of Wall Street financiers.

With a little pressure from Mayer, the newly formed megastudio was named Metro-Goldwyn-Mayer: MGM, or simply Metro. With remarkable rapidity, the studio could boast (as one savvy publicist put it) "more stars than there are in the heavens"—typical Hollywood hype, but not entirely inappropriate for its impressive roster of popular contract players, which eventually included Lionel Barrymore, Wallace Beery, Jean Harlow, Jeanette MacDonald, Norma Shearer, Clark Gable, Myrna Loy and Greta Garbo.[2] More than any other movie studio, Metro was deeply involved in the personal lives of its employees—specifically, its tight control of a tidy public image for each contract player. For Mayer and his colleagues, this was simply a matter of protecting their investments.

From the 1920s to the early 1940s, this studio was the most successful in Hollywood: it never lost money during the Great Depression and released a feature film every week, along with cartoons and short subjects. The eventual decline of the studio was primarily (but not only) caused by the rise of television and by the United States Supreme Court ruling against corporate monopolies, which forced the studios to divest themselves of theater chains; without Loew's movie houses, Metro could not survive.

None of this was foreseen in 1925. That year, 49 million people (more than 40 percent of the American population) paid an average of ten cents to see a total of 576 silent black-and-white films. This was the heyday of stars like glamorous Gloria Swanson and demure Lillian Gish; of audacious Douglas Fairbanks and sensual Rudolf Valentino; of exotic Pola Negri and amusing Marion Davies. Metro was about to produce *The Merry Widow,* with dashing John Gilbert, and soon it would release the epic *Ben-Hur,* which showcased the glossy eroticism of Ramon Novarro.

Along with the established stars and vast numbers of technical workers at various studios, extras for the common crowd scenes in movies picked up their paychecks each week. In 1919, a total of thirty-five thousand people worked in some capacity for the movie industry; by 1925, that number had doubled, and most of the studio workers labored six days every week. Lucille was prepared for hard work when she arrived at Metro, as instructed, on Monday, January 12, 1925. Two months later, she celebrated her nineteenth birthday.

---

2. Later, Metro added dozens more to its long list of contract players, among them Gene Kelly, Jane Powell, Lana Turner, Judy Garland, Ava Gardner, Katharine Hepburn, Spencer Tracy, Grace Kelly, Ann Miller, Esther Williams, June Allyson and Elizabeth Taylor.

LUCILLE FAY LE SUEUR was born in San Antonio, Texas, on March 23, 1906. By the time she registered for the new Social Security program in the 1930s, she had already been accustomed to stating her birth year as 1908; there was, after all, no official document to the contrary, for in 1906, birth certificates were neither mandatory nor routine in Texas. And so, with the encouragement and complicity of studio publicists, she established her birth year as 1908, effectively diminishing her age by two years. According to California law, however, the studio could not have hired a seventeen-year-old in 1925 without parental approval, and this was neither required nor requested in her case. Lucille had applied for a work-study program at Stephens College, Missouri, in 1922, and at that time she truthfully gave her age as sixteen. She certainly could not have hoodwinked anyone at Stephens into accepting her if she was in fact only fourteen years old.

By 1936, magazine articles occasionally reported her true birth year (without correction from the subject or her bosses) and she herself revealed it at least once. The occasion was a meeting in November 1967 with the Trustees of Brandeis University, who named her a Fellow in recognition of "her interest, time and service to a host of civic and philanthropic causes." By that time, she had donated a large cache of personal effects to the university.[3]

The extreme paucity of facts concerning Lucille's parents has not prevented a platoon of writers from spinning fanciful tales about her family and their backgrounds, employment and characters. But very little can confidently be established. Her mother's name was Anna Bell Johnson, and she was born in November 1884, very likely somewhere in Texas. Lucille's father was Thomas Le Sueur, born about 1868 in Canada or (say some sources) in Tennessee. Of the couple's earlier lives and of their marriage, nothing is known except that Tom (as some records identify him) abandoned his wife and children either

---

3. Joan Crawford's adopted daughter Christina always insisted that Lucille Le Sueur was born in 1904, but that cannot be. Lucille's brother, Harold Hayes Le Sueur, was born on September 3, 1903—hence March 1904 would have been impossible as the birth date of the next baby. (The oldest Le Sueur offspring, named Daisy, was born and died before 1903.)

just before Lucille was born or just after—she never provided any information on the matter. Anna then took in laundry and found local odd jobs to support herself and her two children. The little family was grindingly poor and remained so for years to come.

Despite the imaginations of those who have supplemented missing facts with colorful fictions, Lucille's early years remain clouded in obscurity—until 1910, when a census recorded that Anna, seven-year-old Harold (always called Hal) and four-year-old Lucille were living with Anna's new husband, Henry J. Cassin, in the town of Lawton, Oklahoma. Curiously, the Cassin marriage was publicly recorded as Anna's first; indeed, she may never have married Le Sueur.

Lawton, a sleepy town eighty-eight miles southwest of Oklahoma City and the headquarters of the Comanche Nation, was no busy, crowded metropolitan area. But it boasted the Ramsey Opera House, and Cassin was the booking agent and manager for its repertory of musicals, traveling shows, vaudevilles, dance recitals and just about anything that came to town capable of attracting paying customers.

"Daddy Cassin," as Lucille referred to him even after she learned that he was not her father, was the only adult to lavish anything like attention and affection on the little girl. "He was the center of my world—a short, stocky and black-haired man with small brown eyes and a calm manner. A mature man, he was not the type to romp with children, but I could always crawl on his lap—he made room right inside his newspaper. And I knew he loved me." Born about 1867, Cassin called her Billie, a common nickname at that time for children of both genders. For a dozen years, she identified herself as Billie Cassin. "If I could really give credit to the people who helped me the most," she said years later, "I guess he'd top the list."

Cassin often took her to his theater—where, for example, he once featured a classically trained ballet dancer—and, in 1912, treated six-year-old Billie to a performance of something called the "Gypsy Fantasy." They went backstage to meet the dancer, who embraced Billie after the child said that she wanted to dance, too. The young woman gave the child a pair of used ballet slippers and told her that she would have to work very hard. This counsel was at once taken to heart, and Billie began to offer impromptu dance recitals in a nearby barn or on the family's front porch. With no more inspiration than the Gypsy Fantasy, she leaped and whirled, usually to the unlikely tune of the popular song "Wait 'Till the Sun Shines, Nellie," for which she dragooned this or that neighborhood boy to accompany her as impromptu warbler.

"Henry Cassin encouraged me," she recalled years later. "He seemed to think I had talent. This made my mother furious—no daughter of *hers* was going to be a dancer. But his world was real to me. The opera house must have been shabby, but to me it was glamorous. It was the life I wanted."

But her terpsichorean aspirations were interrupted by a painful mishap that summer. Either jumping on purpose or falling by accident, Billie fell from her front porch onto shards of a broken glass bottle. Bleeding profusely, she was gallantly carried inside and comforted by a teenage boy until a doctor arrived. The role of this impromptu Prince Valiant was assumed by a seventeen-year-old high school boy named Don Blanding; he, too, had artistic ambitions, later realized when he became a successful poet, journalist and author of a dozen books. When they next met, twenty years later in Hollywood, Blanding celebrated the childhood incident in a lyric he wrote in honor of the dancer who had become a star.

> *She was just the little girl who lived across the street,*
> *All legs and curls and great big eyes and restless dancing feet,*
> *As vivid as a humming bird, as bright and swift and gay,*
> *A child who played at make-believe throughout the livelong day.*
> *With tattered old lace curtains and a battered feather fan,*
> *She swept and preened, an actress with grubby snub-nosed clan*
> *Of neighborhood kids for audience enchanted with the play,*
> *A prairie Bernhardt for a while. And then she went away.*
> *We missed her on the little street, her laughter and her fun*
> *Until the dull years blurred her name as years have ever done.*
> *A great premiere in Hollywood . . . the light, the crowds, the cars,*
> *The frenzied noise of greeting to the famous movie stars,*
> *The jewels, the lace, the ermine coats, the ballyhoo and cries,*

The peacock women's promenade, the bright mascaraed eyes,
The swift excited whisper as a limousine draws near,
"Oh, look! It's Joan. It's Joan. It's Joan!" On every side I hear
The chatter, gossip, envy, sighs, conjectures, wonder, praise,
As memory races quickly back to early prairie days . . .
The little girl across the street, the funny child I knew
Who dared to dream her splendid dreams and make her dreams come true.

———

THE HEALING OF THE injured foot required a long recuperation, a protracted break from dancing and an absence from elementary school. But Anna disallowed any childish indolence, and soon Billie was literally a working girl—"scrubbing floors for money to help my mother. I didn't have much education, and for years I had an inferiority complex about my background. Maybe that's why I had such a need to accomplish something." The added income from Billie's work was even more necessary when Henry Cassin—perhaps overwhelmed by financial obligations that could not be covered by his wages from the opera house—was accused of embezzlement. He was acquitted in court, but not in the eyes of Lawton's upright citizens, who boycotted the opera house, cold-shouldered him and Anna and forbade their children to consort with Hal and Billie, whose earliest memories were of social ostracism.

By the time the girl was ten, the Cassin household had relocated to Kansas City, where Henry found a less interesting job, managing the New Midland, a shabby residential hotel in a squalid neighborhood. Anna went to work at a laundry service, where she also introduced her daughter to the exacting routine of a drudge. Hal, on the other hand, did not have to work or earn his keep: always his mother's pet, he ignored school with impunity, preferring another pastime—drinking homemade liquor with his buddies.

Irregularly, Billie attended classes—first at a public grade school and then at St. Agnes Academy, where the nuns took pity on the unhappy child whose family did not have the money for full tuition, and offered Billie free classes in exchange for duties such as serving meals to the students and cleaning the rooms of the boarders. Like them, Billie lived at the convent school from Monday to Friday and returned home on weekends, a routine that endured from 1916 to 1919.

The unfortunate result of her teachers' good intentions was to alienate Billie from her classmates, who treated her as did her mother—like hired help. "I agree with whoever said that a miserable childhood is the ideal launching pad for success," she later reflected. But she was also remarkably frank in assessing the times when she behaved imprudently:

> *I never had any close chums. Instead of being pretty, I was "different" {because} my mother wasn't a very good seamstress, so my dresses were always too long or too short. I kept thinking I might be popular if I stood out more, so I did three things—I walked around looking as though I was self-assured, but I came off brassy. I did little things to mother's dresses to make me look different, but I came off {like} a freak. And I worked my ass off learning how to dance, but I became an exhibitionist . . . I was lonely at home and lonely at school, but a lot of it was sheer stubbornness and perverseness. I guess maybe I didn't want to conform, and I paid the price for that.*
>
> *So when I decided I was going to be a dancer, it was for three reasons: I wanted to be famous, just to make the kids who had laughed at me feel foolish. I wanted to be rich, so I'd never have to do the awful work my mother did and live at the bottom of the barrel—ever. And I wanted to be a dancer because I loved to dance . . . I always knew, whether I was in school or working in some dime store, that I'd make it. Funny, but I never had any ambition whatsoever to be an actress.*

During her time at St. Agnes, the Cassin marriage became progressively more troubled. The exact cause of the final rupture is impossible to determine, but one weekend Billie returned home from school to find that Daddy Cassin had simply departed—an event, she recalled, that made her feel "as though the world had ended." After one chance meeting with Billie a few months later, he never saw her again. Henry Cassin died, at about the age of fifty-five, on October 25, 1922, and was buried in Lawton. Bitter, lonely and overworked, the now twice-abandoned Anna subsequently had little good to say about men—an attitude she communicated to her daughter. You had to be careful . . . you couldn't trust any man . . . you had to hide your purse or he'd steal from you . . . you shouldn't believe anything they say, they're all liars . . .

Anna took the children to live in the only place she could find work—in another laundry. "She made arrangements for herself and the two children to live in one unused room behind the laundry," her granddaughter recalled, "[where] it was hot in the summer, freezing in winter. There was no cooking stove, no proper bathroom, and there were three people living in just one room."

Such was their life until Anna took up with yet another man, this time a dissolute character named Harry Hough, who apparently took liberties with young Billie and was caught by Anna in the act of fondling the girl. With that, Lucille was sent off to the nearby Rockingham Academy, where she worked under even more unpleasant conditions than she had known at St. Agnes. The headmistress at Rockingham evidently believed that young girls were best disciplined by corporal punishment. "I was the only working student, and I had to take care of a fourteen-room house, cook, make beds and wash dishes for thirty other boys and girls. The headmistress was really a cruel tyrant, and there was so much work to do that no time remained for studying or learning. I don't remember going to classes more than two or three times a year. But I do remember the broomstick applied to my legs or backside for reasons I don't remember. I was a drudge there the way I was at home, and sometimes I had the feeling that the headmistress was just making an example of me—if the students did something bad, this was what would happen to them."

After Lucille repeatedly begged her mother to bring her home, Anna relented—only to put her back into slave labor, working for long hours as a laundress. Years later, she recalled that there was a complete absence of communication with her mother—a coldness exacerbated by Anna's habit of smacking her daughter's face or arms or legs for any reason or no reason. Hence the two women who most influenced her early years—her mother and the school principal—demonstrated only stern discipline and no positive reinforcement. Lucille's brother, meanwhile, was neither corrected nor punished.

There are numerous accounts of Lucille's schooling. Most chroniclers have stated that she completed the traditional twelve years of elementary and high school and then briefly attended college, from which she withdrew after one term. This wildly overstates the extent of her education, about which she herself was far more honest. "Moving pictures have given me all the education I ever had," she often said. "I never went beyond the fifth grade—I had no formal education whatsoever. When I read scripts, I had to look up words in the dictionary—how to pronounce them and what they meant—in order to learn the lines properly."

After the fifth grade, she was essentially hired to work, and although she had the right to attend classes, there was no time for that. Therefore she quite accurately said that she had "no formal education." Indeed, that lack of schooling was part of the inferiority complex to which she often referred, and for which she tried to compensate during her entire life. Fans provided some endorsement; her awareness of some good performances gave another. But she always felt inadequate, and people who feel inadequate often demand extravagant forms of approval to meet their limitless needs.

Never satisfied with what she had accomplished, Billie pressed forward to what she might achieve in the future. Always attracted to intelligent and creative people (not merely bookish academics), she later embarked on a lifelong program of self-improvement—to which her husbands and friends bore witness; some were even appointed as *de facto* pedagogues.

———

DURING HER TEEN YEARS, Billie became quite popular because she loved to dance and knew how to flirt. A few miles south of downtown Kansas City is Westport, the heart of the region's nightlife. Built along the Santa Fe Trail, the area always had an abundance of diners, cafés and dance halls that attracted crowds of young people, especially on weekends. By the time she was fifteen,

Billie was frequently seen at the Jack-o'-Lantern Dance Hall in Westport.[4] Full of energy and motivated by a desire to forget her dull routine, she danced the nights away whenever possible.

On one evening at the Jack-o'-Lantern in 1919, Billie met a handsome young trumpeter named Ray Thayer Sterling. Three years older and a senior at Northeast High School, Ray was earnest, bright, witty—and, as his classmates said, "sensitive," the code word for "gay." Because she had initially thought of him as potentially her first love (if not her true love), Billie was at first disappointed. But she was eager for friendship, and so Ray became a confidant, encouraging her ambition to be a dancer and aspire to a better life. "Ray was the one I called when anything went wrong," she said long after he died, "and I loved him with my whole fourteen-year-old heart. He wanted me to go out and get my dreams. Once I was in the process of realizing them, I lost him." They maintained an uncomplicated friendship until she left for Hollywood.

In the late spring of 1922, when Billie was sixteen, her mother was offered employment as a dormitory housemaid at Stephens College, a school for women in Columbia, Missouri—120 miles from both Kansas City (to the west) and Saint Louis (to the east). After some fiddling with the details of her previous education, Anna and Billie submitted an application for the girl to enter Stephens that autumn. Once again, it was arranged that she would earn her tuition by waiting on tables in the college dining room.

The work-study deal did not turn out to be the problem, but Billie's complete lack of preparation for university studies did. With nothing more than elementary school in her academic past, she was not an ideal candidate for college courses. "I was simply not equipped," she recalled. "No one could help me, and I was in dire need." Fearful and embarrassed, she packed her suitcase and headed for the railway station. As if on cue, the president of Stephens College, James Madison Wood, also arrived at the station, on his way to a lecture engagement. "I don't belong *here*," she said when he asked her destination.

---

4. This dance hall was still operating in 2009, as the Jack-o'-Lantern Ballroom, at Westport Road and Main Street, Kansas City.

As she spelled out her dilemma, he did not try to convince her to return to college courses: that would have been absurd advice. Instead, he encouraged Billie to develop a realistic sense of her talents and, when possible, always to stay with a project. Although it seemed unlikely, that evening marked the beginning of a lifelong friendship, later maintained by earnest correspondence until his death in 1963. Daddy Wood, as she called him—the father figure who succeeded Daddy Cassin—always followed her career with affectionate enthusiasm.

"In that little talk at the train station at Columbia," she said years later, "Daddy Wood gave me more to benefit me through life, more human education than all the hours in the classroom put together. He'd be surprised to learn the places where I have heard him repeating his words—while I was a member of a cheap road show, while I was kicking in the chorus on Broadway, in cabarets and Hollywood dance halls. I could always hear him say, 'Don't run away; let your record do you justice.' And I've always tried to obey him." They exchanged news and greetings, and once he sent her a signed photograph of himself: "A friend of the Billie who was—and the Joan who now is—and is yet to be." It was among the few personal framed pictures still in her possession when she died.

———

BY DECEMBER 1922, BILLIE and her mother were back in Kansas City. But she refused to return to work in a laundry; instead, for most of the next year, she held down jobs wrapping packages and selling women's clothing at local emporia. "At that time, I weighed one hundred and forty-five pounds of baby fat. I was self-conscious, unsure, and my 'style' was strictly dreadful. I hated my round face, I hated my freckles, my big mouth and eyes. I tried to stretch [myself] as tall as possible, tossed my head in the air, poked my chin out, and dared people to notice me." The challenge worked, and Billie became a popular girl in her neighborhood.

The freewheeling life of the Roaring Twenties characterized young people everywhere, and Kansas was no exception. Young men pursued their dates with sweet talk and stolen caresses—and, in that Prohibition Era, with home-made moonshine and "iced tea," which sounded innocent but packed a wallop. By law, alcohol could not be manufactured, sold or purchased in the United States from 1920 through 1933, but legislators did not take into account American ingenuity: spirits could be obtained almost anywhere without much difficulty, and the consumption of alcohol actually increased during Prohibition. Traveling musicians had bountiful supplies of liquor (and drugs like cocaine) to distract them and to attract pretty girls. And with the proliferation of roadsters and jalopies after the Great War, nothing more than the backseat of a car was required for a romantic evening.

Of Billie's habits and social life at that time, almost no details have survived, and she provided no clues. A few imaginative writers have asserted that, for money, she frequently danced nude at private clubs and even appeared in short loops of pornographic "flickers." But there are neither witnesses nor material evidence to support these claims; still, the absence of facts has not deterred people from concocting tales. It is certain, however, that she was a champion Charleston dancer.

One summer evening, Ray Sterling took her to a dance competition at the Ivanhoe Masonic Temple. After her number, Billie was introduced to the booking agent for a singer named Katherine Emerine, who made the rounds of country theaters and needed a dozen local chorus girls as her "backup," to high-step and croon in unison while Emerine sang and told theater stories. She was about to open in Springfield, Missouri, but her act needed three or four more chorines.

Billie was on a bus the next morning and made a sufficient impression during the two-week engagement that she was invited to contact Kate Emerine again if ever she traveled to Chicago, the singer's home base. Having worked in the show as Lucille Le Sueur, not Billie Cassin, she returned to Kansas City with hopes renewed and forty dollars in her pocketbook, her wages for performing.

Convinced that her aspirations were neither naive nor ill founded, Lucille could not tolerate much longer the tasks of wrapping packages and answering department store telephones for twelve dollars a week. She headed north in search of Kate Emerine before the end of 1923, apparently to her mother's indifference.

Whereas Kansas City in the 1920s had occasional police roundups of petty crooks, the city's newspapers rarely featured headlines announcing riots or murders. The situation was far different in Chicago, where dozens were killed and many hundreds injured in the race riots of 1919, and things worsened in the years following. As labor and economic problems increased after the war, so did the volume of major crime. No one was quite sure whether there were more shotguns than barrels of bootleg whiskey coming into Chicago every day. Al Capone had little difficulty establishing a foothold in the Windy City, where the municipal government seemed to learn much from his strong-arm tactics. Con artists and swindlers like "Yellow Kid" Weil found Chicago a virtual university where complicated systems of theft and exploitation could be learned and perfected. On many streets downtown, there were houses bearing signs that warned "Venereal Disease—Keep Out!" You had to be (in the language of the day) "a tough dame" to survive on your own in Chicago during the Roaring Twenties.

To her dismay, Lucille could not track down the elusive Miss Emerine. Instead, she was referred to a booking agent named Ernie Young, who, during the winter of 1924, placed her as an "entertainment dancer" in some of Chicago's more disreputable strip clubs, for a salary of twenty-five dollars a week. This kind of employment paid for her rent in a tumbledown boardinghouse and kept food on the table, but it might soon have led to disaster if Young had not, after a few days, transferred her to the Oriole Terrace, a Detroit nightclub at East Grand Boulevard and Woodward Street.

This was no sleazy venue. Detroit was, in fact, the home of some of the most important jazz orchestras and influential nightclub acts in American musical history. Beginning in 1922, for example, the Danny Russo–Ted Fio Rito Orchestra (led by the latter, who considered Fio Rito more exotic than Fiorito) established its legendary status through a long engagement at the Oriole Terrace.

Lucille was at once made a frontliner in the dancing chorus of every show at this nightclub, and it was no surprise to the management (or to her) when the Broadway impresario J. J. Shubert regularly took his seat in the audience. He and his brothers owned eighty-six theaters across the United States and took in over $1 million in ticket sales every week. J.J. regularly scouted the country for talent, and Detroit's Oriole Terrace was always a stop on his travels. The new Shubert musical revue, *Innocent Eyes,* was about to open on Broadway, and a lineup of energetic chorines was needed. Not actresses. Not singers. Just pretty background glamour. Off to New York went Lucille Le Sueur.

The previous Christmas, she had been home in Kansas City, with no idea if she really had a future as a dancer. Now, just eight weeks later, she was in New York, ready to begin rehearsals for a Broadway show starring Mistinguett, one of the best-known entertainers in the world.

———

LUCILLE CAME TO NEW YORK at a time when the theatre was enjoying an astonishing postwar explosion. That year, there were 196 new productions in New York—88 dramas, 67 comedies, 26 musicals and 15 revues. Among the notable productions were new works by George Kelly (*The Show-Off*), Eugene O'Neill (*Desire Under the Elms*), George Gershwin (*Lady, Be Good*), Sigmund Romberg (*The Student Prince*), Rudolf Friml (*Rose-Marie*) and George S. Kaufman and Marc Connelly (*Beggar on Horseback*). Katharine Cornell, as Shaw's *Candida,* appealed to sophisticated theatregoers, as did Helen Hayes (in a revival of Goldsmith's *She Stoops to Conquer*) and Ethel Barrymore (in Pinero's *The Second Mrs. Tanqueray*). In addition, the Marx Brothers drew packed audiences, and there were extravagant new versions of Florenz Ziegfeld's *Follies,* George White's *Scandals* and Earl Carroll's *Vanities*—some of them featuring nude models, who were legal so long as they remained motionless onstage. Those who fancied the New York theatre were kept very busy queuing for tickets.

On May 20, 1924, *Innocent Eyes* opened at the Winter Garden Theater, with music by Sigmund Romberg and Jean Schwartz, and a cast of ninety-four performing dozens of numbers. The show ran for eighteen weeks and 126 performances before closing on August 30. Because she was not a headliner but merely among the chorus, Lucille was not mentioned in any news or reviews of the show.

Then and later, neither she nor anyone else provided details of her offstage life in Manhattan. As she said, "Dancing was the main thing. And I dated. I'd learned, by then, that you couldn't take those dates seriously, because the men were just out of college or married or engaged, and having a fling with a chorus girl was the 'in' thing. But those 'Johnnies' treated us to some damned good times."

———

INSTEAD OF TRAVELING TO other Shubert theaters with the national touring company of *Innocent Eyes,* she accepted an offer to remain in New York, where, four days after the final performance, she appeared in the next Shubert and Romberg musical revue—*The Passing Show of 1924,* also presented at the Winter Garden; her salary was thirty-five dollars a week ($440 in 2010 valuation). "I was never good enough to be in the first line of the chorus on Broadway," she admitted. "I was in the second line." The critics found the production mildly diverting but not much more, and the show passed into history on November 22, without benefiting the career of anybody in the company—except one.

Harry Rapf, who worked with Louis B. Mayer, was a producer at Metro and one of the original organizers of the Academy of Motion Picture Arts and Sciences—a clever designation for an institution designed to resist the unionization of every craft working in the industry. In the summer and autumn of 1924, Rapf was in New York, attending shows every night and scouting for young men and women with potential for the movies. Metro had to grind out "product," to supply all of Marcus Loew's 110 East Coast theaters with new pictures every week. Hence the studio was committed to churning out a picture a week, and in fact, they did so. By the summer of 1925, they wrote down a net profit of almost $5 million.

At the end of November, Rapf invited a few chorus girls from the now defunct *Passing Show* to a Manhattan studio for brief screen tests, and Lucille Le Sueur was among them. She was indifferent to the prospect of movie acting, for her sights were firmly set on a dancing career in New York. With almost somnolent indifference, she stood, walked, glanced, smiled and turned this way and that for a screen test that apparently has not survived.

With no promises made by Metro and no immediate prospect of further work in New York, Lucille headed to Kansas City for the Christmas holidays; there, at least, she could count on the encouragement of her old friend Ray Sterling and some former dates only too eager to squire her to parties and dances.

But at Christmastime, a telegram arrived at her mother's apartment, which Lucille had given to Rapf as a temporary address:

> Studio offers you a contract starting at seventy-five dollars a
> week. Leave immediately for Culver City, California. Contact MGM
> office for travel expenses and details.

"When Miss Le Sueur came into my office," Rapf told a magazine editor while she was still packing her clothes in Kansas, "I knew that she had that rare thing—personality. She is beautiful, but more essential than beauty is that quality known as screen magnetism. Even before we made camera tests of her, I felt that she possessed this great asset. Her tests proved it."

And so, on Saturday, January 3, 1925, Lucille Le Sueur arrived in Los Angeles, unaware of a detail that was clarified some weeks later. The "contract starting at seventy-five dollars a week"—which she signed before the end of that month—gave Metro the right not to renew her employment after six months if they found her unsuitable; but if the company did choose to renew the deal, her salary would rise to one hundred dollars a week for the second half year. That was a respectable income (equal to over $1,200 weekly in 2010), but there were no assurances of job security and there were many fine-print demands. Very quickly, snowy Kansas melted away in her memory.

CHAPTER TWO

The Flapper, Flapping
| 1925 |

L UCILLE FIRST CAME to Metro's offices on Monday, January 12, 1925, with two pair of sturdy dancing shoes for the day's assignment. But that week the studio had a surplus of dancers and plenty of what was called "background glamour." Producers were looking for new actors, new *faces* for new pictures. "I got panicky—I'd never thought about acting, but I realized, as I watched pictures being made, that I'd have to do more than dance if I ever got in front of a camera." Nevertheless, there she was, and she signed her contract on Friday, January 16—"as a member of our stock company," as casting director R. B. McIntyre confirmed in a memo to Mayer, Thalberg, Rapf and the payroll clerks.

To compensate for the gaps in her professional preparation, Lucille spent many hours wandering around the Metro lot, wherever scenes were being rehearsed or filmed. She watched actors and spoke to those who gave her a moment of their time, and with her hundred-watt smile and Southern-accented charm, she put questions to cameramen, directors and every technician she could beguile into conversation. In the process, she established some lifelong friendships with, for example, the actors William Haines, Eleanor Boardman and Marion Davies, and another newcomer named Myrna Loy.

"From the day Lucille arrived in Hollywood," according to journalist Adele Whitely Fletcher, who knew her for over a half century, "she worked ceaselessly towards becoming a star. Aware that her youthful plumpness would be exaggerated by the cameras, she jogged every morning before going to the studio—this in a day when no one but athletes had ever even heard of jogging!"

The newcomer was a quick study in every aspect of filmmaking; she may have lacked education, but she had a keen native intelligence. A studio writer, director and producer named Paul Bern noticed her; he was a cultivated German immigrant who quickly became a mentor and guide to Lucille, as he was to other young actors. Bern was known and admired perhaps especially because he made no demands (sexual or otherwise) on those for whom he was both a generous protector and an unofficial tutor.

John Arnold, who had photographed fifty-two films since 1914 and became the head of Metro's camera department, also took Lucille aside and showed her how, with the right makeup and eyeliner, she could significantly improve both her appearance and her chances of success. He also filmed a few brief scenes of Lucille alone, so that she could see what he meant. "I'm not saying I was good," she recalled. "I just wasn't impossible." But she was extremely self-critical about what she saw: "a big mouth" she didn't like, as well as "shoulders wider than John Wayne's, not much in the bosom area, and a lot of bones that showed. The only thing in my favor was my legs and my eyes." But over time and with the help of wardrobe designers, she learned to exploit for the best what she once regarded as handicaps.

She also developed poise and confidence before the camera with the patient help of still photographer Tommy Shugrue, employed by Metro to inundate newspapers and fan magazines with eye-catching photos of contract players, usually young women placed in situations and in attitudes that had nothing to do with any movie at all: the idea was simply to promote the studio and its roster. There were photos of Lucille and others at the seashore, or walking a dog, or tossing a ball, or cheering a team of athletes.

When attractive young men invited Lucille out on a date, she accepted—but only if they went dancing, and only to a place frequented by columnists and photographers, for she knew she had to be seen in order to make an impression. "Everybody was on the make," she said years later, "and I don't mean just for bodies. The men you dated didn't want you—they wanted to be *seen* with you and get noticed." For her part, Lucille was winning dance trophies by the dozen: before 1927, she had collected eighty-four silver cups for dancing the Charleston and the Shimmy.

———

BY THE END OF her first month at Metro, things had changed forever. Lucille was cast as the double for Norma Shearer in *Lady of the Night,* directed by Monta Bell. Shearer played two roles, and when both characters had to appear in a single shot, Lucille stepped in, back to the camera, to play one or the other. "I tried to watch everything Norma did, for she was that wonderful being, a star."[1]

Shearer made no secret that she had set her matrimonial sights on powerful Irving Thalberg, and Monta Bell made no secret that he had his keen eye set on Shearer. But he was no competition for the head of production, who had ordered that Norma was to be meticulously photographed. This Bell did—which was no easy task, for despite her beauty, Shearer was slightly cross-eyed, which challenged cinematographers.

Born in Montreal in 1902, Norma Shearer had already appeared in more than two dozen movies. Her parents were severely disabled emotionally, and her sister, Athole, spent more than forty years in an asylum until her death in 1985. Despite her achievements and favorable public image, Norma lived in dread of inheriting the familial tendency toward mental illness. Her brother, Douglas, however, was not only psychologically healthy, he was also a brilliant

---

1. Also in 1925, Joan worked as an uncredited extra in *Proud Flesh, A Slave of Fashion, The Merry Widow, The Circle* and *The Midshipman*. That year, she appeared in a total of ten pictures.

technician, and from the beginning of the talkies, he supervised Metro's sound department for decades.

Following her affairs with directors Victor Fleming and Monta Bell, Norma had turned her attention to Thalberg, convinced he would be her ticket to better roles. For the present, however, Thalberg was pursuing actress Constance Talmadge.

On February 23, Metro released *Lady of the Night*—along with dozens of photographs of Lucille Le Sueur that were unrelated to the Shearer movie but added to the sexy but inoffensive image Mayer and Thalberg preferred their contract players to project. The publicity department began to receive some mail about the anonymous girl in the still photos, and one enterprising journalist learned that she had appeared without credit in the Shearer picture. With that, Mayer's staff and the editors of *Movie Weekly* joined forces in a contest common in the world of movie publicity, from the earliest days through the 1950s. The ploy was simple, and this time it involved Lucille Le Sueur, whose name Mayer thought was the silliest and least pronounceable he had ever heard. And so the contest—"Name Her and Win $1,000"—was announced on March 27, with the victor to be announced that summer.

⟨———⟩

DURING THE EARLY DAYS of the movie industry—for about twenty years, beginning in the early 1890s—very few actors were identified in the films that were unspooled in penny arcades, nickelodeons and music halls. People worked anonymously in these "flickers," which were considered a form of entertainment for the lower classes, on a par with carnival sideshows. Performers with theater experience feared they would be denied future employment if it became known that they had appeared in these fake pantomimes, and so established stage actors like Sarah Bernhardt and the members of the Comédie-Française appeared only briefly in the early cinema. In addition, the first nickelodeon owners, worried that performers would demand higher salaries, were hesitant to promote them by name.

The first person credited in a movie was Florence Lawrence, a stage performer since childhood who had worked for Thomas Edison's company from 1906 and later appeared in films under the direction of D. W. Griffith, one of the first directors to employ a kind of stock company of players (most notably, Lillian Gish). At the same time, a comic actor, director, writer and producer with the stage name Max Linder made a fortune in and for Pathé Frères in France.

By 1920, movies had become somewhat more respectable fare, and audiences, recognizing their favorite performers from picture to picture, wanted to know more about them. Producers saw financial advantages in creating and promoting certain players they soon called "stars," perhaps because they shone brightly in the darkness of movie theaters. Mary Pickford—"America's Sweetheart," forever photographed in outfits far too youthful for her age—was perhaps the first true American movie star; she had foreign counterparts like Francesca Bertini in Italy, Suzanne Grandais in France and Shotaro Hanayagi in Japan.

The so-called golden era of the studios—a period of twenty years, from the end of the First World War to the beginning of the Second—coincided with the fame, fortune and power of great movie stars, who became absolutely essential in promoting the products. (Directors, on the other hand, were mostly ignored, and for a very long time, few of them—with exceptions like Chaplin and De Mille—had any real clout; most were regarded as secondary to a movie's success.) It became clear with each passing season that neither talent, acting ability nor studio publicity had much to do with the creation of a star: that was the result of the public's *need*. The French philosopher Edgar Morin was on the mark when he wrote, "The imaginary life of the screen is the product of this genuine need for an anonymous life to enlarge itself to the dimensions of life in the movies; the star is its projection. People have always projected their desires and fears in images," and the movies are but the most recent sign of this (literal) projection.

Of course the studios had to recognize what audiences wanted, and they had to respond to this need. The conventional wisdom held that only the stars and producers turned movies into hits, and so Hollywood executives selected young people they felt the public liked and essentially created identities for them—even to the point of changing their names and insisting on certain patterns of conduct in their private lives. Archibald Leach, an acrobat from England, became Cary Grant. Spangler Arlington Brough was renamed Robert Taylor. Ruby Stevens was turned into Barbara Stanwyck. Later, Roy Scherer was rechristened Rock Hudson. Thousands received new identities, and backgrounds were created for them that sounded more interesting, more exotic or more polite than the truth suggested.

Thanks to powerful studio publicists and "talent handlers," the public never knew that so-and-so might be socially inferior or unacceptable according to the standards of the day. Non-Caucasian actors were rarely cast as anything but servants, laborers, criminals or people of low intelligence. Under threat of dismissal from the studio or permanent demotion to minor, stereotyped roles, lesbian and gay actors were forced to go out in public with proper "dates" of the opposite sex—or even to marry for the sake of their careers. This hypocritical requirement is common even in the twenty-first century.

During their off-work hours, women contracted to movie studios were advised not to appear in public without makeup and a fashionable outfit. Men had to behave so that they were regarded as unimpeachable gentlemen, and any studio player could be dismissed for failing to adhere to certain moral standards, sometimes defined in their contracts, or simply invented in a whimsical moment by a mogul. For the sake of image, public appearances and romantic rendezvous were arranged by studio publicists, in concert with fan magazines and the daily press, and journalists were duly alerted in advance concerning the whereabouts of the celebrities.

If a movie star was an alcoholic, a drug abuser, unfaithful to a spouse or found guilty of a crime, the studios could take care of that. Movie executives routinely arranged for media silence, bribed the police and negotiated with newspapers and gossip columnists. In the so-called glory days of Hollywood, the studios thus manipulated the lives of countless thousands. All this control was taken for granted as part of big business.

HENCE THROUGH THE JOINT efforts of Metro and the fan magazine *Movie Weekly,* everyone was invited to submit a new name for Lucille Le Sueur. The winner, as it turned out, would not in fact receive one thousand dollars as the advertising indicated: that was the total amount of money to be awarded. The top prize would be five hundred dollars, with ten other prizes of fifty dollars each for those who submitted the ten next-best names. "She has beauty! She has personality!" shouted the contest headlines. "She photographs remarkably well and is far above the average in intelligence. She is strictly an American type, she is energetic and ambitious, and she has a charm and elegance that stamps her as a daughter of Uncle Sam"—which meant that she was native-born and Caucasian.

Thus the studio trumpeted its find wherever possible. For a behind-the-scenes short subject about Metro that spring, an intertitle—a "card" with dialogue or descriptions inserted between shots— accompanied a brief bit of business: "Our wardrobe designer drapes the beautiful figure of Lucille Le Sueur, an M-G-M find of 1925." They even took advantage of her busy nightlife and her accumulation of dance trophies, sending photographers on Tuesday and Wednesday evenings to the Montmartre Club, where she invariably turned up for exhibition dances, to the Cocoanut Grove on Fridays, to the beach clubs on weekends and to Saturday afternoon tea dances at the fine hotels. This sort of busy nightlife was fine when she was not making a film, but it would soon have to be severely curtailed. Meantime, as she said later, "you never found me dating a boy who couldn't dance."

At first, the publicity actually worked against her. An energetic and tireless figure like Lucille, unmarried but often seen in the company of good-looking young admirers, was presumably a woman of easy virtue. By her own admission, she was certainly no candidate for the convent, but the assertions of wild promiscuity that accumulated after her death are impossible to corroborate.

In this regard, it is interesting to cite one incident in her early career. A particularly salacious letter came to Metro's publicity department, claiming that the sender owned a short pornographic film featuring Lucille Le Sueur. More to the point, the film would be given to newspapers unless Metro bought it for a tidy sum. Mayer asked that the owner have his "representatives" deliver a copy to Culver City; if the person involved in the little movie was indeed Lucille Le Sueur, the man would be compensated in exchange for the film and his silence.

But when Mayer and company saw the bit of celluloid, they laughed loudly. "It's very clear," L.B. bellowed, "that the girl in this picture could be anybody—anyone at all—except our Lucille." A minatory letter was hurried off to the blackmailer, whose house mysteriously burned to the ground the following month.

Harry Rapf was quoted during the several months of contest publicity: "I know she will be a remarkably clever motion picture artiste—but her name is unsuitable for the screen, because it is difficult to remember, hard to spell and still harder to pronounce correctly." In fact, Louis B. Mayer himself wrote those words to his colleagues when he initiated the contest. To give the competition an aura of gravity, the identities of the official judges were also publicized nationwide: Adele Whitely Fletcher, the editor of *Movie Weekly;* Harry Rapf; the movie star Florence Lawrence (real name: Florence Bridgwood), drama editor of the *Los Angeles Examiner;* and Edwin Schallert, drama editor of the *Los Angeles Times.*

Every week until the end of August, the national press reminded the public of the rules to be followed in submitting a name:

1. It must be short or only of moderate length.
2. It must be suitable to the individual, who will use it during her entire picture career.
3. It must be euphonious, pleasing and yet have strength.
4. It must be a name easy to remember and quick to impress.
5. It must not infringe upon nor imitate the name of any other artiste.

Then followed a "biography" of Lucille Le Sueur that made her sound like a Vanderbilt:

1. She is eighteen years old, was born in Texas and is of remote French and English ancestry.
2. She is five feet, five inches tall [*sic*], weighs one hundred and twenty-five pounds, has dark brown hair and large blue eyes and a fair complexion.[2]
3. She was educated in private schools, including St. Agnes Academy at Kansas City, Mo., and followed this education with a diploma from St. Stephen's College at Columbia, Mo.
4. Tiring of the social life of a debutante, she left home to become an actress.

During that spring and summer, while contestants were scratching their heads and sharpening their pencils, Lucille continued to sit, stand, kneel, leap and otherwise pose for stock photos. "Lots of newcomers to films undoubtedly think that posing for [calendar, art and fashion] photos is a waste of time," she said. "It doesn't need to be. I have made a careful study of every single still picture that was ever shot of me. I wanted these stills to teach me what not to do on the screen. I scrutinized the grin on my face, my hair-do, my posture, my makeup, the size of my feet."

In June, Metro at last put her in a picture in which she had a part and was a character, not merely a double. The production was *Pretty Ladies,* starring the famous, bankable and talented ZaSu Pitts, the star of the epic *Greed* and an actress equally adept at tragedy and comedy. Playing "Bobbie," a Follies showgirl in a story about the New York theatre world, Lucille brought real sparkle to her few scenes, despite their silliness. In one sequence, for example, she sat on a block of fake studio "ice" with another showgirl, played by Myrna

---

2. Her height was five feet three inches until very late in life, and after 1925, she rarely weighed over one hundred fifteen pounds. Her natural hair color was red, modified for each picture according to the necessity of the role, the wardrobe and the genre of the movie. Her large blue eyes were her best feature. Often, there were special makeup requirements because of her freckles, which were highlighted by the Southern California sunshine and studio arc lights.

Loy. Lucille's eyes said everything and made her intertitle lines almost unnecessary—as, for example, when she compared her boyfriends to vegetables: "When they're not rotten, they're fresh!" *Pretty Ladies* was the only movie in which Lucille Le Sueur received screen credit under her real name.

Everyone seemed to have the impression that Lucille was a lighthearted, blithe and unruffled personality, recalled Myrna. "Joan always worried terribly. She was the opposite of carefree—she was care-filled, I suppose you would say." She was particularly upset during the filming of *Pretty Ladies* because, as Loy clearly remembered, "she was having trouble fighting off the executives at MGM. Some of them were very powerful, and they were grabbing her and touching her, and she didn't know what to do." This was a common studio activity in the days when *sexual harassment* was an unknown term and men thought they had a right to anything they demanded. Lucille hated this sort of behavior, Myrna continued, "but she was afraid because of the power they held over her career. She and I became friends and stayed friends, which is the most that came out of my first MGM experience."

Lucille's contract was up for renewal during production of *Pretty Ladies,* and Metro raised her pay to one hundred dollars a week, which provided security until the end of the year. She saw this renewal, and the publicity generated by the contest, as signs of the studio's genuine interest in her, and she was not off the mark. Executives offered, and she quickly accepted, lessons in ballroom dancing and waltzing, tutorials in the details of period costumes and manners—and elocution, for there were rumors that sound movies were on the way.

———

IN FACT, THERE WERE so many change-of-name contests afoot in 1925 that, as Adele Whitely Fletcher recalled, the other judges in this case were otherwise engaged and simply did not show up for the final tally and decision. "When they did not appear, I, as editor, chose Joan Crawford as the winning name. Lucille Le Sueur hated that name, until it turned into pay-dirt with the relentless effort and incredible self-discipline she put behind it." Joan admitted as much throughout her lifetime: "I hated that name in the beginning. It sounded like 'crawfish.' But it brought me good luck."

The new name, which made front-page news in American daily papers, was announced to a waiting nation in September 1925, and on the twenty-fifth of that month, Metro drafted a check for five hundred dollars to Mrs. Louise Artisdale, of 149 Dartmouth Street, Rochester, New York. She was not the only one to propose the name Joan Crawford, but her entry bore the earliest postmark.[3]

For many people, then and later, the simple fact of this contest made it seem as if America was in the midst of a very innocent, fun-loving time—but of course it was not. During the week that Metro arranged for Lucille Le Sueur to change her name legally, the Sears, Roebuck mail order department was doing a very brisk business, selling the popular Thompson submachine gun for $175 to any American with ready money. Tens of thousands of these weapons were shipped through the U.S. mail that autumn. The advertisement stated that people would feel safer owning this kind of protection; Sears did not add that the easy availability of these weapons was a boon to murderers, bank robbers, deranged lovers and ordinary lunatics.

And so Lucille had a new name—but her old interests remained. On October 11, while she was completing her next assignment—billed for the first time as Joan Crawford—she was featured in a story printed by the *Chicago Tribune:* "The Montmartre on Wednesday evening played host to several genial picture folk. A Charleston contest, featuring Lucille Le Sueur, known now as Joan Crawford, brought them all up on their feet, as Lucille did some new [steps] wonderfully."

The daytime work was in a picture called *Old Clothes,* in which Joan, costarring with the child actor Jackie Coogan, played a poor young woman who achieves good fortune. Columnist Louella O. Parsons, writing in syndication on November 10 (the day after the picture was released), called attention

---

3. Among many other names considered or listed as runners-up: Diana Gray, Joan Gray, Ann Morgan, Peggy Shaw and Joan Arden.

to Joan as "very attractive, [and] she shows promise." Joan followed this with a brief role as a member of the Ruritanian court, in *The Only Thing.* Years later, she referred to its "compounded stupidity," and just weeks after its November 22 release, it vanished into oblivion.

But an episode during that time was never forgotten. One evening at a club dance, she was introduced to a young man with whom she dominated the floor for several hours. "Startlingly handsome" was her description of her dance partner, "tall, dark, gallant and graceful. My happiness and unhappiness hinged totally on him." He was Michael Cudahy, related to the heirs of the meatpacking business that bore the family name—and he was seventeen years old.

Michael may have been a smooth dancer, but it seemed to have been his only talent. Joan quickly recognized that although he was gentle, he was also weak, undisciplined, utterly without ambition—and a confirmed alcoholic at the age of seventeen. For him, work meant nothing, for he aspired to the life of a playboy. Thanks to a monthly allowance of fifteen hundred dollars and free use of the huge family estate, he had no need of employment in order to live luxuriously. But for Joan, work was the most important thing in life.

For almost two years beginning that autumn, they dated, went out dancing, quarreled and reconciled, went out dancing some more, then quarreled and reconciled again, in an endless cycle of highly neurotic interdependence. "He was the reckless scion of the F. Scott Fitzgerald era," Joan wrote later, "just as I was the flapper of the John Held, Jr., cartoons." The living was wild and dangerous, and theirs was, according to Joan, "a tumultuous romance that could have ruined my life."

What was the reason for her attraction to this deeply disturbed man, and why was she so slow to end their relationship?

For one thing, as she admitted, she had grown weary of her grimy room at the Washington Hotel, and she was only too glad to have opportunities to stay elsewhere. Cudahy could afford to keep hotel suites here and there for impromptu romantic assignations—and he had a home large enough for privacy with an overnight guest.

First impressions are sometimes slow to yield to correction, and Joan saw in Cudahy a striking socialite, well mannered (even, it seems, when intoxicated), a member of a crowd of privileged young things with an apparently endless source of money for frivolities. She had known Good Time Charlies (as they were called) in Kansas City—boys good for a dance, a laugh and a drink—but they were unsophisticated working lads. Stage Door Johnnies in Detroit and New York were always at the ready—but she quickly tired of their absorption with themselves. But Michael Cudahy came from a different, fascinating world of privilege and luxury; in addition, there was evidently a potent sexual chemistry between them.

But Michael was a lost soul. That she did not immediately regard him as downright pathetic shows that she may well have taken him more seriously than he wanted to be taken, and that she saw good qualities and talents, however hidden. He also may have awakened something protective and nurturing in her—and it did not hurt that he was extravagantly rich. But the romance, such as it was, had a dead end, and it took the best part of two years for her to realize that he either could not or would not change—that he firmly denied his alcoholism and was likely to be destroyed by it. Cudahy was an accident waiting to happen.

His family seemed like the bizarre cast of a weird melodrama. Michael lived with his sisters, his mother and a squad of servants in a mansion in the Hollywood Hills, where every window was locked tightly and every drapery was drawn against the infiltration of the merest speck of light. Michael's mother, like a Dickensian madwoman, had not left her house since his birth.

Joan always maintained that Mrs. Cudahy actually liked and appreciated her "because I was the one person who could keep Michael off the bottle," but this was a losing battle, for alcoholics have their methods. Contrary to her impression of Mrs. Cudahy's benevolence, every time this eccentric matron spoke to the press, which was alarmingly often, she referred to Joan only with contempt: an actress—most of all one with so doubtful a background and no social pedigree—was entirely unacceptable as a potential daughter-in-law. For those reasons, Mrs. Cudahy insisted that she would quickly effect an annulment of any marriage the couple might presume to contract. For the present, there was no talk of a wedding—just plans for dining and dancing, fun at parties and weekends at the beach whenever Joan had no Saturday calls at the studio. It all seemed like an endless carousel of amusement, music and high living. But as Joan wrote to Daddy Wood at Stephens, sometimes she grew weary—she felt that this romance was hopeless and that she and Michael were on a treadmill, going nowhere.

———

IN NOVEMBER, THANKS TO recommendations from cameraman Jack Arnold and studio publicist Pete Smith, Joan was assigned a major role in *Sally, Irene and Mary,* the story of three New York chorus girls caught up in a series of whirlwind romances that come to a bad end—especially for Irene (Joan), who is killed in an auto accident. "I loved it," she said. "It gave me a character I could lose myself in, a chance to work with two fine actresses, Constance Bennett and Sally O'Neill, and a very good director, Edmund Goulding. He taught me a lot, and so did Jack Arnold. That picture told me I was doing the right thing, that I just might last."

Goulding had good advice for Joan: "Don't exhaust the audience by overacting." To tone her down and enable her to locate inner resources for an emotion (instead of conveying them by outsize gestures and expressions), Goulding taught her an exercise she never forgot. Between takes, she stepped aside, slipped off her shoes, stood as motionless as possible and tried to feel what strength she could muster even in her immobility.

In addition to Goulding's counsel and Arnold's continuing unofficial tutelage about the best camera angles and lighting for each of Joan's scenes, others involved in *Sally, Irene and Mary* were significant for her.

At that time, Joan went out in public as if she demanded to be seen: her nails were painted blood-red; her hair was bobbed, lacquered and parted in the middle; her makeup was exaggerated; her clothes, on the borderline of frank vulgarity, almost shouted for attention; and she danced everywhere, sometimes all night. Indeed, she seemed to do anything that brought her attention.

Pete Smith, head of Metro's publicity, was assigned to look after Joan. He suggested that she change some things about her appearance, which she readily did. Another publicist tracked her social life, her presence at this restaurant or that nightclub and her winning streaks at Charleston contests, alerting newspapers and fan magazines every time she was out on the town. From the time *Sally, Irene and Mary* was released in early December 1925, Joan Crawford was becoming a national figure—an energetic, fun-loving flapper with just a patina of naughtiness but no scandal.

Perhaps because his family objected, Cudahy thought all this was great fun—but only when it included him. When Joan was photographed with other men, he was inclined to throw things, even though he knew he was not her only dancing partner or her sole lover. "I forgot how to say no," she said years later about her spirited youth.

In addition to Goulding, another helpful colleague was the actress who played the movie's Sally—Constance Bennett, a woman of singular elegance and beauty. Whereas Joan depended on the advice of costume designers, Constance neither liked nor needed them: with her exquisite sense of style, she took care of wardrobe on her own. Whereas Joan knew the value of publicity and always courted the press and the public, Constance was entirely indifferent to reporters and held the masses almost in contempt. From her, Joan learned what not to do and what she could profitably emulate.

Born in 1904 into a wealthy family of actors, Constance was raised in an atmosphere of fine breeding and high style. Her father was the eminent stage and screen actor Richard Bennett, and her two sisters, Joan and Barbara, also became actresses; of the three, Joan Bennett had the longest and most notable career.

Despite her background and breeding, Constance was a hot-headed rebel who did not gladly suffer fools (or most people). An arbiter of impeccable fashion and the quintessential Hollywood hostess, Constance had everything Joan admired and secretly envied, and her wealth, innate good taste and good humor made her one of the most popular women in Hollywood, notwithstanding her notorious temper. She lived in a twenty-room mansion in Holmby Hills (a rarefied section between Beverly Hills and Brentwood), where her guests were among the most famous, the wealthiest and the most powerful people in America.

With everything Hollywood marketed and envied and a gift for both comedy and drama, Constance never really developed an interest in perfecting her talent. At her peak, in 1932, she was Hollywood's highest paid star, with a weekly salary of thirty thousand dollars—equal to $475,000 a week in 2010 valuation—and she remained in the business only to make that kind of money. Openly contemptuous of studios and moguls, she did not care if she worked or not, and finally she withdrew from the screen, turned to the theatre, went out on road tours and developed a nightclub act. An unpredictable nature and the pursuit of a wild private life hindered her career for many years, but after a series of bad marriages, she settled down with a husband she adored, and her life became both serious and—to the astonishment of many who knew her—dedicated to the welfare of others.

That year, Joan learned from Constance a great deal about wardrobe, accessories, makeup and the fine points of being a polite hostess. The two women were never close friends after *Sally, Irene and Mary,* but Joan recognized quality and was unafraid to put questions to Constance, who was amused by the down-to-earth qualities of her costar. She regarded Joan as a midwestern ragtag who could benefit from some polishing, but years later she spoke of her with touching affection and deep admiration.

In her public image, Constance Bennett was the living embodiment of an elusive quality called glamour—a term worth exploring, for very much of Joan Crawford's career was characterized by glamour, glamorous scenes and glamorous photographs.

———

IN ITS ORIGINAL ENGLISH usage in the eighteenth century, *glamour* meant magic or enchantment—specifically, a deceptive, bewitching and dangerous beauty or charm. Linked to the spells of witches and sorcerers, glamour indicated a mysteriously exciting or alluring physical attractiveness, artificially contrived for the purpose of bringing someone "under the glamour," or making them effectively spellbound—that is, bound by a spell. The implication was frankly negative. By the time of Tennyson, "casting the glamour over someone" meant bewitching them by an illusion—causing a kind of haze to fall over someone's sight, so that things are seen in a form different from their reality. A glamorous person, therefore, was not a reality but an illusion, created in order to possess or control the beholder, to manipulate others into forbidden or dangerous actions.

Glamour, then, came to mean a form of falsification—but falsification to achieve a particular purpose: in Hollywood terms, to celebrate a star, or to sell a film. No one is glamorous by nature, and glamour today involves a complicated process of idealization. In Hollywood, there was an enormous effort by technical means to create glamorous, spellbinding personalities, men as well as women. Makeup experts founded schools and systems by which hues and tints were created not only for the consistent representation of a character in a story, but also for separate glamour shots that had nothing to do with a particular movie.

And so photographers set up, arranged and rearranged their lights, retouchers retouched, lighting experts created shadows to glorify the subject and to diminish any of nature's little mistakes. The tricks and effects were innumerable and were often minor works of genius, and the portraits were so painstakingly set up, taken and altered that the end result seemed like something from another world, or at least another sphere of reality. Did any glamour portrait of any star ever really resemble someone you might encounter at the market?

In real life, Constance Bennett was certainly a memorably beautiful woman, but photographs rendered her unimaginably, *impossibly* beautiful. She was not, of course, the only one to bewitch: there were many such women in Hollywood—and men, too. In every case, artifice added to, complemented and sometimes triumphed over nature. That is because Hollywood is, after all, about artifice and unreality. As Ingrid Bergman said, "Everything in Hollywood is fake—the teeth are fake, the clothes are fake, the look is fake—everything!" She then told the story of a movie actor who goes into a studio commissary for lunch and asks the waiter for a piece of pie and a cup of coffee.

The man is told there is coffee, but the restaurant is out of pie. "Well, then, fake it!" the actor replies. "This is Hollywood, after all—anything is possible!"

———

WHILE JOAN WAS OBSERVING and learning from Constance Bennett, she made a lifelong friendship with another player in the cast of *Sally, Irene and Mary*. William Haines was twenty-five, tall and handsome. After appearing in nineteen films in three years, he had become one of the most popular actors in America. "He gave me great advice," she recalled, "and he escorted me to wonderful places." The most critical counsel provided by Billy (as friends called him) was to urge that Joan engage her own publicist, to supplement what Pete Smith was doing at Metro. Before she could insist that she couldn't afford to pay for that kind of service, Billy paid the publicist's fee and put him on Joan's case.

Joan Crawford and Billy Haines were seen everywhere—at fine restaurants and (thanks to his fame and connections) at the best Hollywood parties. After Joan, no one was more delighted about this relationship than Louis B. Mayer, who otherwise thought of William Haines as his biggest headache. Haines was not only exclusively homosexual, he was—horrors!—quite unapologetic about it and very comfortable in his true nature. He was no crusader, but he made no secret of the fact that he shared his life and home with his partner, Jimmy Shields, and he never pretended to carry on a romance with any woman.

Decades later, it is difficult for many people to imagine that there was a time in Hollywood—indeed, in all of America—when no man or woman could be openly gay, and when most homosexuals had to lead lives of secrecy and dread, or contracted absurd, often tragic marriages. Nor was it proper for people to openly befriend homosexuals—that was considered as reprehensible as associating with people of color or criminals. Some things just were not done. To her credit, Joan Crawford never shared any of the prejudices of her time or her profession, and a friend was a friend, gay or not. "Billy and Jimmy had the most beautiful relationship I've ever known," Joan said. "It was the best marriage I ever saw in Hollywood."

As their friendship blossomed, Joan was cast in several more films with Billy—perhaps on direct orders from Mayer himself, who hatched the idea that it would solve the Haines problem and bring enormous favorable publicity to the studio if the two friends married. When Pete Smith's assistant, Howard Strickling, presented the notion to Joan and Billy, their reaction was a loud burst of laughter. The friendship continued unalloyed, but Billy's troubles at Metro were only beginning.

As for Mayer, he had another matter to attend to. He had hired a Swedish actress named Greta Garbo, who had arrived in September, ten days before she turned twenty. At first, he and his producers hadn't the remotest idea how to use her. In December, just after the release of *Sally, Irene and Mary,* she was at work in *Torrent.* After that, in less than sixteen years (until the autumn of 1941), Garbo appeared in a total of twenty-five films for Metro; during the same period, Joan was seen in fifty-four. But by 1927, Garbo was paid $5,000 a week, and four years later, her fee was $250,000 per picture. Norma Shearer and Joan Crawford were fighting for good roles, but Garbo had the largest bank account—and with it, she purchased huge parcels of Beverly Hills real estate that still belonged to her when she died.

The press and the public were convinced that behind the enigmatic Garbo mask was a woman of exotic and erotic mystery. They were wrong. In reality, she was a humorless soul, unformed, without a solid sense of identity or any intellectual curiosity, solitary to the point of being antisocial and in fact quite dull. A completely self-absorbed woman with no real interest in anyone else, she became one of the most famous neurotics of the twentieth century but was mistakenly perceived to be something of a goddess.

"She wanted to be profound," said the writer Peter Viertel, son of Garbo's friend and collaborator Salka Viertel, "but she never realized the way you do it is by getting on with life." Unlike Joan, Garbo could not be approached for a chat by coworkers on the Metro lot: she was regarded with an awe that was almost unimaginable—an attitude she encouraged by her remoteness. For all that, her power and income were immense. Such was the power of glamour alone, disconnected from a life of substance.

Constance Bennett and Greta Garbo were never Crawford's rivals. Except for three films, Bennett's work was at studios other than Metro. As for Garbo, she was the distant foreigner, cast in very different roles from Crawford, who was always recognizably American, solid and quite the opposite of elusive or mystical. But Joan was "a bundle of insecurities," as she said, and her vulnerability led her to always regard every actress as a potential rival. In the decades to come, her fear of losing what she strove so hard to achieve—her creation of Joan Crawford and her dismissal of the embarrassing Lucille Le Sueur—sometimes led to ungenerous behavior she deeply regretted.

CHAPTER THREE

Enter the Prince
| 1926–1929 |

I N 1926 JOAN CARRIED ON her life with her usual high-voltage energy, learning what she could, dancing several evenings each week and campaigning for roles at Metro. Thanks to Billy Haines and her publicity team, Joan was named a WAMPAS Baby Star—not that she was a baby, but rather a "little star" quickly growing up, according to the judgment of the Western Association of Motion Picture Advertisers. (Among the others named that year were Mary Astor, Fay Wray, Janet Gaynor and Dolores Del Rio.)

Joan's salary was raised to $250 per week ($3,000 a week in 2010) beginning in January, and this enabled her to quit the Washington Hotel. She took a short-term lease on a house on Courtney Avenue, above Hollywood Boulevard, and Billy Haines (who had a genius for interior design) offered to help furnish and decorate it. Built in 1924, the house had been briefly occupied by another Metro employee who had quit the business. But Joan soon realized her mistake: the house spread over more than ten thousand square feet—far too much room for a working girl living alone, as Billy pointed out. She decided to occupy only four rooms while she looked for a smaller place closer to Culver City.

Despite his quixotic attempt to marry her off to Billy, Mayer had considerable respect for Joan throughout her long tenure at the studio. Contrary to the attitude and behavior of many stars toward their bosses, she enjoyed a genial and trusting rapport with the man she regarded not only as her employer but also as the owner of Metro-Goldwyn-Mayer—which, of course, he was not.

"He was a fine man, and I admired him. I regarded him as my protector, like Daddy Cassin and Daddy Wood. Mr. Mayer was very important in my life, and I felt he watched over my career." But Norma Shearer had a more powerful protector in Thalberg, whom she married in 1927, thus securing virtually any role that suited her fancy. To her credit, Joan spoke kindly of Norma: "Professionally, she was good—a little aloof, but not bad, considering she was royalty, the queen of the lot."

Joan's roles in twenty-seven silent films between 1925 and 1929 provided a solid and valuable apprenticeship for the sixty feature talkies that followed from 1929 to 1970. When sound arrived, it was clear that she had an expressive voice free of regional inflections, and while she appreciated superbly crafted dialogue, she learned that less is more—that glances, gestures and images should be the primary means of telling a story, and that talking pictures should not be (as Alfred Hitchcock memorably said) mere pictures of people talking. From directors of her silent films like Edmund Goulding, Eddie Cline and Jack Conway, Joan learned how to minimize actions and reactions, playing subtly rather than grandly. And from dancing, she knew how to use her arms and legs fluidly and gracefully, without sudden shifts or awkward poses.

———

IMPRESSED WITH HER PERFORMANCE in *Sally, Irene and Mary,* the comedian Harry Langdon paid Mayer handsomely to borrow Joan for a role in his independent picture *Tramp, Tramp, Tramp,* made early in 1926. Not as enduringly famous as Charlie Chaplin, Buster Keaton or Harold Lloyd, Langdon wore clown-white makeup that exaggerated his wide gaze, affecting a preadolescent meekness at the ripe age of forty-two. That year, he was in the midst of a busy if somewhat confused career that was eventually ruined by an enormous ego unsuspected by those who saw only his mild on-screen character.

A team of writers worked on the story and script, which was little more than an excuse for Langdon's goofy brand of physical, sad-sack humor and his wide-eyed obsession for a shoe magnate's daughter—Joan, who was nothing more than window dressing in the picture. She was seen only briefly until the climactic tornado, a triumph of special effects in which Harry saves her from being whirled away forever. "Joan Crawford is a nice leading lady with little to do," observed *Variety*.

"I was just an MGM contract player and had to take whatever was thrown at me," Joan recalled. "I was earning a weekly salary and ways had to be found to keep me busy, no matter how unsuitable and carelessly conceived the part." *Tramp, Tramp, Tramp* was the first time Joan was loaned to another company during her time at Metro. This was a common practice in Hollywood during the days of contract players, when studio bosses realized a huge profit by allowing other producers to borrow a star—who was then paid only the fee contracted for with the home studio.

"Whatever was thrown" at her was a perfect description of the next assignment—*Paris,* released in May 1926. On paper, it seemed to have everything right: story and direction by Goulding, photography by Arnold and exotic Parisian sets courtesy of Metro's carpentry shop and art department. In her role as a low-life dancer, Joan insisted that she "overacted like a simpleton," but *Photoplay* hailed her performance as "exquisitely played."

———

THAT SPRING OF 1926, there were two developments in the Crawford-Cudahy affair. First, Michael's mother summoned reporters from the *Los Angeles Times* and said once again that if her son and Miss Crawford "ever go through a ceremony, the union will promptly be annulled. My son is only eighteen years of age and I am his legal guardian, so I can say that this marriage would be annulled if he ever did decide to marry this girl." She added, without the slightest hint of humor, that Michael would probably go to school in England during the coming summer. That day, he was on the polo field, and when reporters tracked him down, he tipped his hat politely, spurred the horse and galloped away without a word.

Joan had no such easy means of escape when a journalist located her at Metro. "No, I'm not married," she said on May 5. "It is true that Michael and I love each other and plan to be married some day, but we haven't taken that step yet."

The second development, a direct contradiction of her last statement, was perhaps inevitable. "Michael and I agreed to disagree," Joan told the *Los Angeles Times* on June 7, announcing the end of their engagement (by which was meant their affair). "His mother's objections had nothing to do with it," she continued, "nor had any other person. We decided that we do not love each other enough to marry, that's all. I still think Michael is very wonderful and we may go out together sometime. But as for anything serious, no." In fact, this marked the end of the entanglement.

This was a prudent decision on Joan's part. Six months later, still under the legal age of twenty-one, Michael Cudahy attempted to marry the actress known as Marie Astaire (real name: Esther von Brusberg). He was arrested in Santa Barbara and sent home to his mother. On July 12, 1929, he was arrested for drunk driving and causing injuries to the occupant of another vehicle.

This mishap occurred six days after his first legal marriage, to the nineteen-year-old actress Muriel Evans. That union was soon dissolved, and Michael subsequently married a dancer named Jacklyn Roth. He again revealed himself to be an unsuitable mate, and the second marriage ended in 1937. In 1941, at the age of thirty-three, Cudahy married Marjorie Conover, a former Mack Sennett bathing beauty. Three months later, he suddenly abandoned her and entered the U.S. Army. In 1945 he returned from war service to life in Hollywood, where—at the age of thirty-eight, on February 15, 1947—he died at Hollywood Hospital. The cause was "a chronic liver complaint," according to the *New York Times,* which added: "He was known in the film colony as a playboy"—true, but poor journalism. As for the discarded wife Marjorie, a deranged Hollywood real estate salesman murdered her in 1952. Joan may certainly have reasoned that she was well rid of this tragic, self-destructive man in 1926.

———

"I'M SO SORRY I made such a dreadful mistake," Joan wrote to a friend, referring to her next picture, *The Boob*. "You don't have to tell me it was a terrible picture—I won't even go to see the preview!" Her judgment was accurate: it was a dreary attempt at humor, in which she had the small role of Jane, "one of Uncle Sam's revenue agents," according to the intertitle card. Helping to round up a gang of escaping bootleggers, she appears very late in the picture and merely stands by, looking official. The critical consensus: *The Boob* was "a piece of junk."

Joan's memories mostly had to do with her director, William A. Wellman, later perhaps best known for *The Public Enemy,* the first version of *A Star Is Born* and *Nothing Sacred*. Wellman had been a hell-raising juvenile delinquent, and he never kicked the habit. In Hollywood, he was predisposed to offend actresses especially, by rudely grabbing, pinching and fondling them. "He was a horny wise-guy with little respect for women," according to Joan. Wellman's astonishing justification: "She had a reputation in those early days as quite a wild slut, so what did she expect?"

———

EIGHT FILMS WITH JOAN Crawford went before the cameras in 1927. "I worked my ass off that year, didn't I?" she asked rhetorically many years later. "MGM was a goddam factory!" In *Winners of the Wilderness,* set during the French and Indian Wars, Joan portrayed a general's daughter, but she felt overwhelmed by the lavish eighteenth-century costumes. Its January release was followed two weeks later by the premiere of *The Taxi Dancer,* notable as the first time Joan received top billing. The title refers not (as commonly thought) to a prostitute but to a young woman paid to dance with paying partners at a club—the so-called ten-cents-a-dance girls who socialized with male dancers. "I was better than the picture," she said, and most reviewers agreed: "Joan Crawford rides high over the inferior material. Here is a girl of singular beauty and promise, and she certainly has IT"—a reference to novelist Elinor Glyn's term for sex appeal. Joan's wardrobe and character were simpler in *The Understanding Heart,* first shown at the end of February, in which she played a lookout for the Forest Rangers who becomes involved in a sizzling love triangle that blazes during a raging fire. *Time* magazine dismissed the picture as "so befuddled that it is incomprehensible."

But Joan's sense of herself and her career was much clarified by an important introduction to a key Hollywood figure that season. Gloria Swanson had long been Joan's idol—not just as an actress, but as a model of how a star behaved. "I have decided," Gloria had said, "that when I am a star, I will be every inch and at every moment a star. Everyone from the studio gateman to the highest executive will know it." These words became virtually Joan's motto, her design for living.

Swanson had originally wanted to be an opera singer, but she abandoned that aspiration at seventeen, when she married twenty-nine-year-old Wallace Beery—a terrible mismatch that ended after three months. After work at several other studios, Swanson began working with Cecil B. DeMille at Paramount, and together they shifted the image of the ideal American woman from Pickford and Gish—heroines of innocent romance yarns—to the new woman of the 1920s, who was provocative, sensual and sophisticated. During that decade, Swanson was the world's most photographed woman.

Joan noted that Gloria dressed as elegantly offscreen as on—a custom enforced by Swanson's Paramount contract, which stipulated that she must appear stylishly outfitted in public. By the time the two women met, Swanson was in fact the most copied movie star in the world—and Joan was among the copiers as soon as she could afford to be.

From her idol, she learned not only about wardrobe and manners, but also how to compensate for a poor education by immersing herself in good reading and high culture. At that time, Swanson was married to the French aristocrat Henri de la Falaise (who later married Constance Bennett). This marriage, too, was not a success, and although they did not divorce until 1930, Gloria began a notorious affair with Joseph P. Kennedy in 1927.

Crawford observed that Swanson lived for her public, her publicity and her fans. She saw that Gloria kept records of the names and addresses of all her admirers, filing their letters and copies of her replies—practices Joan religiously emulated for the rest of her life. Before long, like Gloria, Joan was very much aware of her own fame and did everything she could to maintain her image as a star, "every inch and at every moment." Both women ultimately came to realize that fame and stardom were serious threats to a healthy private life.

———

"WORKING WITH LON CHANEY [in *The Unknown*] was both traumatic and delightful," Joan recalled. The star of *The Hunchback of Notre Dame* and *The Phantom of the Opera* was a quiet, somewhat remote but generally friendly man off-camera. But during filming, no one had greater concentration, and no actor required more of himself.

The Unknown, directed by Chaney's friend Tod Browning, is the bizarre story of Alonso, a Spanish circus artist who performs remarkable tricks despite the fact that he is "the armless wonder." This apparent deformity, however, is a hoax: Alonso's arms are actually bound underneath his clothing—a ruse to hide his identity as a crook sought by the police, who are after the notorious man who has a hand with two thumbs.

The cruel ironies of the story have two levels.

Alonso is in love with his assistant, Ninon (played by Joan), who has a pathological fear of men's arms—thus she shrinks from the embrace of the circus strongman, Malabar (Nick Kerry), who promises to wait patiently until she overcomes this disturbing phobia. Her pathological terror leads Alonso to a horrific act: he has his arms surgically amputated, confident that now he need never fear being revealed as a wanted man and secure in his conviction that Ninon will fall in love with him.

Armless forever, Alonso returns to the circus after a long recovery from the gruesome operation. He then learns that Ninon has finally conquered her obsessive fear and is blissfully married to Malabar. Mad with despair, Alonso attempts to kill his rival by having horses tear his arms off during a dangerous act, but this fails and Alonso is himself killed.

Watching and working with Chaney, Joan became aware for the first time of the difference between, on the one hand, merely *performing* a role, by standing in front of a camera and going through memorized motions, and, on the other hand, really *acting* a role. In the final scenes of *The Unknown* (released on June 4), when Alonso realizes that his enormous sacrifice has been for nothing, Joan recalled that Chaney "was able to convey not just realism but such emotional agony that it was both shocking and fascinating." Her role in the picture was small but difficult, for she had to find the proper means to make Ninon both phobic and sympathetic—an effect she achieved by replicating Chaney's quiet concentration. "Joan Crawford is one of the screen's acknowledged artists," wrote a New York film critic. "Certainly her performance in this picture is a most impressive one."

———

HER NEXT FILM, *Twelve Miles Out,* concerns a young woman (Joan) and her aging fiancé (Edward Earle) who are kidnapped and taken out to sea by a fugitive bootlegger (John Gilbert). A rival bootlegger boards the ship, and he happens to be an old buddy of the one now in charge. A fierce rivalry for Joan ensues before both die, ending a weak romantic triangle.

John Gilbert, then madly in love with Greta Garbo, was doomed to disappointment when she summarily abandoned him. Concerned with little else than her response to him, Gilbert was indifferent to both Joan and the movie. If Joan had hoped that working with Metro's romantic star might continue the kind of serious acting education she had enjoyed with Chaney, she was certainly disappointed.

Two more pictures followed in quick succession, produced during the summer and early autumn of 1927—both of them with her friend Billy Haines. The first was *Spring Fever*—"a waste of everyone's time and money," according to Joan. She was on the mark, for it was indeed an insipid comedy of manners with shallow characters and nothing at stake. "God, golf is dull on film!" she added—but director Edward Sedgwick was mad for the sport, which monopolizes the picture. Joan played a rich society girl, falling for a poor shipping clerk (Haines) who is transformed into a successful golf pro. With wealth now on both sides—*voilà!*—they are free to marry without social embarrassment. Of working with Billy, Joan had only happy memories despite the project: "He would take you in his arms in a love scene, joking so that you had to brace yourself not to laugh. What made a Haines picture was always [Billy] himself, the symbol of eternal, cocky, lovable youth."

But their second collaboration that season was vastly superior to *Spring Fever*. *West Point* was in fact one of the most astonishing and hilarious movies made at the end of the silent era.

Joan was cast as Betty Channing, daughter of a hotel owner; she pops into the story every now and again as the girlfriend of Brice Wayne (Haines). Made with the cooperation and technical advice of the U.S. Military Academy at West Point, the movie was filmed on location in New York's Hudson Valley. On the surface, it's about the ambivalence of wealthy playboy Brice toward the disciplined life of a West Point cadet, his mockery of its military folderol and his eventual heroics as the academy's star football player in the big game against Navy.

Billy and Joan had enormous fun making this movie. He flirted with the cadets who were cast as extras, while she led one or two boys astray by inviting them off campus for a bit of canoodling. The two actors' skylarking, practically under the noses of the academy's top brass, was exploited in the story's sassy tone and content. But the actual theme of *West Point* became (with the tacit approval of director Edward Sedgwick) that of a highly eroticized friendship between Brice and his buddy Tex McNeill—a pale, lovesick, androgynous lad, acted to fey perfection by nineteen-year-old William Bakewell.

West Point moves along its surprising course, presenting Brice and Tex as a loving couple: indeed, Brice is far more interested in Tex than he is in Betty, and Tex is oh so grateful that Brice "has fixed it so that we can be . . . er, ummm . . . roommates," as the intertitle reads. At several points, Tex swoons, faints, sobs and chokes up with sentiment over Brice, who responds with much fluttering of his long, fake eyelashes. "We'll take our time doing things," Brice tells Tex with a wink.

Tex's big scene occurs when, confronting classmates, he defends Brice's antics. Later, when Brice visits Tex in the hospital following an accident, the two men hold hands during the entire sequence, gazing dreamily into one another's eyes. Otherwise, Brice displays similar undisguised adoration only when he stares at the American flag. With the change of gender, in other words, *West Point* is a classic Metro love story.

But how could this picture have been released in its final edited form during the tenure of Louis B. Mayer, who was regularly giving Billy Haines hell about his life with Jimmy Shields? How could *West Point* get past Mayer, who was constantly trumpeting Metro as one big, happy family while the studio turned out films that were supposedly good for everyone?

For one thing, Mayer was much preoccupied that year with Greta Garbo's initial contributions to the studio's fortunes; for another, Billy was very big box office—his name is alone above the title here—and audiences, blissfully ignorant of the actor's private life, named him the most popular movie star of the year. Mayer knew the value of a dollar.

Acting together in the first twenty minutes of the picture, Billy and Joan affected good comic chemistry—and then her character conveniently disappears, so that the two men can enjoy all the romance of the story. She returns, at the finale, only to be kissed and to accept a marriage proposal, which is patently absurd. "Joan Crawford is quite charming as the girl who, for some unexplained reason, finally learns to love Brice Wayne," wrote the senior critic of the *New York Times,* who may have guessed what was going on. The picture, Joan rightly recalled, was "a throwaway for me." But she loved working with her best friend, who had "great naturalness and charm and an overwhelming sense of humor."

A minor accident occurred during production, and the studio publicists cannily turned the news story into a free advertisement for the picture. On August 29, a driver was delivering Joan and Billy to the military academy from their rooms at the nearby Thayer Hotel. A large truck sideswiped their car, forcing them off the road and causing Joan to sustain bruises to her knees and forehead; Billy was only shaken. Back at the hotel, they rested for a few hours and then Joan tapped at Billy's door. "The show must go on!" she called cheerfully. "Why?" asked Billy, who suggested that they repair to the hotel bar.

———

WEST POINT WRAPPED TWO days later, and the company returned by a long, scenic train route to Los Angeles. When they arrived, on September 5, news of Marcus Loew's death in New York had just come over the wires, and rumors swirled about the future of Metro-Goldwyn-Mayer, but business continued as usual.

A week later, Warner Bros. announced that on October 6 there would be a screening in New York of *The Jazz Singer,* the first feature-length motion picture with synchronized images, dialogue and sound effects. A nationwide release was to follow in February.

It's a common misconception that every studio at once scrambled to make the transformation from silent to sound movies. But that is not accurate. For one thing, there were two rival sound systems. Warner's Vitaphone process required a painstaking technical link between the theater's motion picture projector and the machine used to play the recordings accompanying the movie. On the other hand, there was a superior, direct sound-on-film process developed by Fox Studios, but it needed an expensive new type of projector. Of major importance was cost: it was estimated in 1927 that the addition of sound at least doubled a film's budget. There was also the issue of expensive new movie-theater equipment. Under orders from Loew's board of directors, therefore, Metro-Goldwyn-Mayer temporized, for the New York executives believed that sound was just a fad that would fade.

From 1927 to 1930, the studios, which had limited equipment and few technical wizards, had to make hard decisions about which films to produce as talkies and which to make as silents. There was also the problem of the international market, a dilemma that confronted studios worldwide. Intertitles could be inexpensively made in any language, but foreign-language sound versions required an entirely separate film to be made: after each scene was photographed, it had to be repeated. (Subtitles were developed later.) While Mayer awaited further instructions from New York, production had to continue; in fact, Joan appeared in nine more silent movies until her first talkie was released nearly two years later. By then, Joan Crawford legally (but not professionally) had another name.

———

ON OCTOBER 17, PAUL BERN escorted Joan to the West Coast premiere of John van Druten's play *Young Woodley*, first produced in London, later on Broadway and now at the Belasco Theatre on South Hill Street in Los Angeles. Writing many years later, Metro's former publicist Katherine Albert recalled that Paul Bern "began the awakening of Joan's mind. He taught her things she had not known existed—the beauty of words on paper, the feeling for musical harmony, the appreciation of form and color on canvas." As Joan said, "He recognized something in me that other men did not care to see—that I had a brain."

The title role in the play that evening—of a sensitive schoolboy who imagines himself in love with an older woman—was assumed by the seventeen-year-old son and namesake of the popular movie star Douglas Fairbanks. Renowned for his athletic performances in pictures like *The Three Musketeers, Robin Hood* and *The Black Pirate,* the senior Fairbanks was also a cofounder of United Artists, which he had formed with Charles Chaplin, D. W. Griffith and Mary Pickford, who became the second Mrs. Douglas Fairbanks. The first, young Douglas's mother, was Anna Beth Sully, daughter of a once wealthy but now impoverished industrialist. Years later, Douglas Fairbanks Jr. described his mother as a woman of "passionate possessiveness. She longed for—but seldom got—the kind of smothering devotion that she lavished on her own loved ones." With his famous father, on the other hand, "there was no great warmth, nor did he seem to know or care much about my professional progress. My parents divorced when I was ten, and my mother took me along when she went to London and Paris, where I had the occasional tutor—but lessons were haphazard; my education was virtually nonexistent."

With the cachet provided by his father's name, however, young Douglas—tall, handsome, polished—found that all sorts of doors readily opened to admit him. In London, he enjoyed the company of aristocrats, statesmen and even some members of the royal family, and in Paris, he met the likes of Gertrude Stein, Ernest Hemingway, Jean Cocteau, Maurice Chevalier and Cole Porter.

As a teenager, Douglas easily made friends everywhere, and famous women tapped at his door, even without invitations. By the time he was playing the title role in *Young Woodley,* he had lost both his naïveté and his innocence. He had appeared in silent films from an early age, "but I was lazy and never quite reached my capabilities." However severe that critical self-assessment, Douglas Fairbanks Jr. certainly had a varied, busy and productive ninety years. (From 1923 to 1933, for example, he appeared in no fewer than forty-five motion pictures.)

Paul Bern took Joan backstage to meet the cast after the performance that October evening. She had met the young leading man before: he was a friend of Michael Cudahy, and they had been introduced at several of the Cocoanut Grove's Friday dance competitions—which, as Douglas recalled, were often won by Joan and Mike. The day after their backstage meeting, she wrote Douglas a note detailing the fine points of her admiration for his performance—and because she included her address and telephone number, he rang and she invited him to her house for tea. "She was a few years older than I, but that was fine with me—and quite in accordance with my continuing preference for older women."

During their first visit together (as he recalled), Douglas "hammed it up, trying to appear an intellectual artist, and she played the part of an overwhelmingly impressed country girl who saw glamour in her future. After an awkward but pleasant hour, I got up to leave. I asked if I might have a photograph of her in exchange for one she had requested that I bring of myself. She produced a large 11-by-14 portrait, inscribed 'To Douglas—May this be the start of a beautiful friendship, Joan.'"

On December 9, Douglas marked his eighteenth birthday; by that time, he and twenty-one-year-old Joan had already embarked on a passionate affair that was, on his side, "neither serious nor exclusive." In that aspect of the program lay the seeds of future trouble. Still, his initial impression was of "a vital, energetic, very pretty young girl, quite unlike anyone I had known before. Her looks were not classic, but despite an irregularity of detail, her features projected an overall illusion of considerable beauty, [and] her figure was beautiful. It was fine-trained by years of dancing and a continuing devotion to keeping fit. I started off entranced by her."

For the first time, Joan thought she had met a man she could marry, but without parental permission Douglas was stymied, and the couple presumed they would have to wait until he was twenty-one. "She built up a fairy-tale prince in her imagination," Douglas added, "and I played up to it for all it was worth. I postured too much, made outlandish statements and read classical poetry aloud. If she had been even a little bit more sophisticated, she would have seen right through to the affected, infatuated young ass that I was, [but] I began to wear her like a flower in my button-hole."

Very many people, then and later, presumed that Joan Crawford saw Douglas Fairbanks Jr. as a ticket to the upper realms of Hollywood society. But such a judgment is not merely cynical: it fails to recognize that Joan already had far greater fame and that Douglas, notwithstanding his many minor movie roles, was nothing like a star. In fact, it was he who stood to benefit from their association, as he acknowledged years later. "To be honest, in her own way, she taught *me* a great deal and pushed me to a fuller height as my own self and away from the person hiding his shyness behind such affectations as imitating Barrymore and pretending to an unreal aestheticism."

As for matters monetary, she could not have had any such ulterior intention, for the senior Fairbanks did not support his son but instead had set up a delayed and modest trust fund for him—"and so I was not the rich young heir everyone imagined," as Douglas admitted. More to the point, her income far exceeded his for the entire time of their relationship and marriage. For all that, the magnetism between Douglas and Joan was immediate, intense and multileveled. As they both said years later, the relationship was based on the kind of passionate physical chemistry typical of youthful ardor.

At her suggestion, he called her Billie (the name used by only a few of her oldest or closest friends), and he was her "Dodo," a riff on his being the second Douglas. She absorbed everything he had to say about art and literature, and about Paris, London and New York. It would be unreasonable to imagine that seventeen-year-old Douglas had the depth of understanding only maturity can bestow—but his enthusiasm was contagious. Very soon Joan said that she, too, wanted to travel to the great cities of the world and to compensate, however she might, for her background, her poor education and her ignorance of cosmopolitan society. "She always harbored an inferiority complex," Douglas added, "and she used it as a whip to spur herself onward and upward."

Joan's appreciation of him naturally flattered his boyish ego, but there were other reasons for him to feel attracted to her. "She really always saw the best in people, and she was ready to take people as they were. And I admired her for her brave attitude toward life. She told me about her awful childhood, but she described it matter-of-factly, without pity. I had never known anyone with that kind of background. You just had to admire what she overcame, and what she was accomplishing at that time."

Douglas Sr. and Mary Pickford invited the young couple to Pickfair—the vast Pickford-Fairbanks mansion in Beverly Hills to which all of Hollywood society wanted an invitation. At first, there was "a warm reception," as the young man recalled, "and Mary did all she could to make the clearly shaky young girl feel at home." But when it became clear that this was a serious affair, the elder Fairbanks was not enthusiastic—"but he was gentleman enough not to show it." On the other hand, when Anna Beth met Joan a few weeks later, she was "condescending" and described Joan to her family and friends as "my son's current chorus-girl fling."

"The most important contribution that Billie made to my evolving character," Douglas Fairbanks Jr. continued, "was her insistence that I break away from home and Mother. The greatest gift Billie gave me (far better than anything I ever did for her) was the encouragement to be courageous. She made no bones about telling me that I'd 'never be a real, responsible, grown-up man' as long as I let myself be controlled by Mother." Joan was on the mark, for Anna Beth Sully Fairbanks still handled all her son's financial affairs, took his salary, and then parceled out an allowance to him—until Mike Levee (Joan's and Doug's new agent) took over the management of their respective financial affairs.

———

THE NEW YEAR 1928 was even more crowded and productive than 1927. With her salary raised to fifteen hundred dollars a week before the end of 1928, Joan sped through no fewer than six more silent pictures. She was also speeding quite literally in January. Driving from home to Culver City in her new white coupe—a Christmas present from Mayer—Joan bumped a pedestrian who happened to be an employee of Cecil B. DeMille. The woman sustained a minor injury, and before anyone could cry "Lawsuit!" Joan was slapped with a complaint for reckless endangerment. Metro handled the matter out of court, the police were mollified, and the injured woman limped quietly away, comforted by a check for several thousand dollars.

Joan's reason for the dash to the studio was the completion of *The Law of the Range,* a hilariously bad Western with Tim McCoy, in which she played a sweet, old-fashioned young thing caught between a villain and his virtuous twin brother—in other words, a romantic triangle yet again for the popular Miss Crawford. Miscast and uncomfortable, Joan seems to have been assigned this picture because, emboldened by her affair with Douglas, she frequently irritated Irving Thalberg by demanding better and stronger roles. Not above acting like a headmaster, the production chief instead showed her who was boss by giving her precisely what she did not want.

With her usual pluck, Joan turned her next film, a silent version of the successful Broadway musical *Rose-Marie,* into something of a holiday. Since there was location work that January in the Sierra Nevada range (doubling for the Canadian Rockies), she invited Douglas to join her when he could. "I felt uneasy as a French Canadian, but the critics didn't notice." In fact, they did:

"Miss Crawford does rather a fine piece of work," wrote one. "There is depth to her portrayal." Another observed that, "as one of the most admired of the new leading women, this is just about the first time that she has been permitted to be anything but statuesque and patrician." She brought her real-life alchemy of passion and vulnerability to the character, but her skill could not save the picture, about a turgid love triangle, a motif that was now a Crawford trademark. In addition, Rudolf Friml's original score was nowhere to be heard.

Her next two pictures had a similar story structure. In *Across to Singapore,* produced quickly in February, both Joan and Ramon Novarro were, as she said, woefully miscast. In *Four Walls,* which followed, she was a crook's gun moll, converted to righteousness by John Gilbert. The critics were impressed by this very different kind of role: her performance was "splendid," cooed *Variety,* and the *New York Evening World* reported that "she simply walks off with the picture, stealing it right from under the nose of John Gilbert . . . This will go a long way toward lifting Miss Crawford to a point nearer the top in Hollywood circles, a point toward which she has been rapidly climbing in the last year or two." That "top point"—the first of many in her long career—was reached in the next picture, which achieved a success no one at Metro anticipated.

Filming of *Our Dancing Daughters* began that spring—but after a few days, it continued without Joan. The reason for her delay in joining the cast was Metro's dramatic proposal that she submit to dental surgery, to adjust her jawline and to straighten, cap and replace a number of her teeth. This has always been a common beautifying procedure in Hollywood and elsewhere, and Joan Crawford was but one of many stars who underwent various operations for the sake of their careers. But in the 1920s, such surgeries carried significantly greater risk than they did many decades later. Her sojourns in hospitals, all paid for by Metro, were scheduled with more reference to the doctors' appointment books than the studio's production schedule. This explains why Joan's appearance varies in *Our Dancing Daughters.*

On its release, however, the picture made Joan Crawford the equal in star power to Greta Garbo at Metro-Goldwyn-Mayer. It also gave her an international prominence and respect she had not hitherto enjoyed; henceforth, all her pictures were easily marketed at healthy profits outside the United States.

The plot was concocted to exploit the wild lives of young people at the height of the Jazz Age—and therefore to entice that very same audience into theaters. "Dangerous Diana" Medford (Joan) is a wealthy, vibrant society girl—but she has neither the tarnished past of one friend (played by Dorothy Sebastian) nor the frank greed of another (Anita Page), who connives to steal Diana's boyfriend, Ben (John Mack Brown). After the avaricious girl becomes a faithless wife to this upright fellow, she falls down a flight of stairs in a drunken stupor and dies. Now Diana and Ben are free to live happily ever after.

The movie was made as a silent, but it was released with musical recordings that were distributed to theaters to accompany the scenes of Joan's Charlestons and Shimmies and for the sound effects of cheering and shrieking by the story's silly partygoers. There were also recordings of occasional bits of offscreen dialogue, but the movie had no all-talking sequences.

Needlessly complicated, shallow in characterization and lacking any sense of pacing, *Our Dancing Daughters* is important only for what it reveals about a performer who is both star and actress. She rose above the material with inventive, wordless wit, finding subtle body language and facial expressions to convey what the lack of spoken dialogue could not; and she made credible the personality of a girl who has no reason to suddenly emerge as almost heroically unselfish. Modest about her achievement, Joan said simply that the film was "about a way of life I knew as a flapper who shakes her windblown bob and dances herself into a frenzy, a girl drunk on her own youth and vitality . . . But it was a field day for me: the script department was told to write strictly for me, and the picture had good dancing, good comedy lines, [and I had] good support from Johnny Mack Brown and Nils Asther. I loved every minute of it."

So did the critics. The *New York Mirror,* for example, was not alone in proclaiming that Joan "does the finest work of her career." As *Time* magazine noted, a month after the movie's premiere that September, "Hundreds of young women [and their boyfriends] crowded the theaters where this picture was showing." Long lines formed and tickets were sold for standing-room patrons. Within a week of its release, Joan's name went up on the marquees. Her fan mail increased to thousands of letters each week, magazines and newspapers hounded the studio for interviews with her, and even she could not remain detached. "I drove around with a small box camera, taking pictures of 'Joan Crawford' in lights."

Her publicity continued with another news story that ran nationwide at exactly the same time as the picture's release. Douglas and Joan both issued announcements of their engagement, but they provided no date for the marriage. A year or two was added to his age and subtracted from hers when the proclamation was made.

On September 19, Douglas helped Joan move from her rented house at 513 North Roxbury Drive, Beverly Hills, to a new, larger residence fit for a movie queen. Located at 426 North Bristol Avenue, in the western sector of Los Angeles known as Brentwood, this was a lavish estate consisting of a rambling house of eighty-one hundred square feet, situated on a tract of land spacious enough for a pool and guesthouse. Then and later, this was not exceptional for the neighborhood; among many others, Bette Davis, Cole Porter and Tyrone Power had nearby residences that equaled or even surpassed Crawford's estate.

At the same time, Joan was busy at work, playing a gypsy girl who falls in love with a roguish prince, in a disappointing film called *Dream of Love,* based on a nineteenth-century French play by Scribe and Legouvé. She dismissed the finished movie as "another load of romantic slush"; as one New York critic observed, this was not "the right script material for such a fresh and vital actress."

The studio's on-set photographs of Joan, taken during the production of *Dream of Love* and reproduced in magazines and newspapers worldwide, surely helped attract the public, and much of this had to do with her costumes— from sultry gypsy outfits to exquisite evening dresses and ball gowns. For this movie, and for twenty-nine more Crawford films in the next dozen years, the designer Adrian was responsible for what she wore.

Adrian Adolph Greenburg, who changed his name to Gilbert Adrian and was known professionally simply as Adrian, was Metro's chief costume designer from 1928 to 1941. During that era, he was responsible for the on-screen image of hundreds, including Greta Garbo, Norma Shearer, Jean Harlow, Greer Garson, Katharine Hepburn, Hedy Lamarr, Judy Garland, Joan Crawford and Janet Gaynor (whom he married in 1939). He also designed much of Joan's personal wardrobe. "Adrian had a profound effect both on my professional life and personal life," Joan said later. "He taught me so much about drama. He said nothing must detract. Everything must be simple, simple, simple—just your face must emerge . . . [and] he was so expert that he never made me feel as though I was being used as a clothes-horse in the pictures."

———

THE PHOTOS AND THE news of Joan's success were particularly welcome to her family in Kansas. In October, her mother and brother wrote to her that they had decided to leave everything behind and live in sunny California. In early November, Hal and his new bride, Jessie, arrived at North Bristol Avenue, followed by Joan's mother two weeks later. "That's been quite a burden," Joan wrote to a friend on November 22, "getting a place for them to live, and getting my brother and his wife jobs."

Her family could not have arrived at a busier time in her life, as the letter explained: there were "thousands of exhibitors here at the studio having lunch, reporters from the four corners of the earth interviewing me, Mother's birthday this week, Thanksgiving, starting Christmas shopping, more lawsuits, signing new contracts, still getting my house furnished . . ."[1]

"If you can make it in the movies, with that funny face of yours and all

---

1. The exact meaning of "more lawsuits" is impossible to determine. Some have claimed that Joan was cited as the corespondent in several divorce cases, but there is no documentary evidence to support these assertions. The phrase probably refers to the protracted legal tangle over the auto accident described above.

those freckles," Hal said to Joan, "then I sure can." He had not worked more than a day or two in his life, and now he was twenty-five. But he thought his good looks augured a surefire career as a movie star.

"When sorrows come, they come not single spies but in battalions," according to Shakespeare. So it was for Joan, beginning that season. Hal drank, he often stayed out all night with Joan's car, which he scratched, dented and finally wrecked—and more than once, Joan awoke in the morning to find Jessie absent and some stranger sipping coffee at the kitchen table, after spending the night with Hal in his room.

She introduced her brother to the head of casting at Metro, but there was nothing for him until 1935, when he landed a job as an uncredited extra. After several months of this unpleasant intrusion, Joan found Hal and Jessie an apartment, paid the rent and hoped for some distance and peace. The following year, Hal began to complain that Jessie wanted an independent life; Jessie countered that Hal didn't like being a husband, which suggested all sorts of unspoken problems. They were divorced in August 1929, after less than a year of marriage.

"Hal was a parasite and a drunk, and he made my life miserable," Joan said many years after her brother's death. "For over thirty years, I supported those two free-loaders [Anna and Hal], and I can count on one hand the number of times they said 'Thank you.' Hal was chronically mean, and nothing lasted long—not his jobs, not the men and women in his life. Liquor, then drugs, and always his distorted ego, took over. I supported that son of a bitch until he died." Joan's daughter Christina saw Hal's decline for herself years later: "Mostly he seemed to be in constant trouble with women, with drugs and drinking, and finally with ill health. My mother bailed him out."

Joan's mother remained at North Bristol longer than Hal—until claims were made by several Los Angeles department stores where Anna (Joan recalled) "was spending money as if it were going out of style—hats, shoes, bags, clothes—she never showed me the bills, she just charged everything to my name and address—five hundred dollars at one place, four hundred at another . . ." Joan paid the stores, and then she found her mother a comfortable apartment; she also continued to provide support throughout her mother's long life.

"She was old and tired," Joan recalled years later, "but she was a good woman—even though she ignored me when I was a kid. She found life a lot easier during her last years. She was, you might say, intimidated by my friends, by anyone who was famous, and she preferred to stay out of the way. I let her live her own lifestyle, and that style included Hal. But I simply wouldn't have him around—so her loyalties had to have been divided."

Not long after Joan helped her mother move into an apartment, Anna legally changed her surname to Crawford.

CHAPTER FOUR

Enter the King
| 1929–1930 |

M ISS CRAWFORD IS as gorgeous as ever and offers a vivid performance," according to one newspaper critic, writing in early 1929. He was referring to *The Duke Steps Out,* Joan's assignment for late January and early February; in it, she was (as she said) only "background" for William Haines, who played a professional boxer in love with a California coed. Nevertheless, the picture made a fortune when it was released in March, and the two friends again received good notices.

Following that tedious exercise, Joan joined every major MGM player (except for Garbo, Novarro and Chaney, whose contracts excused them) for an appearance in *The Hollywood Revue of 1929.* This plotless musical was designed to outshine even *The Broadway Melody,* which Metro had released in early February—that was the studio's first all-talking picture and the first sound film to win an Academy Award as best picture.

Produced by Harry Rapf, *The Hollywood Revue* was devised to showcase Metro's talent roster. Not entirely on pitch, Joan sang a solo ("I've Got a Feeling for You"), and her dance number, filmed without cuts and released unedited, was a bit clunky. She was also included in the final sequence, which burst into Technicolor while Metro's stars crooned "Singin' in the Rain." For this number, everyone was outfitted in yellow slickers and drenched with a downpour of water; they seem by turns surprised, amused or annoyed with the inundation.

———

THAT SPRING, JOAN AND Douglas secretly finalized plans for a June wedding in New York City, where Anna Beth was living with her lover, Jack Whiting, a Broadway musical comedy performer. Because his mother had agreed to witness the nuptials, Doug could marry at the age of nineteen; Joan turned twenty-three in March.

Details of the forthcoming nuptials were not released to the press, and Joan had to ask permission to be absent from the studio: "It was Louis B. Mayer's rule," recalled the Metro contract player Pamela Blake, "that no one should leave town unless one had his say-so." This was duly granted, and then Mayer came up with the idea to cast the happy couple together in a movie—not a sequel to *Our Dancing Daughters,* but a movie made in the same spirit and style, about jazz babies speeding, drinking and dancing their way from party to party and affair to affair. The result, written and photographed hastily, was *Our Modern Maidens,* and Mayer decided to delay its release until late summer, the better to exploit the upcoming Crawford-Fairbanks wedding.

The picture was Joan's last silent film and her only one with Douglas. She thought it would be great fun to name her character "Billie" so that he would address her in the story as he did offscreen; the writer and director did not object. After the movie's opening quarter-hour montage of wild parties, the story gets down to its somewhat tired melodramatic business. Billie is engaged to Gil (Douglas), whose diplomatic career can be hurried along if she flirts with Abbot (Rod La Rocque), a man with good political connections. While she does so, Gil falls for a girl named Kentucky (Anita Page)—briefly but ardently, and with enough time to get her pregnant. The wedding of

Billie and Gil is interrupted by Kentucky's announcement of her imminent maternity, which gives Billie the chance to be brave and self-sacrificing— conduct for which she is eventually rewarded by being reunited with Abbot, a far better catch. Gil, of course, does what was once called The Right Thing and slinks away to marry Kentucky.

The protracted silliness of the movie nevertheless had its compensations during production. During one of the party sequences, Douglas was permitted to include his expert pantomimes of John Barrymore, Lon Chaney and John Gilbert—a skit that concludes with a hilarious imitation of his father as Robin Hood, complete with a feather in his cap. As for Joan, she was given ample opportunity to dance and even to join a jazz band, wielding her drumsticks like a pro.

The picture wrapped at the end of May, and Joan and Douglas left immediately for New York where, on the morning of June 3, they were married at Saint Malachy's Church, beloved of actors because of its location in the theater district. As promised, Anna Beth was present with Jack, who apparently found the happiness contagious: three weeks and three days later, they, too, were married.

Mr. and Mrs. Douglas Fairbanks Jr. quickly returned to work in Los Angeles, where reporters met their train in crushing numbers. The newlyweds were then invited to a very warm reception at Pickfair, where "Billie cried with relief," as Doug recalled.

On September 14, he accompanied Joan to Grauman's Chinese Theatre on Hollywood Boulevard, where, according to the hallowed movie-star tradition, she embedded her hand- and footprints in the stone court. "May this cement our friendship," she inscribed above her dated signature.

Douglas was not asked to do the same. "I had no particular desire to be a personality like my father," he said, "nor was I equipped to be one. I was determined to be my own man." So saying, he began rehearsals for a revival of Philip Barry's play *The Youngest*. Joan made herself a sort of volunteer theater attaché, carrying out the duties of box-office cashier for every evening performance, selling tickets and helping Douglas with his makeup. When word of her presence circulated, the play sold out, and the engagement at the Vine Street Theater had to be extended.

———

"NEITHER BILLIE NOR I had much opportunity to settle down in the conventional sense," Fairbanks recalled, "we both worked too hard and hectically . . . [and she] let nothing stop her admirable though humorless dedication to professional advancement. Never, before or since, have I known any other professional who expended more personal energy on self-improvement courses and on her relations with her fans and the press as did the girl known as Joan Crawford. She went to dance classes once or twice a week, took swimming lessons and daily exercises and massage. Her powers of concentration were immense."

For Joan, everything related to her career. "But I was interested in a wider variety of other people and things," said Doug—and this caused considerable tension between them—as did, for him, the fact that his salary was half of hers.

"He wasn't as ambitious as I was," according to Joan. "He had a dozen talents and indulged them all in his easygoing way, but he'd never had to fight his way up the way I had, and he had no taste for it. I wanted Douglas, but I wanted work, too, and the rest of the time with him. I took my work with deadly seriousness."

Joan certainly had to do just that for her next picture, *Untamed,* her first talkie. Because many film actors had poor diction, or voices that were too high or too low, or had accents they could not lose, a large number of them could not negotiate the new sound barrier and lost their jobs. At that anxious time, Metro engaged the noted Italian voice professor Mario Marafioti to help those with real or imagined problems. Having coached Enrico Caruso, Marafioti was in a good position to do the same for screen actors.

"I didn't know enough to be afraid," Joan said years later, but she did as instructed and made an appointment to see the professor.

When she told him that she wanted to learn how to speak for the movies, he handed her a copy of his book, *Caruso's Method of Voice Production: The Scientific Culture of the Voice.* "Read it, child," said the professor. "Study it."

Joan was puzzled. "Learn to talk from a book?"

"Study the book. *Then* we begin."

"But Dr. Marafioti—I start a talking picture tomorrow!"

He shrugged.

She politely said good-bye and never saw him again.

"So I just went and did *Untamed,* with Bob Montgomery"—the first of six films in which the pair costarred. (Coincidentally, Robert Montgomery was a great friend of Douglas Fairbanks Jr.'s.)

———

"BELOW THE EQUATOR'S PATH across South America, the Valley of Zoro lazes through sunswept days and awakens to welcome each tropic night with dance and song." With that florid opening title card, *Untamed* begins. Intertitles occur occasionally in this movie, which was also released as a silent for the benefit of the many theaters not yet equipped for sound.

Untamed is the unlikely story of Alice "Bingo" Dowling (Joan), who has been brought up in the tropical jungle and knows little of civilization—this we gather while watching Joan leap into a wild and sultry "savage dance." Soon her father dies in her arms (after the longest death scene since Mimi's in *La Bohème*). Bingo then learns that she is heiress to millions, earned from Daddy's oil prospecting in the tropics. Her uncles then decide she is "not yet housebroken" and needs a little polish, so they send her off to New York. On board ship, Bingo meets the handsome but impoverished Andy (Robert Montgomery), who honorably refuses to marry her because he's poor and she's terribly rich. What a guy.

Manhattan does grand things for Bingo, and before we know it, she has perfect diction and manners, wears a wardrobe designed by Adrian and sings beautifully while Andy plays the guitar or she plays piano. She also wins dance contests and soon has New York society in the palm of her hand. She finally wins Andy, who is given a job in the oil business and so will match her dollar for dollar. Joan's performance in *Untamed* was praised for her clear and unaffected voice, but the movie did little for anyone's career.

———

THE NEW YEAR 1930 began with a few weeks of free time, and so Joan and Douglas attended to some of the many tasks in the home he now shared with her on Bristol Avenue—"where everything had to be spotless all the time," as he recalled. Then and later, large residences in Hancock Park, Beverly Hills, Holmby Hills, Bel-Air, Brentwood and Pacific Palisades were built, enlarged, torn down and replaced in a lavish and often wacky mélange of styles inside and out.

The Crawford-Fairbanks house had, depending on which contemporary magazine article one trusted, ten or fourteen or seventeen or twenty-four rooms. Excluding the pool house and the later addition of a movie theater, the original residence seems to have consisted of twelve extraordinarily spacious rooms and four baths, including servants' quarters over the garage. An issue of *New Movie* magazine thus described the place:

The house, which they call "Cielito Lindo" or "Beautiful Little Heaven," is of Spanish architecture, white with a red tiled roof. It is set far back off a road that winds up into the green foothills. {There are} grilled doors, tiled borders, wrought iron stairways, artistic balconies and arched doorways. Cool pepper trees and tall palms supply shade, and there is a gaily-flowered patio. The interior furnishings are Early American, with rare old prints, Chippendale chairs, grandfather clocks, hooked rugs, Queen Anne chairs, Maplewood beds, curio racks, old glass, pewter bric-a-brac and Miss Crawford's collection of two thousand dolls . . .

The walls and beamed ceiling of the living room are finished dull white. The carpet is tan. The draperies are of brown glazed chintz and a flower design of tan, brown and red. In the dining room, white walls set off the apple green rug. Miss Crawford's bedroom has a great canopied bed with three hundred yards of antique rose taffeta. Her husband's bedroom is

of genuine maple, with every window valanced [sic] *in the same wood[1], and
there is a play-room {i.e., a den} furnished with black and white linoleum,
a gilded baby grand piano, a modernistic davenport, a victrola and radio,
all the latest novels, and a card table.*

Like the fictional Auntie Mame, Joan went through a dizzying array of
design and decorating styles. Previously, she had decorated the Beverly Hills
house in what she and Billy Haines later called "Cocktail Chinese" décor.
Then came Early American, followed by Italian Baroque. But with Billy's help,
things eventually settled down. She soon got rid of her massive doll collection,
softened the living room colors, replaced gaudy brocades with modern white
sofas and English antiques and chose Wedgwood blue for the accent color. The
"play-room" lost its black-and-white hospital appearance, and a white Steinway
grand replaced the old piano. The effect was eclectic, but basically the style
was eighteenth-century English.

———

AND SO, WHILE DECORATORS, painters and deliverymen labored that February of 1930, Joan worked on her next assignment, shot mostly in the
northern reaches of the San Fernando Valley. *Montana Moon* is certainly the
low point in her early career—a bundle of Western-movie clichés with an
impossible plot in which she plays Joan Prescott, an East Coast debutante
who travels to the wilderness, incautiously weds a real gosh-a-mighty cowboy (again, John Mack Brown, later Johnny Mack Brown) and then abandons him. On the way back to New York, she is overtaken by bandits and
saved by her husband, to whom she darn well happily returns. There are
also, incredibly, two Yiddish vaudevillians among the wranglers, and lots of

---

1. For many years, if one believed the American press, spacious houses provided separate
bedrooms for husband and wife, even if the couple (occasionally or always) used only one.
For publication, however, spouses always had to appear as if they were roommates, chastely
separated by walls.

cowboys baying at the eponymous moon. "It was awful," said Joan, and she was right.

Almost immediately, and doubtless with some relief, she started work on something more familiar. The characters in *Our Dancing Daughters* had grown up (but not much) to become *Our Modern Maidens,* so it was perhaps expected that they would turn into *Our Blushing Brides.* (That year, some wit asked if the next installment would be *Our Dizzy Divorcées.*)

As so often, the title bore no connection to the story of Jerry/Geraldine (Joan), Connie (Anita Page) and Frankie (Dorothy Sebastian), who dream romantically of the proverbial better future while sharing a cramped Manhattan apartment and working at tedious jobs. Alone among her roommates, Jerry is cool and sensible, rejecting the advances of Tony (her employer's son). Frankie marries a crook, while Connie leaps into bed with Tony's caddish brother, who abandons her, thus precipitating her suicide. At the somewhat damp finale, Tony and Gerry are duly united.

The highlight of *Our Blushing Brides* is a musical fashion show featuring Joan as a model and Adrian's designs as the wardrobe that every woman simply must have. This sequence, at the structural midpoint of the movie, suddenly turns the remaining action very grave indeed—themes of infidelity are introduced along with abandonment and suicide. It's hard to avoid feeling that after the wardrobe extravaganza, the writers and the director felt that they had to take seriously the fact that the Great Depression was at its peak.

Critics reserved their praise for Joan: "It would all be quite lamentable if it were not for the humorous and intelligent acting of Joan Crawford . . . She carries the burden of dramatics in this photoplay and comes off splendidly and intelligently." Even as the collapsing economy continued to affect lives all across America, people put down their nickels and dimes to see *Our Blushing Brides,* which cost $337,000 to produce and within weeks grossed more than $1.2 million.

Joan's appearance was memorable in this otherwise unremarkable movie—not least of all because of "her clever use of those huge saucer eyes," as Douglas said. "She knew how to use her makeup to carefully exploit her eyes, and she knew that if she held her head down and looked up, they seemed even larger."

But her talent went deeper than mascara and canny glances. Her performance in *Our Blushing Brides* was an important step forward in her career, and Mayer and company took notice. Joan had dropped her silent-screen mannerisms, and she credibly conveyed the character's emotional dilemmas and inner struggles with subtle expressions and small gestures; in fact, the picture may be the first full example of her effort to do less and imply more. "Joan Crawford displays a dramatic power and a fascination that overcomes all the little inconsistencies of plot and locale," wrote a Hollywood critic. "We all know that she can dance, sing and make whoopee, but she can also be serious and has great potentialities as a tragedienne. It is time that MGM gave her an opportunity for deeper characterizations." That time would come soon enough.

But first, Joan began work on a musical called *Great Day,* a production that was suddenly abandoned and forever shelved by Metro after important scenes had been filmed. It had not been successful on Broadway the previous year, but it had a few songs by Vincent Youmans that quickly became standards—among them, "Without a Song" and "More Than You Know." At the insistence of Thalberg, who conceived the movie as a lavish extravaganza that would improve on the stage version, Metro bought movie rights. The screenplay was finalized, and the casting, sets and wardrobe designs were completed. Publicity for *Great Day* began, too, and still photos were taken of the principal actors in full costume on several sets. After long and complicated rehearsals, filming began in July.

But Joan was horrified when she went to see the early "rushes," unedited scenes hurriedly developed for the review of a few executives and stars. "They were God-awful," she said, and ran at once to Mayer, who had left the entire production to Thalberg. "I am dreadful," she told Mayer. He went to see for himself. Whether in fact her performance was as frightful as she claimed can never be confirmed, but after he sat through some of the scenes, Mayer put through a call to Joan: "You're right—stay home." On his order, the production was at once shut down, and except for a few photos, all traces of *Great Day* vanished forever from Metro's archives (including the processed film, negatives and all documentation). This represented a studio loss of almost three hundred thousand dollars (over $4 million in 2010 valuation).

The true reason for Mayer's drastic action may not have had to do with Joan's performance, but with the picture's bloated budget, which was increasing daily—a situation that Mayer had already complained about to Thalberg. Joan's displeasure occurred at just the right time, for now Mayer had his chance to bring the boy wonder down to earth from his high perch.[2] As for Joan, she was (at least outwardly) placid about the whole affair, not to say sanguine. "The time had come to move forward," she recalled. "I wanted to be a serious dramatic actress. I'd proved I could play the dancing girl I'd once been, and so I told Mr. Mayer, 'Now let's have something new!' "

———

BEFORE THAT COULD HAPPEN, Joan took advantage of a rare hiatus, and she and Douglas repaired to a luxury resort known as the Norconian Club, three hundred fifty miles outside Los Angeles. When they returned home, she continued her redecorating chores and interviewed potential servants. "Douglas had been reared in style," she recalled, "but I had not. I came from a poor family, and I came up the hard way. It was Douglas who taught me graciousness and introduced me to a way of life I had never known before, with servants and cars and secretaries."

Some of her education in this new way of life also derived from visits that year to her in-laws at Pickfair, to which the young couple were now more regularly invited for Sunday luncheons and pool parties. "I was out to tear up the world in the fastest, brashest, quickest way possible. And then I saw myself through the Pickfair eyes, and every last bit of my self-confidence dropped away from me. Shyness overwhelmed me, and I got a terrific inferiority complex. Immediately, I set out to change myself in every way." Thus began Joan's

---

2. For a fascinating essay about the abandonment of *Great Day,* see www.legendaryjoancrawford.com/greatday/html.

transformation to society doyenne, a self-imposed metamorphosis sustained with her usual single-minded energy.

She longed to be regarded as the proper companion for her wellborn husband and more than merely tolerated as a daughter-in-law. And so she emulated Douglas's every refinement. She studied French, engaged a vocal coach and learned opera arias, she learned to dress with better taste, and she toned down her hair color from its natural bright red to a sedate chestnut brown. She also read voraciously, picking up a book whenever she had a quarter hour to herself at home: the Romantic poets, the classics, history, the nineteenth-century novelists, Shakespeare, H. G. Wells and more.

All this effort to pursue what Douglas called her "self-improvement courses" was done with absolute seriousness. Vincent Sherman, one of her later directors and lovers, understood that after her marriage to Douglas, "she wanted to develop herself artistically and culturally. She was looking for identity, dignity and importance—and a more serious life."

As word of the "new" Joan Crawford circulated and changes became visible in her appearance and audible in her conversation, she found to her disappointment that everything she did was counted as loss. In her early days in Hollywood, the gossips dismissed her as merely a hey-hey girl from the provinces; now that she was discussing literature and the arts, she was called high-hat. When Joan chatted with the crews at the studio, people said she was posing and accused her of currying favor; now that she conversed with visitors like conductor Leopold Stokowski or Lord Louis Mountbatten, she was tagged as a snob.

In these circumstances, she simply could not win, and eventually she stopped trying to convince people that she was at heart a woman who took life, like her career, seriously. Like many celebrities, she began to find it difficult to trust others and so did not make friends easily. In this regard, it is easy to understand why she often doubted people's motives: did they like her for herself or for the cachet attached to her name and fame?

Fairbanks admired and was encouraged by his wife's intellectual, cultural and social ambition, by her wide tastes and interests, by her acceptance of people on their merits and not their social standing and, perhaps most of all, by her admiration for him.

One of the things that pleased me so much about Billie was her estimation of me. Everything I did and said, everything I suggested and recommended she received with attention and respect. Besides that, a part of her always depended on me. Whenever we were out in a crowd, she clung to me like a frightened child. People did not know that Billie was really a terribly vulnerable person, all during her life. A lot of her so-called toughness was part of the pose, part of being "Joan Crawford." Only when she clung to me and I held her, protecting her from the crowds she never trusted, could she stop shivering with fear.

When we went up to Pickfair to visit my father and stepmother, he did not really have contempt for her—she was convinced that he did, and she was sure he rejected her because she was from the wrong side of the tracks, so to speak. No, what my father really resented was that the public now knew that he was old enough to have a married son and even to become a grandfather. Mary {Pickford} didn't share that resentment, and in fact she became a very important influence in my father's progressively warmer attitude toward Billie and me.

During the Crawford-Fairbanks marriage, there was a moment Joan never forgot—and it came from her father-in-law. One afternoon at Pickfair there was a discussion about acting in silent movies versus talkies. There was a long pause, and then Douglas Fairbanks Sr. said quietly, "Feelings are for silent pictures—thoughts are for the talkies."

This was perhaps the single most important aphorism Joan Crawford took to heart for the refinement of her craft, and she thought the statement was worth years of formal dramatic training. Indeed, it expressed and confirmed what she had begun to practice, perhaps without awareness, in *Our Blushing Brides*. From this remark, she began to understand that the open, often grand gestures of silent pictures, once taken for granted, were meant to express feelings *in the absence of dialogue*—but that in movies *with* sound, it was important to convey thoughts visually rather than to rely on words. With the subtlest reactions, the blink of an eye, the lift of a brow, a tilt of the head, a slight movement of the lip or a finger, so much could be conveyed—partially by means of the judicious close-up, but mostly through the skill and sensitivity of a gifted motion picture actor who understood that, in the movies, less is more.

———

JOAN WAS ALWAYS HONEST (and sometimes too generous) in assigning credit for her successes to directors, and especially to Mayer and his colleagues, of whom she said, "They took me out of the chorus line and made me a star, with all the money and preferential treatment that went with that magic word 'star.' And when I decided that I could actually become a serious actress, they tried their damndest to make me one. They helped me with coaching and had the guts to give me good, demanding parts."

That kind of challenge, that longing to be "a serious actress in something new," as she said, finally came with her next project—a dark and complex movie called *Paid*. Her role had at first been given to Norma Shearer, who became pregnant just as filming began; Thalberg then insisted that his wife stop work until the baby's birth. "*Paid* was my first really heavy dramatic role," Joan recalled, "and I did a good job—a damned good job, thanks to Sam Wood [her director] and a script by Charlie MacArthur." This was the third (and not the last) filmed version of the successful 1912 Broadway play *Within the Law*.

However one assesses Shearer's talents, it's virtually impossible to imagine her in the role of the brooding, furious and finally redeemed Mary Turner, a shop clerk sent for three years to prison for a theft she did not commit. Vowing vengeance, she is released, joins a band of thugs and almost fulfills her promise by hatching all sorts of nefarious schemes. But she is, of course, converted by the love of a good man—and saved from a life of desperation and crime by the memory that she had vowed never to return to jail.

This was a character and a performance unlike any Joan had previously played. "If I have to do one more of those three-girl, dancing-daughter stories, I'll kick somebody," she said at the time. "I like the drab. I like to play human beings in the gutter." *Paid* gave her just that opportunity.

She affected a haunted appearance, at first dry-mouthed and fearful when introduced to the dangers and consequences of prison life—particularly in the provocative scene in a communal shower and later, in the company of crooks. Joan's performance more than carried the film: she lifted it above clichés to the point of almost unbearable pathos. This was a multileveled portrait, unerringly right, never overstated but always restrained. Her glances communicate her feelings; her voice is always on a pitch proper for the moment.

Shot in only thirty-one days, *Paid* demonstrates that Joan could indeed, as she hoped, "be a serious dramatic actress," and this was her "something new." *Time* magazine, usually not so enthusiastic about her, summed up the general critical response: "Joan Crawford can hold her own with any of Metro-Goldwyn-Mayer's other actresses, including Greta Garbo." The picture contributed vast sums to Metro's accounts, and Joan received an envelope from Mayer: "In appreciation of the cooperation and excellent services rendered by you, we take great pleasure in handing you a check in the amount of $10,000." This bonus, Mayer added, was in addition to the salary stipulated by her contract (then two thousand dollars per week).

No such good fortune attended one of Joan's costars, Marie Prevost, who had been a Mack Sennett bathing beauty before she undertook a series of light comedies and melodramas. Marie's sense of humor lightened several bleak moments during the production of *Paid,* and her performance as another jailbird was funny, disturbing and affecting. She continued to work for a few years, but producers—failing to appreciate her gift for mimicry and low comedy—told her that she ought to lose weight (although she was far from obese).

Depressed, Marie dieted mostly on alcohol. Eventually, she could not find work, and soon she was living in dire poverty. When Joan learned of her predicament, she tried to help, sending regular checks and sometimes delivering them in person. In 1937 Marie died alone in a derelict room in a seedy part of Hollywood. Her death was due to acute alcoholism and malnutrition, and her body was not discovered for several days, after neighbors had complained about the constant barking of her pet dachshund. Marie Prevost was thirty-eight years old.

———

DURING THE FILMING OF *Paid,* Joan continued to improve her acting skills. She began to study an entire script, not only her part—"in order to learn the overall story, and particularly my evolution as a character in relation to that story. I changed from A to B to C as the film progressed for the audience, but as far as the shooting schedule was concerned, I had to be A on Monday, D on Tuesday, B on Wednesday and so forth. So there I was, mini-talented and scared, but determined to make it—so I worked hard."

By the time *Paid* was released—oddly, during Christmas week 1930—Joan had also completed work on *Dance, Fools, Dance,* a far more violent movie than its irrelevant title suggests. Produced in November and December at a cost of $289,000, the immediate box office receipts were over $900,000. (No wonder that Joan was Mayer's house special: her pictures essentially paid for the more expensive Garbo and Shearer productions.) Directed by Harry Beaumont, who had worked on four Crawford pictures and would direct two more, *Dance, Fools, Dance* is an important film from several viewpoints and warrants detailed consideration—not least because it was the first of eight films in which Joan's costar was Clark Gable.

Gable had appeared in seventeen movies, mostly as an uncredited extra or in minor parts. But his career now seemed stalled and his prospects hindered by virtual anonymity, and roles in three short-lived Broadway plays from 1928 to early 1930 did not help. At twenty-nine, he had just been divorced from his first wife; he would soon marry the second of five, this one the wealthy daughter of a Texas millionaire. In *Dance, Fools, Dance,* Gable at last landed a significant supporting role, while Joan had sole billing above the title.

She also contributed to the development of the story and final screenplay. Writer Aurania Rouverol had no trouble with the two opening sequences. But on the production's rushed schedule, she found it impossible to transform her own story into a movie, and to write credible and engaging dialogue. She needed help, and Joan—with more than thirty movies behind her—was willing and able. In fact the script of *Dance, Fools, Dance* owes almost everything to her.

———

THE MOVIE OPENS ON a private pleasure schooner, and at once Joan, as the spoiled socialite Bonnie Jordan, sings and dances for a full four minutes ("Oh, he is a gay caballero . . ."). Surrounded by her rich young friends, she then whines, "If something doesn't happen soon, I'll die." Well, she need not go that far: a young man calls out, "All right, everybody—stand by, and off with your clothes." That's the cue for dozens of pleasure-seekers to strip to their underwear and dive into the water. Later, Bonnie's equally rich boyfriend, Bob (Lester Vail), goes to her cabin and proposes marriage, but she is diffident: "I believe in trying love out—on approval." The moonlight swim sequence and this kind of dialogue could never occur in a Hollywood movie four years later, when the stringencies of the Production Code and its concomitant censorship went into effect.

The holidaymakers return home to their mansions and their waiting servants in Chicago. It's the autumn of 1929, and Bonnie and her brother, Roddy (William Bakewell), are idle and rich—infallible signs of this are her chain-smoking and his bootleg whiskey, even in the era of Prohibition. Moments later, their fabulously wealthy father, on whom they depend for everything, drops down dead after learning that the stock market collapse has wiped him out. Bonnie and Roddy are now completely penniless, and their lawyer tells them they will survive only by going out and getting jobs. Boyfriend Bob enters to offer his condolences when he learns of Bonnie's financial predicament, and he offers "to do the right thing"—which means, of course, that he will marry her because they have been lovers.

But Bonnie wants her independence, and she is willing to face the world and find work: "I'm going out to get myself a man-sized job. I'm not afraid! You'd be surprised what she can earn when a young girl sets her mind to it." Roddy, on the other hand, is a shiftless idler for whom *work* is only a four-letter word; he prefers to start drinking at breakfast and remains in an alcoholic haze throughout the day and evening. It would be fine with him if Bonnie became the full-time breadwinner.

Dirt-poor but plucky and resourceful, she lands a job as a newspaper reporter and is soon appreciated for her hard work and good humor. "You don't know the thrill of making it on your own," she tells her brother in the cramped flat they now share, "and I don't mean by trading on your name and running to parties all the time."

"I'm on the verge of big money," Roddy replies, "and I'll soon have you running around with the old crowd again." He fails to add that his money comes from bootleg whiskey, and that he will soon be linked to a notorious gang of crooks. At this point, Joan's hand in the development of the script, and specifically of Roddy's character, is clear: Roddy became only a slightly fictionalized version of Joan's own brother, Hal, to whom William Bakewell bears a striking physical resemblance.

"Run around with the old crowd?" Bonnie asks. "I'm not sure I want to run around with the old crowd again."

"Why not?"

At this point, Bonnie answers for herself—and for Joan Crawford: "I used to think anything I did was all right. I was Bonnie Jordan—*in society*. Society! What is it but a lot of people who are for you when you're on the up and up, but what would one of them do for you when it came to a showdown? Nothing! It isn't *who* you are, Roddy, but *what* you are that counts!"

Unknown to Bonnie, Roddy now goes off to make his fortune with a gang of criminals headed by the notorious Jake Luva (Gable, without a mustache), who uses his fancy nightclub as a front. Roddy is accepted into Jake's mob because of his social connections and does very well selling liquor illegally. At the same time, Bonnie is assigned to cover the rackets in a series of stories for the newspaper.

The second act of the movie now begins, as Jake's cronies murder members of a rival gang. "Seven mowed down with machine guns in a garage!" cries the paper's editor—an obvious reference to the real-life Saint Valentine's

Day massacre the previous year, when seven men were gunned down in a Chicago garage. This scene at the news headquarters is clearly critical of the media frenzy to get big stories with pictures—the more violence and blood, the better for selling daily papers.

Roddy is in shock: he drove the getaway car for the Luva gang and is sickened that his job has led to murder. He then talks too much with a visitor to Jake's club, unaware that the man is none other than a reporter, Bert (Cliff Edwards), Bonnie's colleague at the newspaper. Luva orders Roddy to kill the reporter—which he does in order to save himself.

The police are after Bert's killer, but the newspaper wants to track him down first: "Nobody knows the Jordan girl is working on our paper—and they'll never suspect a girl!" says the editor, sending Bonnie to infiltrate the mob and smoke out the killer. And so Bonnie goes undercover, assumes a false name and becomes a dancer at Luva's club.

But Jake falls for Bonnie. "You're going to have a little supper with me tonight—up in my room," he whispers to her seductively as they dance. "We've got to get better acquainted."

"I'd love it—I'll go and dress now," she replies, as both of them smile knowingly.

"Don't be too long," he says—and then Gable bluntly draws Crawford toward him, hip-to-hip, groin-to-groin. She was obviously not expecting this bold sexual advance, for she tries to conceal a grin of surprise and mild shock—and glances toward the director and cameraman, expecting to hear "Cut!" But the film kept rolling.

When Bob recognizes her at the club, Bonnie tries to throw him off the track: "I'm just a cheap little dancer in a nightclub." He departs, and when the phone rings in Jake's private apartment, Bonnie answers and recognizes Roddy's voice. What can she do about him, now that she knows her brother killed Bert? She sneaks away from Jake and confronts Roddy, who admits his crimes.

The third act begins as Jake and his gang discover the truth about Bonnie and threaten to kill her and her brother. There's a shoot-out that leaves Jake and his henchmen dead and Roddy dying in his sister's arms as she chokes back her sobs. She then calls the newspaper and reveals the truth. At the end, Bonnie quits her job and welcomes back boyfriend Bob, with whom she dashes away.

Dance, Fools, Dance remains one of the best early sound movies made in Hollywood before Motion Picture Code censors took out their pencils and scissors. Lacking the extreme ugliness of the Warner cycle of crime thrillers like *The Public Enemy* and *Little Caesar,* it was crisply directed, convincingly designed, economically paced and expertly acted—and it has lost little of its impact with the passing of time.

Joan had mastered the full range of emotions for a character that is variously an idle socialite, a career woman and a betrayed sister, and her appearance and performance indicated that she was a modern American woman who could endure and overcome crisis after crisis. There was good reason, after *Dance, Fools, Dance* was released in February 1930, for the American public to vote her its most popular actress that year, and she remained in the top ten annually until 1936.

Her glow of sexual availability and her neatly tailored wardrobe do not isolate Joan as Bonnie from the "ordinariness" of Depression-era America—and that was the difference between Crawford and Garbo, and between Crawford and Shearer. Somehow these other women seemed to be in a world apart, glamorous and remote no matter what their roles. Joan, on the other hand, was working from the interior, from her own experience, and here she had a character she understood.

At that time, there was no "Method" style of drama, nor was there any mainstream or prevalent school of acting with exercises on which she might have drawn. Without coaches or classes, Joan simply went from project to project, doing the truth of things rather than analyzing her way through them. At the age of twenty-four, she already knew a great deal about raw life—and about refined life, too. With experience and feelings, however formative, jumbled and conflicted, she somehow realized that she could use just about everything and everyone to improve her talents, and that her talents might become art. Nothing was more important to her than her career, and her will to maintain it would in time become both her blessing and her curse.

CHAPTER FIVE

Virtuous Vices

| 1931–1932 |

THERE WAS SOMETHING desperate about the production of *Laughing Sinners* from day one. At times it seemed to the cast that it was almost cursed, which was a very strange feeling to have when the movie was supposed to celebrate good old-fashioned American religious frenzy.

Metro had purchased movie rights to Kenyon Nicholson's play *Torch Song*, which had nothing to do with the 1953 Crawford picture with the same title. It had been a failure on Broadway, but the studio needed product, and so *Torch Song* was exported to Hollywood and became Joan's next assignment; filming began in early February 1931. Her costar, as the man who saves a girl thrown away by a traveling salesman, was again John Mack Brown.

The picture began as *Torch Song* but was soon rechristened *Complete Surrender,* which implied something both criminal and erotic (or at least romantic). But the title was the least of their problems, for things began badly and turned even worse. During the first week of filming, Joan was singing "Brighten the Corner Where You Are," in a scene designed to provide moral uplift, when suddenly, a thirty-nine-year-old supporting actor named Norman

Phillips collapsed at her feet and was pronounced dead. After a moment of silence and the removal of the body, the show went on. But halfway through production, Mayer and his colleagues realized that they had a major failure on their corporate hands. The story was trite and humorless; Joan's dyed blond hair was badly lighted in almost every sequence; the sound was muddy; and Brown's scenes with Joan looked like *tableaux vivants.* Brown was an attractive and cooperative fellow, but unfortunately he was not a gifted actor, and, except when cast in cowboy roles (which he loved), he seemed like a very handsome cigar-store Indian.

Joan's previous movie had just been released nationwide, and distributors now had firm booking dates for her next. What to do? Mayer insisted that Brown would have to go, and Joan hastened to the rescue: she would be willing to work overtime and weekends with a replacement—so why not Clark Gable, whom audiences and critics liked in *Dance, Fools, Dance?* Rearrangements were made in record time, and the movie's title was changed again, to *Laughing Sinners.* But nothing helped. The story and screenplay were still creaky to the point of collapse; Joan's hair was blond in some scenes and dark brown in others; plausible emotions were absent, and facile sentimentality abounded; and poor Gable, still far from his tenure as the confident, controlling romantic hero of his later movies, was literally unbelievable as the earnest savior of woebegone women. "He seems slightly puzzled to find himself banging a Salvation Army drum," as *Time* put it.

Only Joan triumphed. "Miss Crawford has seldom looked so radiantly alive and beautiful," wrote Andre Sennwald in the *New York Times,* adding that she had replaced the overly intense and self-conscious quality of some earlier performances with "a vibrant and breath-catching spirit." Neil Hamilton, in the role of the unctuous traveling salesman who tosses her aside in favor of the boss's daughter, explained Joan's success despite the failure of *Laughing Sinners:* "Regardless of the script, she invested everyone else in the picture with that same sense of responsibility—to make a film that was as good as it could possibly be. I have never known anyone who works so hard on a performance, to bring it up to its highest level, or who was more conscientious about her acting. It wasn't just about stardom with Joan—she wanted to be good, she wanted the picture to be good, and she wanted you to be good, too."

For her, the most memorable element of *Laughing Sinners* was her costar: "I hit off a few sparks, on screen and off, with an up-and-coming young actor named Clark Gable." Soon after, the sparks burst into flame.

———

AS CAMERAMEN AND DIRECTORS came to realize, blondes photographed brilliantly against dark backgrounds, and that year, Metro's publicists reported that audiences reacted more than favorably to women like Jean Harlow, Carole Lombard and Constance Bennett. And so the stoppers again came off the bottles of dye for Crawford's next picture, *This Modern Age*.

Joan was cast in the role of Valentine Winters. She travels from New York to Paris in search of her estranged mother, Diane (Pauline Frederick)—who is not, as presumed, a wealthy society doyenne but rather a kept woman, living in her lover's mansion. Shocked at first, Val soon becomes part of a fast set and is courted by a dissolute young alcoholic rake named Tony (Monroe Owsley). He tries to make love to her but is rejected: "In Spain," she says languorously, "they call that baloney." Val learns to drink and smoke, to race around Paris in grand "driving machines" and to wear Adrian's slinky wardrobe with easy grace. "Make virtue out of vice," she muses dreamily. "Never take anything seriously, and always be amusing." With that kind of talk, we know she is in for a comeuppance.

A more honorable young fellow then appears—Bob (Neil Hamilton)—but his impossibly stuffy parents cause trouble. The usual complications, conflicts and confessions occur, and Bob finally tracks down Val and whisks her away from boozy Tony—after the happy reconciliation of mother and daughter.

The movie, alas, has neither center nor focus. Was it planned as a romantic comedy and then refashioned into a morality tract? Either way, *This Modern Age* was certainly no highlight of the early Crawford years, and her performance had a rare quality of inattentiveness, as if she felt unwell in some scenes. As she recalled years later, "There were many times when I said, 'I was just lousy in that—I wish I could do the whole thing over!' "

———

IF JOAN WAS INDEED tense and preoccupied during most of 1931, as she seemed to Doug and some colleagues, she certainly had reasons.

For one thing, her agent encountered difficulties in finalizing her contract renewal, and for some time she feared that she might be dropped from Metro's roster. The parties finally came to terms, and Joan signed for three thousand dollars a week, with raises scheduled so that, by 1936, she would receive three times that amount—which made her one of the top dozen wage earners in the United States.

But her troubles were not over when the financial issues were settled. Joan's brother, Hal, continued his louche life and irresponsible antics—very like the character Tony in *This Modern Age,* except that Hal had no money and always depended on Joan. After his divorce from Jessie, he met Joan's light-ing stand-in at Metro, a Texas firebrand named Kasha Haroldi, who aspired to stardom; after a stormy courtship, she and Hal were married on September 6 that year—an event that Joan hoped would bring some stability to her brother's life. Hal's behavior could bring Joan undesirable negative publicity, and Louis B. Mayer regularly reminded her that a good family image was indispensable for the studio's stars.

A third reason for Joan's anxiety had to do with the shifting fortunes of her marriage, which after two years showed signs of unraveling. About her career, she was single-minded, and nothing took precedence over it. But in her constant attempts to guide and control her fame, she was unwittingly becom-ing its servant—and sometimes its slave.

Doug, on the other hand, had many outside interests and sources of diver-sion, not to say of pleasure. He liked to read, paint and write, and he readily accepted invitations from friends for weekend parties or brief excursions. On such occasions, the predictable occurred. "I take no pride in admitting that I was not true to Billie," he said years later, "and unfortunately she found out.

We had married when we were very young, and I was still very curious and surrounded by temptation. There were a lot of incidents when I did not resist."

That year, Laurence Olivier and his wife, Jill Esmond, had come from London to work in Hollywood. Doug and Larry became fast friends and frequently toured Hollywood's most exotic nightspots. One such place was the Russian Club, where they were seen carousing with the balalaika players, clinking endless glasses of iced vodka with strangers and vowing to restore the Romanoffs to the Russian throne. One night, a vaudeville performer they had seen at Grauman's Chinese Theatre offered them cocaine, and in a reckless moment they accepted—once only, they swore, finding it a very unpleasant and disorienting experience.

Coincidentally, the Olivier marriage was in a precarious situation, too— for reasons arising from Olivier's ego and Jill's fundamental ambivalence about heterosexual marriage. (Despite her expressed outrage when Olivier abandoned her for Vivien Leigh, Jill Esmond later settled down and lived happily ever after with a female companion.)

"It was a wild, wild place in those days," Olivier said of Hollywood in 1931, where he spent long nights away from his wife and in the company of actresses like Lili Damita or Elissa Landi. "And Bob Montgomery, Doug Fairbanks and I were the wildest." That summer, Doug told Larry that a rich and beautiful woman had fallen in love with him and had asked Doug to do the introductions. This was a practical joke: Doug knew no such woman, but he engaged a studio extra to join Larry for a drink. When the couple met, however, a genuinely fervent attraction occurred. Doug, continuing the prank, then arranged for their assignation at the home of a cooperative friend. When Doug was certain that Larry and the extra had settled in for the night, he signaled a burly stuntman he had also hired, who burst in on the couple, shouting, "What are you doing with my wife?" Olivier promptly keeled over in a faint.

Follies like this continued all that summer of 1931, while Joan was feverishly exploiting an interval from work to further decorate her home, improve her French and spend long hours with her vocal coach. Meantime, Doug and

Bob Montgomery chartered a yacht for a fishing weekend near Mazatlàn, Mexico, where more mischief was planned. When Larry arrived, he was greeted by grim, armed soldiers and hustled off to the local jail. Thinking they expected a bribe, Olivier tried to explain that he had no cash. After several anxious hours, Doug turned up, explained that he had invented this jolly caper with the assistance of a Mexican magistrate and spirited Larry away to catch marlin. Young Mexican ladies were never far from their yacht.

"I fought to keep my marriage going," said Joan of this time.

> *I remember the time an actor who was supposedly a great friend of mine {perhaps Robert Montgomery or Laurence Olivier} kept pumping such verbal rubbish in my husband's ear as, "I know some really cute girls over at the studio."*
>
> *This actor proceeded to get my husband drunk, and they went out on a double date. I got wind of the fact, but I wasn't worried about the actor—I was worried about my husband. After all, the girl in question might have blackmailed him or involved us in a pretty huge scandal. I found my husband with this cutie, {and} I took him home and sobered him up. He was apologetic and grateful. I myself was terribly hurt, but by holding on and fighting, I saved our marriage—at least for a while.*

The fourth and perhaps the most compelling reason for Joan's apparent and occasional apprehension that year can be summarized in three words: *Clark Gable* and *Possessed*—the title of their third collaboration within a year, and the movie that changed their lives forever.

———

"HE WAS, I THINK, a genius who really became appreciated properly only after Thalberg shook things up and convinced Louis B. that the director could be a creative asset, not just the man who kept the budget down and the picture on schedule."

Joan was speaking of her director on *Possessed*, Clarence Brown, who by

1931 had already directed over twenty pictures (three starring Garbo) and would work on four more with Joan. "He helped me so much," she continued, and "I think he helped all the actors in his films. He made you 'right' and convinced you that you *were* 'right,' and he picked up on subtle things the producers missed entirely. At Metro, I think he was the first director to leave his stamp on a picture, and most of us recognized this, but we were afraid to say so out loud, because the producer's ego wouldn't stand it."

Like many successful movies of that time, *Possessed* was based on a hit play—in this case, Edgar Selwyn's *The Mirage* (1920) and a silent-screen version of it—but now it had the added advantage of an exquisitely crafted screenplay by Lenore Coffee. In no more than seventy-five economical minutes, the movie tells the story of Marian Martin (Joan), a poor, small-town girl working in a paper-box factory, who aspires to much more than her situation provides.

For decades before the average age of moviegoers dropped below sixteen, it was a fact proved by polls, studies, interviews and surveys that American women overwhelmingly determined which motion pictures couples and families paid to see, and therefore which were box-office hits. *Possessed* struck a powerful, responsive chord among Depression-era women of 1931, deprived of prospects and caught in frightening economic circumstances. On their neighborhood screens was Joan Crawford—sensual yet strong-willed, vulnerable but determined, and willing, as Marian says, "to use whatever men find attractive about me" to succeed.

In a way, Marian Martin *was* Joan Crawford. Her natural hair color was restored for *Possessed,* a picture that curiously but clearly parallels her own ascent from deprivation to prosperity. Like Marian, Joan "belonged" to no one: she rose by sheer force of will, and women in her audience found something important in that for them and for their lives. It wasn't so much about greed, sexual enslavement or upper-class prostitution; it was about hope, possibility and determination—and, at the final fade-out, about redeeming love. *Possessed* is not merely a movie with a pretty face.

This entire complex reality comes together in a moment of sheer, wordless movie magic, superbly created by Clarence Brown and his cinematographer,

Oliver Marsh. Trying to cross over from "the wrong side of the tracks" in her small town, Marian is delayed by a passing train. From the platform, she watches in wide-eyed wonder as the passenger cars move by, each window revealing—like a movie screen—the actions and very different lives of the people within, "on the other side" of life as Marian knows it.

First, she sees cooks preparing a fine meal in the train's kitchen. In the next car, a waiter sets an elegant dining table. Then she watches as a uniformed maid irons a woman's silk lingerie—and then, in the next car, a lady takes up her silk stockings while her husband shaves in a private bathroom behind translucent glass. Next, a couple in evening dress dances languidly— and so the train passes. All this is shown without dialogue, as the movie simply presents a montage of Marian's hopes and fantasies, projected onto the lives of others who came from elsewhere and were heading to a better place of which she could only dream. *Possessed* was a motion picture made by adults, for adults and with adults.

Weary of her dead-end circumstances, Marian tells her swaggering sometime boyfriend, "You don't own me—nobody does! My life belongs to me!" She then turns to her impoverished, careworn mother: "If I were a man, you'd think it would be right for me to go out and get anything I could out of life and use anything I had to get it. Why should men be so different? All they've got is their brains, and they're not afraid to use them. Well, neither am I."

Marian goes to New York, where in a moment of happy accident, she meets a wealthy, divorced lawyer named Mark Whitney (Gable), who vows never to risk a broken heart again in marriage. "I left school when I was twelve," she says, apologizing for herself. But Mark transforms naive, unpolished Marian into a sleek, bejeweled Manhattan sophisticate, setting her up as his mistress in high style and creating for her a false identity as "the widowed Mrs. Moreland." But she is more than his mistress: they are completely devoted to each other, and after three years they are still committed to their passionate relationship.

But things change. Bravely and unselfishly, Marian quits her life with Mark when she learns that she would be a liability to his political aspirations. Trying to save his feelings, she pretends that she has been nothing but a heartless adventuress after all: "Inside, I'm still exactly what I was when you met me—a factory girl, smelling of sweat and glue—common! That's what I am—*common*—and I like it."

Before filming began on September 21, Joan asked to meet with Lenore Coffee. Joan had read the screenplay and recognized that, whether Lenore knew it or not, Marian's story was Joan's, and she wanted to elaborate the fine points for the writer's benefit. In this regard, it is crucial to recall that Joan Crawford never pretended to be anything but a small-town girl, uneducated, rough and untutored, whose good fortunes were handed to her by Metro-Goldwyn-Mayer. "They gave me everything I had," she said more than once. "I came from nothing, but Hollywood took me from nothing and gave me everything good that I've learned and that I have. And I will always be grateful for that. I could have done nothing on my own."

WITH MARIAN GONE FROM Mark's life, he turns to politics. But trouble emerges in the form of Mark's rivals, eager to sabotage his career as potential governor by spreading the scandal of his earlier private life with the notorious Mrs. Moreland. Marian, who now considers herself a doomed outcast in any case, saves the day. In a torrential rainstorm, she makes her way to a massive rally for Mark and, when he is challenged about "Mrs. Moreland," she interrupts his accusers and rises to address the crowd: "I am 'Mrs. Moreland.' I was in his life once, but I'm not any more. He belongs to all of you who are here tonight . . . Was he a murderer, a thief or a liar? No, worse—he loved a woman and she loved him—but now Mark Whitney belongs to you. Keep him!"

Trying to hide her sobs, she dashes out into the rain, toward the city train station—thus closing the story's circular structure. Mark races to join her, and as the rain drenches them, he embraces her protectively: "I don't care what they do to me back there," he says. "If I win, it'll be with you. And if I lose, it'll still be with you." So ends *Possessed,* a far more emotionally appealing and visually convincing story than a summary can convey. "Miss Crawford adds another excellent performance to her list," according to one major critic. "It's the best work she has done since *Paid*," noted another.

Remarkably often it has been claimed that Joan Crawford's popularity and stardom in the 1930s were based on her repeated assumption of roles as a poor shop-girl who rises to "make good" in a man's world. That view is more than a simplification—it is downright inaccurate. Twenty-five Crawford films were released during the 1930s, but she portrayed a store clerk in only two (*Our Blushing Brides* and *The Women*). Her career was defined by the creation of a far greater diversity of characters than is commonly asserted.

In *Possessed*—completed in twenty-six days and released on November 21, 1931—Joan Crawford is not a shop-girl but an exhausted factory worker. (There are extant photos from a sequence filmed but eventually deleted, in which Marian is shown working in the paper-box plant—perspiring, insignificant and dwarfed by machines, steam and industrial equipment.) And she does not "make good," unless by "good" is meant luxury and material security. The final appeal to the audience's better instincts (and their contentment) is provided by an ending in which enduring achievement is bestowed through love and sacrifice. The false "Mrs. Moreland" finally no longer exists, and Marian Martin regains an authentic life by doing good, not by having goods. It helps that the love of her life realizes this and is willing to make equivalent sacrifices.

Joan's performance derived not only from her deep understanding of Marian Martin, but from a careful composition of thoughtful reactions and restrained actions, nothing delivered with obvious calculation. Marian's anger became credible, her vulnerability touching, her passion provocative. With *Possessed*, Joan took her place in public esteem as an actress who made complex adult emotions real.

There can be no doubt that her altered relationship with her costar helped, especially in their love scenes. Indeed, during the preparation of the picture, in early September, Joan Crawford and Clark Gable began an affair that endured, intermittently but immutable devotion, for thirty years.

Both Crawford and Gable came from humble backgrounds. Both had lost a parent. Both had been day laborers at an early age, and both were profoundly insecure, presenting to the world the camouflage of a tough edge, the better not to be hurt. But there was a difference. At Metro, Joan trusted Louis B. Mayer, whereas Clark was always suspicious that a boss or a rival might suddenly replace or displace him.

Crawford and Gable contracted and dissolved their respective marriages, and they each endured the public's fickleness and occasional indifference. Through the vacillations of time, experience and maturing, they found a level of quiet confidence in their mutual support. "Our relationship was private, between us," Joan said. "It was a glorious affair, and it went on longer than anybody knows. It was sublime, probably more exciting because we felt like kids who'd gotten into the cookie jar while Uncle Louie [Mayer] was in the other room."

"Joan was an outlet for Clark," recalled Metro publicist James Merrick, who knew both stars for many years. "He could talk about all his problems, and she listened and offered the right comments and usually the right advice. Outside of Carole [Lombard, Gable's wife from 1939 to her death in 1942], she was the only person who really got through to him. A lot of us thought they would marry, and I think they came close a couple of times, but . . . it wouldn't have worked [because] she was stronger than he was, and Clark knew he had an image to protect."

But there was another element in the relationship that helps to understand both the longevity and the status of their affair. "We were both peasants by nature," Joan said, "not well educated, and so frightened and insecure that we felt sort of safe and home again when we could get together." Both of them, as she admitted, "loused up marriages, and we had images to protect." In addition there was a so-called morals clause added to standard studio contracts—a stipulation requiring actors to display virtually blameless behavior in their private lives, at the risk of finding themselves unemployed. Divorce and remarriage were one thing, but an openly conducted affair was quite another.

As Joan said, "We both felt that sooner or later, probably sooner, the public would say, 'To hell with them,' and we'd sink right back into oblivion . . . [but] we gave each other courage and taught one another how to laugh." There was also the matter of Gable's promiscuity—"with more [women] than the studio wanted to admit," as Joan said. But she endured his peccadilloes as he did hers. Douglas chose to ignore the intrigue, for he had embarked on his own free-wheeling lifestyle. "I was faithful in my fashion," he said years later, admitting that he was not, "and I took pains to be as circumspect as I knew how."

———

AN IMPORTANT DEVELOPMENT IN her career occurred in the autumn of 1931, when a group of devoted admirers organized the Joan Crawford Fan Club, formed under the tireless leadership of Marian L. Dommer. With military efficiency, the adoring Miss Dommer edited a Joan Crawford newsletter, charged annual dues of fifty cents for membership in the Club and spent $250 a year of her own money to keep the group functioning. (One of the charter members was an unknown fifteen-year-old named Charles Johnson, later famous as the movie star Van Johnson.)

"We have members in all sections of this country," Miss Dommer wrote in her replies to inquiries about membership,

> as well as in many distant parts of the world—England, Ireland, Australia, Scotland, South Africa and even Java included. Miss Crawford takes a keen interest in all of our activities. Not only does she send personally autographed pictures to all of our members, but she writes a long letter to the members for each edition of our club publications—and she also answers your questions about her in "Joan's Question Box," a regular feature of the magazine . . . which also includes club news, gossip and the latest news of Hollywood, New York and London, the entertainment centers of the world. We do have a regular editorial staff . . . and we cordially invite anyone to submit articles to our magazine. Among our contributors to each edition are Jerry Asher and Katherine Albert, two of Miss Crawford's best friends, both professional writers . . .
>
> Membership entitles you to a personally autographed picture of Miss Crawford, a membership card, membership list, six issues of The Crawford

News, *which is published every other month, and all other club privileges. The dues are fifty cents a year for domestic members and seventy-five cents, or three shillings, for foreign members.*

The Joan Crawford Fan Club endured for over twenty-five years.

———

THE YEAR 1932 BEGAN with a flurry of activity. Thalberg had the idea to gather as many of his major players as possible into one lavish and expensive movie. The studio owned the rights to a play called *Grand Hotel,* which had ended its Broadway run in December, and by January a film of it was rushed into production with a cast featuring Greta Garbo, John Barrymore, Lionel Barrymore, Wallace Beery and Joan Crawford.

Grand Hotel is one of the most famous movies of its time, but perhaps only because of its cast. The picture is neither tightly paced nor credible; in fact it is, as a major critic observed that year, "dull to the point of complete enervation." It might well have benefited from the excision of forty-five minutes, but its bloated grandeur and vast sets provided spectacle, and *Grand Hotel* won the best picture Oscar (but no other award, which is noteworthy).

Part of the problem was supposed to have been its major attraction— Garbo, who very nearly destroyed the picture with her overacting. Her performance as a maddeningly self-absorbed ballerina was delivered without nuance or recognizable feeling, and at every moment she fell back on tired, silent-screen, over-the-top gestures. As always, Garbo was remote and demanding at work, insisting that her love scenes with John Barrymore be filmed with only the director and cinematographer present—a requirement, of course, that gave everyone the impression that she and the scene were terribly important. There was no doubt that the camera adored her face, but that does not necessarily make for a great actress, and in *Grand Hotel,* Garbo proved that she was, as critic George Jean Nathan wrote that year, "one of the drollest acting frauds ever press-agented into Hollywood eminence."

Garbo's unintentional parody of a highly strung artist was in sharp contrast to Joan's entirely unaffected performance; indeed, Joan was the only other female star in the movie. She created a portrait of a stenographer willing to remain after hours for more than the usual tasks, a pretty young woman who finally learns the value of elementary human kindness and offers it unselfishly. As for Barrymore, Joan recalled that the actor's tragic alcoholism made him "unstable, and he couldn't care less about the picture. I was in awe of him, but he was cross and sometimes unkind." During these early years of her career, Joan learned the value of good relations with both actors and crew, and to that end she was invariably prompt. She also began the habit of offering presents to the crew at the end of filming—a gesture no one interpreted cynically at the time.

———

WHILE JOAN WAS COMPLETING her scenes in *Grand Hotel* in January and early February, she also attended preproduction meetings for her next assignment, *Letty Lynton,* "which was even more of a smash for me, personally. It was a hell of a story and script and had a character I could really come to grips with. If there is ever a Joan Crawford retrospective, I hope they show this one." Her enthusiasm, if not the quality of the final production, was justified, and those who knew her that year acknowledged the intensity of her efforts and the quality of the result. Robert Montgomery, assigned to his third film with Joan, recalled that he "felt sorry for her at times, because she really worked much, much too hard. She was intensely concerned with making something important of herself." *Letty Lynton,* loosely based on a brilliantly crafted novel by Marie Belloc Lowndes, contains one of Joan's most deeply felt performances.

Before production began, Joan and Doug made a quick trip to New York, for she had heard rave reviews about Sydney Guilaroff, a twenty-five-year-old hairstylist who was working at a Manhattan salon and who was consulted by a number of film stars. "I studied her beautiful face with her fantastic bone structure," he recalled shortly before his death in 1997, "and I gave her a sleek and smooth hairdo, brushed back behind her ears." Joan was delighted with the result and returned the next day with a photographer. She wanted precisely this look for her character in *Letty Lynton.*

Over the next two years, Joan frequently traveled by train from California to New York so that Guilaroff could design styles for each upcoming picture. With a photographer standing by each time to document the hairdo, Joan returned to Metro with instructions. "Finally," recalled Guilaroff, "Louis B. Mayer complained about Joan always leaving Hollywood before she started a film, and he asked her why she insisted on me. The next thing I knew, I was aboard the Sunset Limited and headed for MGM and a new life." Thus began the career of the most famous coiffeur in the history of Hollywood. From 1934 to 1990, he worked on more than four hundred pictures, designing hairstyles (and often makeup) for almost every woman at Metro and many men, too. Sydney Guilaroff insisted that he owed his career to the recommendation and loyalty of Joan Crawford.

———

LIKE THE NOVEL BY Marie Belloc Lowndes, the film *Letty Lynton* was inspired by the case of Madeleine Smith, a young woman in nineteenth-century Scotland. She was accused of poisoning her lover but was finally freed when a jury returned a verdict of "Not Proven," a judgment peculiar to Scottish law. The Belloc Lowndes novel fictionalized the true-crime history and turned the matter of a rather straightforward crime of passion into something more complex and psychologically acute than any of its later dramatizations, of which there were several. The novelist also created, as she wrote, "accessory characters . . . far more profoundly affected in their lives than even the chief actors in the drama."

The production began oddly. Clarence Brown, who had directed Joan so sensitively in *Possessed,* at first encouraged the makeup team to give Joan an appearance that all but duplicated Garbo. In the early scenes filmed that February, Joan bore an astonishing resemblance to the Swedish actress, and Joan even began to recite her lines in deep tones, with long pauses. "I'm going into seclusion," she announces with marmoreal remoteness, just as Garbo had twice said, "I want to be alone," in *Grand Hotel.* But after four days of filming two brief sequences, Joan reverted to more natural rhythms, created her own Letty, and the specter of Garbo vanished.

As the title character, she portrays a wealthy and bored socialite, first seen in Montevideo, Uruguay, the final stop in her yearlong cruise with an elderly female companion. Letty is very much bored with her oily, manipulative lover, Emile Renaud (Nils Asther), whom she waves off with the airy dismissal "I never kiss anyone before one o'clock in the afternoon." En route to New York, she meets the handsome and wealthy Hale Darrow (Robert Montgomery), who is far more appealing and acceptable than his predecessor. Everything seems well ordered for the two wealthy young people—until the first (now jilted) boyfriend blackmails Letty by threatening to publish her love letters to him unless she returns to his bed.[1]

Desperate, Letty goes to Emile's hotel suite, intending to take poison in his presence. She empties a vial of arsenic into her champagne, but before she can drink it, Emile drains her glass. "Yes, I did it," she hisses at him as he lies dying. "I meant it for myself, but I'm glad I did it, you dirty, filthy mongrel—I'm glad I did it!" At the finale, Hale and her mother provide Letty with handy, mendacious alibis for her whereabouts on that fatal night, and she is free to go forward with her marriage.

Letty Lynton transfers to the screen none of the novel's ironic gravity or drama, and all that remains is the possessive lover, the incriminating letters and the death by poison. But the movie does offer a superb Crawford performance that combines her trademark vitality with a sense of stern inevitability—not a shallow pantomime, as Garbo had delivered in *Grand Hotel* and which, at first, Clarence Brown thought might be apt for *Letty Lynton*. Once again, Joan found her own voice—for example, in a long dialogue in her shipboard suite with Montgomery, as they sit in opposite lounge chairs to discuss their aspirations. Both performances are full of subtle tensions and suppressed romance. She fears the exposure of her past, while he dreads that he will be an insipid companion. But Robert Montgomery is otherwise only a supporting

---

1. In an important shipboard scene, Joan wore an Adrian-designed outfit whose subsequent popularity put it into both the myth of movies and the folklore of fashion—the so-called Letty Lynton gown, a floor-length dress of white organdy with a ruffled hemline. Metro announced that tens of thousands of copies were made and sold in stores across America; this was completely untrue, but their story provided great publicity for the movie.

player; the picture is Joan's. She makes murderous intent and perjury seem the stuff of every socialite's day.

———

SHE WAS COMPLETELY OFF the mark in dismissing her next effort, for which she was loaned out from Metro to United Artists. As the notorious Sadie Thompson in Lewis Milestone's film of Somerset Maugham's *Rain,* she was, she insisted, "simply awful [in an] unpardonably bad performance . . . I was wrong every scene of the way." This complete miscalculation of her achievement may well have been caused by the overwhelmingly negative fan mail Joan received about the movie: even her admirers were unable to see that the actress wearing tawdry clothes, portraying a woman of easy virtue who sneers at male hypocrisy, was not that woman in real life. The public's negative reaction was a classic example of moviegoers rejecting a performer because they did not like the role: "our Miss Crawford" was playing the role of (gasp!) a prostitute, and the vast majority of the critics and public would have none of it. And Joan, always responsive to her fans as well as the reviews, nurtured an inappropriate contempt for her performance, which is actually one of the finest of her career.

The dreary exterior sets for *Rain* were constructed on rugged Catalina Island, twenty-two miles southwest of Los Angeles, which also provided close proximity to the deserted beaches needed to resemble the faraway South Pacific. Filming was a round-the-clock hardship for cast and crew alike: artificial rainstorms were provided by the studio's special effects wizards, but violent squalls actually slammed the island almost constantly. Accommodations were modest, tempers grew short, and there was nothing to provide comfort or amusement. Joan counted the days until her assignment concluded. But her colleagues never saw her impatience turn to temper. At work, she behaved much as she did at home: "I do not recall her occasional anger ever boiling over into a temper tantrum," insisted Douglas.

Notwithstanding her low opinion of her achievement, Joan's Sadie Thompson is a fully limned character. "Your God and me could never be shipmates!" she cries out to the sanctimonious Reverend Davidson (Walter Huston), who contemptuously sets out to reform her. During her long speeches, which rise to real moral outrage over his condemnation of sinners, Joan sustained an admirable, vivid intensity that was never merely shrill. The problem is not in her character, it is that Davidson thinks of God as an accountant, which Sadie cannot. "And the next time you talk to him," she tells the preacher, "you can tell him from me that Sadie Thompson is on her way to hell!" (We know she doesn't believe this, but it's what he wants to hear, and she wrongly thinks that it's one way to shut him up.) Joan knew when to cry out, when to pull back, how to underplay and how to reveal a soul battered by confusion.

With that, Reverend Davidson begins to recite and to repeat, several times over, the Lord's Prayer—in which at last she joins him, whispering the hallowed, half-remembered phrases. So begins Sadie's conversion and the emergence of Davidson's repressed libido—both eventualities doomed when he rapes her, then walks toward the sea and slits his own throat. Author Maugham, director Lewis Milestone and Joan Crawford were quite aware of who was finally redeemed: Sadie, who utters the words of forgiveness and compassion even after her trust has been dreadfully exploited. Told of Davidson's death, she turns aside. "Now I can forgive him for what he did," she whispers. Moments later, when Davidson's widow says, "I feel sorry for him—and I feel sorry for you," Sadie has the last line: "Well, I feel sorry for just about everyone in the world, I guess." Joan's delivery—plangent, weary, without sarcasm—concludes the film on a note of quiet, pacifying wisdom.

Rain, destined for a negative reception until wiser reactions were offered decades later, was finally completed in June. In her haste to quit the uncomfortable filming conditions, and perhaps to avoid traveling by ferry back to Los Angeles, Joan agreed to ride with a crew member in a small airplane. But the quick trip was also a frightening one. As they approached the mainland, a sudden, strong wind hit them violently for a few disorienting seconds. Joan and her pilot landed without incident, but she announced that it would be her last journey by airplane. She kept the promise for twenty-three years.

———

BY JUNE 1932, JOAN had completed three demanding and important pictures. With her salary at almost four thousand dollars a week, Mayer and Thalberg would normally have rushed her into a new assignment, if for no other reason than to realize a continuing return on their investment. But *l'affaire Gable* was now an open secret in Hollywood. With the whispering campaign growing louder each day, Metro could not rely on the continued silence of the press— and once the general public knew about the romance between these two married actors, the careers of both would be jeopardized, and the studio would suffer major losses.

To separate the lovers, Louis B. Mayer cleverly announced that MGM was offering Mr. and Mrs. Douglas Fairbanks Jr. a belated wedding gift. In 1929 their work schedules had denied the couple time for a honeymoon, but now they would have one—a trip to Europe. They were to travel in grand luxury, and by happy coincidence, their companions would be the Oliviers, who were weary of Hollywood and had work waiting for them in England.

And so, in late June, Metro's publicists escorted the two couples to New York, whence they boarded ship for London. "Jill kept mostly to herself during the trip," Doug recalled, "and it was clear that their marriage was as strained as ours. But Billie, who was extremely sensitive and always dependent on the good estimation of others, took Jill's coolness and apartness for outright rejection. She felt certain that the Oliviers just didn't think she was good enough to be seen with them. Of course, Larry could be a terrible snob, but I must say, he was Mr. Congeniality—terribly nice to both of us."

Olivier, who was soon to begin working in London on a picture with Gloria Swanson, put many questions to Joan about her idol—and that helped to thaw the chill of the trip. Recalled Doug: "Larry told me—privately, of course—that he thought Billie was very bright, very observant about people, and that what she had to say about Hollywood was right on target and very helpful to him. I was proud of her."

But there was really no help for the Fairbanks marriage, and the delayed honeymoon became in fact the calculus for eventual divorce. "I am sorry to say that I crept out of our suite at night to visit another lady traveler," Doug later admitted. He was not so naive as to think that Joan was unaware of this—just as he was aware of her relationship with Clark Gable.

Things did not improve in London. The round of parties and West End shows to which they were invited provided pleasant distractions, but Joan felt ill at ease among British theatre folk, aristocrats and members of the royal family—a society in which her husband moved gracefully and in which he counted many friends.

Away from her normal round of hard work and achievement, Joan became acutely nervous, and by mid-July she begged Doug to book their passage home. As he recalled, Joan "couldn't wait to get back to work. She was so frightened and felt so alien. She thought the public would forget about her, and that there would be no more good roles for her if she stayed away too long. Of course this was nonsense—six weeks wasn't too long—but there was no convincing her. She wanted the security of what she could recognize."

CHAPTER SIX

Mrs. Tone
| 1932–1937 |

I WAS ALWAYS an outsider," Joan said years later of her time in Hollywood. "I was never good enough—not for the Fairbanks tribe, not for Mayer, not for his so-called film society." In fact, these people did not regard Joan Crawford as "never good enough." That was a judgment she applied to herself.

Although the source of every feeling in adulthood ought not to be blithely sought in childhood experiences, it is certainly true that Joan's lifelong tendency to see herself as a social reject derived, at least in part, from her unhappy background. She preferred, therefore, the image of Joan Crawford that she herself refined, developed, altered and maintained by sheer force of will—and that image was not, despite the opinions of her critics, far from the reality. This had not so much to do with the roles she played on-screen as with the person she chose to be in real life, off the screen—someone who was ultimately a success, a living example of Cinderella who became a movie queen, not a mere princess. And this image was not a fiction—although there was no charming prince with whom she lived happily ever after.

Evidence that she was "good enough" for moviegoers—people who mattered to her more than any others—was waiting when Joan returned home from England in the summer of 1932. The *Motion Picture Herald,* a trade publication, reported the results of its recent poll of movie exhibitors in America, who were asked to identify "the biggest money-making stars of 1931–1932." Joan Crawford was listed third, after Marie Dressler and Janet Gaynor but before Greta Garbo and Norma Shearer.

Apart from any consideration of her acting talents, Joan was celebrated in the many magazines of America. With the country enduring the worst years of the Great Depression, the glamour industry thrived as the single most visible escape mechanism—not only in the movies but also in the press and the fan monthlies. Metro continued to commission idealized, glorified and dramatized photos of the stars, none more than Joan Crawford, who posed for many hours each month for master still photographers like George Hurrell, Clarence Sinclair Bull, John Engstead and Laszlo Willinger.

"She liked to pose," recalled Hurrell, Metro's senior stills photographer and the head of its portrait gallery. He collaborated with Joan on more than fifty photographic sessions over the course of a decade.

> *She was very pliable and gave so much to the stills camera. She really worked at it. She would spend a whole day, changing into perhaps twenty different gowns, different hairdos, changing her makeup . . . In a sense, she used {these changes} to present a new image that might possibly work for her whole screen personality. Every time, there was a different kind of lighting or different backgrounds or poses. Crawford had the closest face to Garbo's—perfect proportions. Crawford had strong jawbones, her cheekbones were good, and her forehead and her eyes were good . . . She had a classic beauty and a kind of spirituality—practically everything she did was a picture.*

After Joan's death, Hurrell defended what some called her excessive vanity. Recalling that on an average day he took more than a hundred different photos of her, Hurrell added that after they had worked together for eight or ten hours, he pleaded exhaustion. "But she never wanted to stop—she said, 'Let's get one more, just for luck!' She was the most decorative subject I ever photographed. There was a strength and vitality about her that always shows in the finished print. If I were a sculptor, I would be satisfied with doing only Joan Crawford, all the time."

Nobody wakes up in the morning looking glamorous. Hence the photographed Joan Crawford, like any other actress in Hollywood, was fundamentally a highly technical fabrication that transcended the ordinary. Something in the subject's face had to be there to build on, but photographers were not paid to document: their skill was glamorizing. Most movie fans probably knew this when they admired and collected the photos, but admire and collect they did. In a way, it was the very otherworldliness that made the photos desirable.

———

HOWEVER IMPORTANT THEY MIGHT HAVE BEEN to the studio's fortunes and her own, photos of Joan were always an adjunct to the moving pictures. But during the late summer and autumn of 1932 there was no immediate project at Metro that seemed right for her, and the studio had to do something fast, for she was now being paid forty-five hundred dollars a week and had a long-term contract.[1] In addition, the advance word on *Rain* was not good: the picture was, however appropriately, dark, its setting was unattractive, and its action was violent. Nothing about it was pretty, and on its release it had nothing for Depression-era audiences, for whom life was dreary enough, thank you.

In March, the *Saturday Evening Post* had published William Faulkner's story "Turn About," and director Howard Hawks snapped up the movie rights. It was just his kind of material—a story of military men in war-torn London, saving the world mostly through their skills with fighter pilots. After Faulkner and Hawks came up with a screenplay, Thalberg was interested—but only if a love story could be mixed in, specifically for Joan Crawford in

---

1. Garbo was receiving nine thousand dollars a week and Norma Shearer six rhousand, but Crawford was way ahead of Gable, whose salary was twenty-five hundred.

the role of an Englishwoman who has promised to marry one man but falls in love with another.

When Joan was told the studio's plans for her, she demurred. This was going to be a buddy picture, all the characters but one were English, and the story was set in Europe. Foreign accents were not among Joan's gifts, as she reminded her bosses. Other writers composed subsequent drafts of the screenplay, and by the end of November the project—renamed *Today We Live*—was ready to go. Joan reluctantly received her work schedule.

She may have felt more optimistic when she learned that Gary Cooper was among her leading men: at that time, he was a major star at Paramount who had already worked with Marlene Dietrich, Claudette Colbert, Helen Hayes and Tallulah Bankhead. The other actors included Robert Young, who had appeared in a dozen movies, and Franchot Tone, thus far seen in only one.

Today We Live must be ranked not only as the low point in the career of Joan Crawford but also as one of the most dreadful movies ever made. Cooper was the only player to be cast as an American, so he did not have the burden of affecting a British accent. But Young, Tone and Crawford were not so fortunate, and the result is beyond ludicrous. Not for one moment is Joan credible as an English country gentlewoman named Diana Boyce-Smith (for some unknown reason, everyone calls her "Ann"), and the script was almost comically bad. It told of Diana's engagement to a childhood friend (Young) who is replaced in her affections by a tall American stranger (Cooper); woven in and out of the action is Diana's brother (Tone). Joan's accent comes and goes—and when it comes, she stumbles and hesitates before saying almost anything.

In this rancid soup, audiences knew that the story was set in England because everyone said things like "How veddy, veddy good of you" and "Stout fellow now, girl!" and "That's a good job, what?" and "I say . . ." But they did not, for the most part, understand what they were hearing, for the dialogue consisted of a crazy kind of elliptical speech that made the characters sound like Indians in a Hollywood Western. At one point, a man introduces himself and his sister by saying, "Brother. Sister. Mine." The movie's language has all the charm of a first-year foreign language class, for characters do not speak in complete sentences: instead, they say things like "Gone yesterday. Forgot. Or didn't say. Can't tell where . . . Thought so. Your letters." Subjects and pronouns vanished, and present-tense verbs were rarely employed. This was not lifelike adult speech, nor was it poetic diction—it was simply arty, self-conscious baby talk that had no effect but to confuse audiences. Because of this nonsense (and a twenty-five-minute sequence of aerial fighting), moviegoers stayed away in droves, as Samuel Goldwyn said in another context. How could they do otherwise, when word got around that the movie featured sentimental episodes starring a fighting cockroach?

The two-hour-long picture has all sorts of unexpected oddities. When Robert Young's character loses his eyesight, he and Franchot Tone (as his best buddy) stand at the open door to Joan's bedroom while she sleeps. "Now look at her while I'm touching you," Young says to Tone. Just what was going on here?

Perhaps because Joan was smitten with Franchot Tone, who played the role of her brother, she never recalled just how bad the picture was. That discovery was left to the audience, but neither they nor the critics were fooled, much less impressed; the film was a failure in every regard.

———

TODAY WE LIVE WAS completed in early 1933 and released on March 3, the eve of President Franklin D. Roosevelt's inauguration, which injected a dose of optimism into the American psyche. At the end of April, while the new administration was activating bold economic measures, Joan shared the front pages of newspapers with her announcement that she and Doug had submitted papers for a legal separation. "There will be no divorce," she said, but two months after that, Mr. and Mrs. Douglas Fairbanks Jr. filed for divorce; the final decree became effective on May 13, 1934. "Doug had married Joan Crawford the chorus girl," she said years later, "and maybe that's the woman he really wanted—not the pretender to the throne. I was recreating the sort of life he'd had with his parents, and he didn't like either one of them very much. In any case, I am convinced that an actress should not marry."

It was particularly poignant that husband and wife had by this time become good friends if not compatible marriage partners—and they would remain good friends for the rest of their lives. Joan had seen something of a more refined life with Doug, and he was grateful that she had removed him from parental pressure and urged him on to a more mature independence. But for the present, they had to put some distance between them: Doug left Bristol Avenue and continued to pursue other ladies and other interests, while Joan was almost immediately seen around town in the company of this or that eligible man.

But life was always earnest for her, and she knew what she had to do—return to work, and in something that would be a surefire success after the failures of *Rain* and *Today We Live*. Always on good terms with Mayer, she went to him (not to Thalberg) and begged for a good role in a good picture. Mayer was sympathetic—not only because Joan was an expensive investment and he much needed a successful project for her, but also because he liked her common sense and dedication to hard work.

As it happened, Metro owned the movie rights to a novel by James Warner Bellah that had been serialized in the *Saturday Evening Post* earlier that year—the episodic and sentimental story of a burlesque dancer who rises to respectability, wealth and fame, with predictable romantic complications before the happy ending. This seemed the perfect vehicle for Joan, but at first she was hesitant. She finally accepted after Mayer invited her to participate in the story's development from page to screen. The production retained Bellah's title—*Dancing Lady*.

At the same time, Mayer's son-in-law, producer David O. Selznick, had just arrived at Metro from a tenure at RKO, and he was assigned to handle the production of *Dancing Lady*. Selznick had no great fondness for musicals, but he saw at once that the script lacked precisely what would make it a success for MGM and Crawford—sequences of dancing and singing stirred generously into the story. Warner Bros. had just released the musical extravaganza *42nd Street,* which was so lucrative that it very quickly saved that studio from bankruptcy. The moral of the story was clear: Metro would have to prepare *Dancing Lady* very carefully indeed if it was to be successful.

The screenplay went through several drafts, but Joan was still dissatisfied and on the verge of telling Mayer that she would prefer not to do the picture—until Selznick invited her to a script session and cannily told her, "Joan, I think you're right. I don't think this is really the right picture for you—it's such a tarty role. I think it's more Jean Harlow's style." His remark had the desired effect: "Look, Mr. Selznick," Joan replied with a touch of acidity, "I was playing hookers before Harlow knew what they were. And let's not hear any talk about style, because I know more about that than she ever will." Selznick then clinched the deal with Joan by telling her that Clark Gable was available to be her leading man, and by agreeing to her request that the important supporting role be given to Franchot Tone, who was then being photographed as Joan's escort around town.

But these actors were not dancers, and the picture needed a good dancing partner for Joan. Selznick quickly solved that problem, too. One of his last deals at RKO had been to sign the stage star Fred Astaire to a movie contract, beginning August 1. Telephone calls were made, telegrams were sent, Selznick's legendary elaborate memoranda were dictated—and on July 15, three days after he was married in New York, Fred Astaire arrived in Culver City for two weeks of work on *Dancing Lady*. Fred had briefly appeared in an on-set cameo in a 1915 silent picture, when he was sixteen, but *Dancing Lady* would be his real movie debut.

Joan knew that the scenario was very like her own life story—the tale of a poor but determined hoofer who, like cream, rises to the top—and she had decided to celebrate the connection between the movie and her life before the press did so in uncomplimentary terms. On the first day of production in late June, Joan expeditiously completed the opening scene of the movie, which she had developed with the writers and with director Robert Z. Leonard—and had based on her time as a Broadway chorus girl for J. J. Shubert. As dancer Janie Barlow, she and a group of burlesque showgirls are hauled before a judge after performing a remarkably inoffensive striptease number. With tough humor, she explains that this was the only work she could find that allowed her to dance. Joan's performance was managed wittily—it was grit with a smooth velvet surface—and no one could find fault with either the girl in the story or the one on the screen.

The picture was planned to take only four weeks, but more than four months were needed to complete it.

First, Clark Gable fell ill with a strange infection that defied certain diagnosis. A few days after he returned to work, he collapsed and had to be hospitalized for an emergency appendectomy. There were complications, and his recovery kept him away from the studio until the end of August. This, of course, necessitated rearranging the shooting schedule and recasting several roles played by actors who now had other commitments. Fred Astaire's participation was a stroke of good fortune, as his scenes were conveniently moved forward in the production schedule.

Misadventures accumulated. Dancing with Astaire (who was playing himself) as the camera rolled, Joan overdid a scene in which she was supposed to interrupt the action of the story because of a leg cramp. But in fact she fell awkwardly and badly sprained her ankle. The production schedule was so tight, however, that this incident was left in the finished film, and a line of dialogue was added to explain it. Game girl that she was, Joan returned to the studio that same day— cooperative as always, despite the discomfort of her taped and painful foot. She worked for seven hours, doing close-ups for a major dance number that now had to focus on her face instead of on her usually agile feet. But a week later, she had to withdraw for several days—and again shooting was interrupted—when she learned that she had sustained a hairline fracture. "I am holding up production with a sprained ankle," she wrote to a friend in New York on September 9, minimizing the diagnosis. "It is the same one I've broken three times and it's painful as the very devil."

Despite all the production setbacks, *Dancing Lady* shines with good humor, engaging songs, lively dancing and an astonishing polish, justifying Selznick's belief that Metro could out-Warner Warner when it came to musicals. The picture provided a major boost to the careers of Crawford and Selznick; it introduced Fred Astaire to the moviegoing public; for the first time, people saw a trio of boorish louts who became wildly successful as The

Three Stooges; and, in a small scene, Eve Arden appeared with Joan (as she later would, in more important roles in *Mildred Pierce* and *Goodbye, My Fancy*).

The picture opens in a burlesque house and concludes on a legitimate theater stage, bookending ninety minutes that fly like a greased eagle, mostly because of the appealing performances and the witty dialogue. Joan was perhaps never before more lovingly photographed; her hair was lightened, softened and parted; her makeup was more natural, emphasizing her eyes; and Adrian's wardrobe for her was not as outrageous as in *Today We Live*. Her tap dancing was spirited—at least in what remained of the footage taken before the accident—and her acting was alive with nuance and the kind of unexpected humor that made the romantic triangle of Crawford-Gable-Tone less sticky.

Gable, thin after his illnesses and sometimes all but unable to stand up straight, wears his pencil-thin mustache for the first time in a Crawford picture, and audiences loved them in their fourth collaboration together. As for Tone, he had little to do but feign adoration of Joan and appear both sophisticated and drunk most of the time—characteristics too often replicated in his offscreen life. Another of Joan's contributions to the screenplay was the development of Franchot's character, a snob forever tutoring Janie Barlow on proper grammar and the best way to dress. Those moments of corrective etiquette were lifted right out of the Crawford-Tone relationship.

Dancing Lady took far longer to complete than Metro had planned, and the four months of production were unusual in those more disciplined and economical years of meticulous movie preparation and six twelve-hour days each week. But the healthy box-office returns in December immediately wiped out its $780,000 cost and brought in nearly twice that much in profits. However riddled with problems during filming, this surprisingly entertaining picture justified Mayer's faith in his son-in-law as a Metro producer, and Joan was blissfully restored to the critical and popular favor she coveted. Unlike *Rain,* this was a movie the public took to its heart.

THE YEAR ENDED WITH an announcement from the family. On December 2, Kasha Le Sueur bore a baby girl, soon christened Joan Crawford Le Sueur. "I admire my sister-in-law more than any woman I know," Joan disingenuously remarked to a reporter. "But if they let me have that baby, I'll adopt it right away." This seemed like a shocking thing to say, but Joan knew, as the newspaper-reading public did not, that Hal and Kasha were soon to separate and, as she told friends, she was deeply worried about the fate of the child.

In her subsequent divorce complaint, Kasha stated that Hal was indifferent to her and "not interested in being married"—the same charge his first wife leveled, which may have implied all sorts of unmentionable details. Kasha then departed with her baby, who was, years later, known as Joan Lowe when she appeared occasionally as an ensemble dancer on Broadway (most notably in *Funny Girl,* in 1964). Despite Auntie Joan's claims, she did not raise her niece as her own child, although she contributed financially to the baby's welfare.

Offscreen, it was evident that over the years, Joan had learned a great deal from Metro's hair, makeup and lighting experts. As Annette Tapert has demonstrated in an important book on the history of Hollywood glamour, actresses like Claudette Colbert and Norma Shearer never altered their particular signature looks. But Joan reinvented herself and changed her appearance according to the styles of each decade and the requirements of each role. In this regard, one of her most memorable talents developed over the course of forty years: her skill in knowing how to accentuate her large, expressive eyes, enhance her sensual mouth, exhibit to best effect her pronounced cheekbones and angular jawline and—thanks especially to Adrian—emphasize rather than camouflage her broad shoulders.

Joan's cleverness at the vanity table and in selecting her wardrobe made her one of movie history's unique and uniquely beautiful women. "I was a flapper in the age of flappers," she wrote later, "and I became a sophisticated lady in the age of sophistication." And she used in life what she learned in the movies: that wardrobe is like a supporting player—the face registers emotions, the body moves to express reactions. "Underdress," she advised her fans. "Play down the accessories. Leave the startling hat or jewel at home. But for a public appearance, give them something stunning."

From 1933, in response to Mayer's injunction that she ought not to go out casually attired, Joan adhered to a self-imposed convention: she promised that no one would see her in public unless she looked like Joan Crawford, the movie star. No one ever did. As she famously remarked, "If you want the girl next door, go next door." Convinced that this was as much a matter of respect for her craft as it was for her fans, it also had something to do with pride. "No actress living works harder at her job," according to publicist Cameron Shipp, who knew her for thirty years and was echoing Douglas Fairbanks Jr. Similarly, Helen Louise Walker, a journalist who knew her well for twenty years, wrote that Joan "cares more than anyone I have ever known about what people think of her."

One "startling jewel" she had to leave at home in 1933 and thereafter was a large, outlandishly expensive blue-white diamond ring that seemed to flash scarlet. This was a present from none other than Franchot Tone, with whom she was (as the saying goes) romantically involved from the time of *Dancing Lady*—an affair that interrupted her fervent dalliance with Gable. She was by then a trusted soul mate and confidant for Gable, and although they would from time to time be lovers again, their relationship after 1934 was often a deep, noncarnal friendship.

—————

FROM THE START OF the Crawford-Tone affair, Joan considered him "a different fiber" from anyone in Hollywood, her first husband included. But here she was in many ways off the mark: the two men were in fact very much alike, even in appearance, and her attraction to Tone suggests a kind of repetition compulsion—a desire to revise a situation in which she had once stumbled. "Franchot was the son of society, of wealth," she said—but so was Doug. The difference lay mainly in the direction and arc of their mature years. Doug lived creatively and prosperously to ninety, leaving a legion of friends and admirers, while Franchot went through several fortunes and died penniless at sixty-three.

Franchot's theatrical experience, however, had been substantial. Born in February 1905 in New York, Stanislas Pascal Franchot Tone was the son of a scientist who became an enormously rich corporate director. While studying languages at Cornell University, Franchot acted in plays, and after graduating and rejecting the family's offer to enter their prospering business, he went to New York to pursue a career in the theatre.

From 1928 to 1933, Tone appeared in no fewer than fifteen prestigious Broadway productions, in which his costars were the likes of Katharine Cornell, Sylvia Sidney and Ruth Gordon. He was a charter member of the influential Group Theatre, founded by Lee Strasberg, Harold Clurman and Cheryl Crawford, and he worked with Elia Kazan, Clifford Odets, Stella Adler, Sanford Meisner and Lee J. Cobb. His achievements onstage soon attracted the interest of Metro-Goldwyn-Mayer, and he quit New York for Hollywood.

In *Today We Live,* Franchot gave an awkward, mannered performance for which his stilted faux-British accent was no help. But in Joan's eyes, he could do no wrong. "I saw him watching me [during the shooting of *Today We Live*], his great, thinking eyes so penetrating, a little crooked smile on his aesthetic face . . . and his well-trained, scintillating mind stimulated mine." At her home after their workdays, he read Shakespeare, Ibsen and Shaw aloud to her, and while she hooked a rug, he hooked her. "He taught me to respect my own mind—not just to absorb things emotionally, but to *think* . . . [and] we both started studying opera. He was imaginative and charming."

When *Dancing Lady* was completed, Franchot whisked Joan away to New York, to see the Group Theatre's production of Sidney Kingsley's play *Men in White*. After the final curtain, Franchot whispered to her: "Here's where we'll be someday—you and I, Joan—in the *theatre,* where you belong." She was flattered and excited by his confidence and respect. Perhaps she should also have sensed a certain danger. "His dignity, culture and charm were entrancing," she continued. "So why fight it?"

For two years, Joan and Franchot were a couple in every way except legally. He was Professor Higgins (if not Svengali); she was Eliza Doolittle (if not Trilby). For much of the time, the uneducated, always insecure Joan was receiving more from the polished, confident Franchot than she could have dreamed—or so she said. She seemed not to know, nor did she acknowledge (as did he), that he had come to Hollywood completely ignorant of the demands and skills necessary for film acting. In short order and with her typical intensity, she gave him the equivalent of a four-year course of study in studio lighting, voice modulation, makeup, subtle reactions— everything she had mastered while appearing in four dozen films during the previous eight years. To the press, she repeated that she would not marry again, and the more she insisted, the more Franchot pressed his case. He was with her when she received notice of her final divorce decree from Doug, in May 1934.

That news came just as Joan and Franchot were completing their third collaboration—*Sadie McKee,* produced from February to April. In this uneven movie, which hovers between romantic melodrama and low comedy, the hands of many writers were all too evident, for the plot has twists past counting. Joan played the title role of a housemaid for a rich family. She goes to New York, survives three troubled relationships and becomes remarkably mature and self-sacrificing before she is rewarded with serenity, wealth and true love.

Episodic though it is, Joan had several poignant scenes and a few deliciously comic moments in which she mimicked being riotously drunk, and her final scene is moving without arch sentiment: at the bedside of a dying former lover who abandoned her, she is forgiving and compassionate, avoiding all traces of movie mush. As for Franchot, he still seemed uncertain, overacting rather childishly for the camera; in addition, the role of a privileged playboy was wearing thin for him and moviegoers. "I was pretty unhappy with the way the picture was cut," Joan wrote to her friend Genie Chester in New York on May 17. "Perhaps it will make sense, but I doubt it."[2]

From *Sadie McKee,* she hurried at once into *Chained,* another picture with Clark Gable. At the same time, Mayer and Thalberg put Franchot in *The*

---

2. Genie Chester, the daughter of the chairman of General Foods, had polio as a child and was afflicted with severe lameness throughout her life. She had been Douglas Fairbanks Jr.'s best friend and became a lifelong friend and confidante to Joan, too.

Girl from Missouri, a Jean Harlow comedy. Completed in July, *Chained* was essentially a comic-romantic piece about a love triangle in which Joan falls for a wealthy rancher (Gable) while she is the mistress of an equally wealthy but married tycoon (Otto Kruger) whose wife will not agree to a divorce. Absurdly titled and drenched in high fashion, *Chained* is nevertheless noteworthy in relation to two events in Joan's life.

Just as the production began, a weary man arrived nervously at Metro-Goldwyn-Mayer's front gates, announced himself and was shown to the soundstage where Clarence Brown was about to film close-ups of Joan sipping a cocktail. While key lights were rearranged, the visitor was taken over to meet the star. He was, he said shyly, Thomas Le Sueur, her father—a man she perhaps knew was still alive but of whom she had not the remotest memory. After a few moments in the hot spotlight of a movie set, he faded back into the darkness of her history as the baby girl he had abandoned. They never met again.

A far happier event during the production of *Chained* involved Joan and Clark. For all his efforts to separate them, Mayer now behaved with astonishing perversity, insisting that they be reunited romantically on-screen. In this picture, the two friends shared several unusually long dialogue scenes, set in a ship's swimming pool and at lunch. The script they received for these sequences consisted of inconsequential remarks intended to be mere filler but disguised as exchanges—and after the two actors had seen their lines, they agreed to take matters into their own hands. When the scenes were filmed, Joan and Clark improvised their own dialogue, ad-libbing hilariously to the point that they both broke up with laughter—as did the crew and, later, audiences. The swimming scene was particularly effective, as they glided smoothly back and forth through the water, chatting, politely arguing and giggling uncontrollably.

Wisely, Clarence Brown kept his camera rolling, and these scenes are forever memorable for what they reveal about the comic inventiveness and expert timing of two professionals who had become quite comfortable working together—and who were gifted at devising spur-of-the-moment lines and gestures to lift the movie out of its nearly terminal torpor. If only for these moments, *Chained* continues to reward viewers decades later. Clarence Brown had been right and Joan wrong when she protested, at the start of production, that she believed she was "too stiff" to play comedy. "Joan, goddammit," he told her, "you're one of the three actresses in this town who can do anything, so do it!" And so she did, although she never learned whom else Brown had in mind.

———

CRAWFORD AND GABLE HAD no need to improvise lines for the next assignment, their sixth together. The script (yet another romantic triangle) was the work of Joseph L. Mankiewicz, adapting a Broadway play of the previous year. He worked with Joan as the writer and/or producer on no fewer than nine Crawford movies, and their collaboration was memorable. "Whatever I can contribute technically to a characterization," Joan said years later, "I learned through the years working with Joe Mankiewicz. He was first a writer, then a producer-writer, and we worked closely together—it was one of the happiest times of my professional life. As we worked on new scripts, I was allowed to sit day after day during writer-director-producer discussions, listening to each new development of the story and the characters."[3]

Production of *Forsaking All Others* began in September, just weeks after the premiere of *Chained*. Franchot had hoped to be included in the new picture, but Metro kept him busy elsewhere; in 1934 he appeared in six films, most of them on loan-outs to other studios. But he was indifferent to the roles and begged Mayer to put him back to work again with Joan. He also bristled when he learned that the role he had coveted in Joan's next movie had gone to Robert Montgomery.

Forsaking All Others expanded the limitations of action imposed by its theatrical antecedent and simultaneously exploited the new screwball comedy

---

3. Joseph L. Mankiewicz produced seven Crawford vehicles for MGM: *The Gorgeous Hussy, Love on the Run, The Bride Wore Red, Mannequin, The Shining Hour, Strange Cargo* and *Reunion in France*. In addition, he wrote two: *Forsaking All Others* and *I Live My Life*.

genre, with its variations on the abandoned bride, an unsuitable groom and, eventually, the right man—all of it punctuated by satiric sideswipes at the idle rich and slapstick races through the countryside. Mankiewicz and director W. S. Van Dyke sharpened the story of a woman who has been pursuing the wrong man since childhood—until he becomes the right man, and then the wrong man again. None of this confusion mattered: it was the breakneck speed of the story and the sheer, sleek, art-moderne beauty of the actors and the sets that audiences loved. "This is one of Miss Crawford's best performances," noted the critic for *Variety,* pleased that the "tongue-in-cheek moralizing" of her recent movies was not to be heard.

From the opening scenes—a long sequence in which Joan receives an almost sadistically tough workout from a German masseuse while welcoming friends—she dealt neatly with any objection that she could not handle comedy. Her timing was deft, her gestures modulated, her voice more varied in pitch than previously.

The production posed no problems—but when the script and the edited picture were presented to the recently formed board of Hollywood censors, *Forsaking All Others* ran into trouble. The administrators of the Motion Picture Production Code fumed when they heard the words *tramp* and *sex appeal* and they demanded more polite language; otherwise they threatened to withhold their seal of approval, which meant that very few theaters would screen the movie. In addition, the censors did not like very proper scenes in which people took showers, even if only their heads were photographed. Nor did they approve of unmarried characters staying in the same hotel, unless they resided in separate suites and preferably on distantly separated floors. But somehow they ignored lines like "I could make a fire by rubbing two Boy Scouts together"—spoken on a cold and rainy night by Montgomery when he needs firewood. Van Dyke, Mankiewicz and producer Bernard Hyman yielded to the censors on a few minor points, but they simply ignored most of the foolish objections. The film went out with a seal of approval and made a fortune.

WITH FOUR LUCRATIVE PICTURES behind her (*Dancing Lady*, *Sadie McKee*, *Chained* and *Forsaking All Others*), Joan was in a good position to renegotiate her contract with Metro; her agent easily arranged this at Christmas 1934. Her three-year deal guaranteed her seventy-five hundred dollars weekly for the first year, eighty-five hundred dollars weekly for the second and ninety-five hundred dollars weekly by 1937 (the equivalent of $142,500 a week in 2010). If she completed more than nine films between January 1, 1935, and December 31, 1937 (which she did not), she was to receive a bonus of fifty thousand dollars—which Mayer paid her in any case, in appreciation of her intense and dedicated professionalism.

———

AT HOME, JOAN BEGAN to host formal dinner parties, with every element invariably supervised by Franchot: the right wines for each course, the proper table service and the best background music, provided by a harpist, pianist or string trio. "He contributed greatly to my cultural and intellectual development," she said in 1951, "and I don't mind admitting it one bit. Franchot helped me cultivate a strong liking for literature, art and opera. When I was going through that stage, I had as many people of culture and taste [to my home] as I could possibly manage."

Thus continued what Doug Fairbanks had called Joan's lifelong commitment to self-improvement. But for all her consorting with "people of culture and taste," she never forgot—and was usually more comfortable with—the average, unknown, behind-the-scenes workers who crossed her path. Joan befriended film crews and technicians as she did executives, remembering their birthdays, asking about their families, paying hospital and doctor bills for the indigent and providing financial assistance to help families who were ill or had fallen on hard times—as so many did in the 1930s. These generous acts were done quietly, and anyone who publicized her generosity was soundly chastised.

Some people, then and later, called Joan's benevolence nothing but grandstanding or enlightened self-interest: the recipients of her kindness, ran this argument, were people who would remember her, support her, benefit her, be grateful to her—most of all, they would *like* her. That may indeed have been part of the mix of motives; as Thomas More famously said in the sixteenth century, "Only God is love straight through." But Joan was very much aware of her own good fortune, and she felt compelled to help others when she could. In the last years of her life, such actions became a pronounced and constant habit.

These random deeds could be criticized as exaggerated or even the invention of publicists were there not one compelling piece of evidence to the contrary. In 1934 Joan contacted Dr. William Branch, a member of the surgical team that performed her dental and facial operations of 1928, for which there were follow-up procedures in 1932 and 1933. Joan asked Branch to help her devise a unique program by which she would underwrite the hospital expenses for destitute patients who had once worked in any capacity in the movie business. These people were to receive all necessary care at the Hollywood Presbyterian Hospital, where she endowed several rooms and a surgical suite. All the bills were sent to her and she paid them quickly and privately, without referring them to her business manager.

The arrangement was made on condition that her name not be used, and that she receive no credit or publicity for her charity in any way; years later, when this bequest was discovered and Joan was openly praised, she feigned ignorance of the entire matter. "In the two years after 1937, more than 390 major surgeries were completed," according to a confidential hospital report made in 1939. "Joan Crawford paid the bills, she never knew the people for whom she was paying, and she didn't care."

———

ALTHOUGH *FORSAKING ALL OTHERS* was a major hit for the studio, Joan had no illusions: she rightly saw that it was a bundle of clichés, however glossily assembled. In fact, the films in which she was cast from 1934 through 1938 were invariably tedious, notwithstanding their visual appeal and Joan's performances. The unfortunate downward spiral continued full throttle with *No More Ladies.*

Frank Capra's *It Happened One Night,* released early in 1934, had established screwball comedy as the most successful form of escapist entertainment at the height of the Great Depression. Audiences loved to see the rich satirized and the poor elevated, and they loved romantic endings. Capra's movie provided all this and more, and when Oscar time came, awards were handed out to him (best director), to Claudette Colbert (best actress), to Clark Gable (best actor) and to Robert Riskin (for best screenplay). *It Happened One Night* was also named best picture of the year, and at once it seemed as if every studio in town was racing to produce screwball comedies. But this genre was not Metro's forte, as *No More Ladies* revealed.

The script was based on A. E. Thomas's mildly successful 1934 Broadway play about a society lady who tries to reform her unfaithful husband by making him jealous. The first drafts of the screenplay, hurriedly submitted in early 1935, were so flat and unamusing that the project was handed over to a platoon of screenwriters for rewrites and polishing. The best of these was done by Rachel Crothers, a highly successful Broadway playwright with a keen gift for character and for pointed and witty dialogue. Her script was then turned over to others for a redraft. When the redoubtable Miss Crothers saw the finished film, she complained to MGM and to the press that her work had been butchered beyond recognition and demanded that her name be removed from the screen credits.

Despite the fact that Joan should have felt comfortable working for the fifth time with Montgomery and the fourth with Tone, she was uneasy from the start about the silliness of the script for *No More Ladies.* She also felt that her performance lacked the whimsy that is the first requirement of a screwball character. Then director Edward H. Griffith came down with pneumonia, and George Cukor was engaged to complete the picture, which he did at the end of April.

Cukor already had major credits for directing Katharine Hepburn in both *A Bill of Divorcement* and *Little Women* and for guiding an all-star Metro cast in *Dinner at Eight.* But at first Joan was having none of him. "I could be a headstrong bitch," she admitted some years later. "I didn't let Cukor help me, and I interpreted the part wrong. It was another of my personal mistakes."

The truth is that ultimately she did indeed allow Cukor to help her—insofar as the script permitted him to help—and she repeatedly sought his tutelage after he got her through the difficult final scenes. Still, she was found wanting by the critics: "not a distinguished performance," wrote one when the movie was rushed into distribution that June; *Time* added that she had "the appeal of cold turkey."

Despite her anxieties during the production, Joan was notably helpful to a young actress named Gail Patrick, to whom she gave expert advice on makeup, wardrobe and especially on the right way to pose for glamour photographs. "There was a time when I'd have been grateful if anyone had helped *me*," she said. "Newcomers to films sometimes think that it's a waste of time to pose for publicity photos. But I've made a careful study of every single still picture that was ever shot of me. I wanted these stills to teach me what not to do on the screen. I scrutinized the grin on my face, my hair, my posture, my make-up—everything. I learned—so can others." Gail Patrick did, and felt forever in Joan's debt.

No More Ladies is almost unwatchable, full of stock characters (a wealthy drunk and a crusty but benevolent grandmother) and a cast that variously wanders about in tuxedos or in impossibly chic gowns designed by Adrian. That year, Joan was fitted with a new set of false eyelashes so outrageously long and thick that they cast deep shadows on her face and gave the cameramen headaches. Some wise cosmetician eventually trimmed the lashes, probably after complaints from leading men with scratched faces.

———

JOAN SAW TROUBLE BREWING again when she was handed the script of her next assignment. Based on a short story with the off-putting title "Claustrophobia," it was planned as another screwball comedy but turned out to be an arid, airless account of a society girl who tries to land a handsome archaeologist for a husband. At first Joan had asked Mayer to cast Franchot as her leading man, firmly believing that he would raise the quality of the picture and that together they could make the romantic comedy credible. But Franchot was already cast in Gable's next picture—*Mutiny on the Bounty,* which began filming in early May.

Instead, the role of the archaeologist went to Brian Aherne—a tall, handsome British leading man with substantial credits on Broadway and in Hollywood. Titled *I Live My Life,* it began filming in early June and was completed in mid-July. "It was formula stuff," said Joan, dismissing the picture; the critics agreed.

Her freedom from this chore happened none too soon for Joan, who had heard disturbing rumors about an offscreen romance elsewhere. After his seafaring epic with Gable, Franchot had been loaned to Warners as Bette Davis's costar in *Dangerous.* On their first meeting, Davis was smitten with her new leading man, and very quickly a real-life skirmish was set in motion, without the tone of screwball comedy. Joan was on the scene as soon as word of this affair reached her: she disengaged Franchot from Davis's arms and took him back home, convinced that only matrimony could tame his wanderlust.

Thus it happened that, for the first time, Joan put her private life front and center. With Mayer's good wishes, she took an unofficial leave from Metro, and in late September she whisked Franchot off to New York. There, he was happily reunited with his friends at the Group Theatre, the couple attended Broadway premieres, and Joan made her radio debut in an adaptation of *Paid.* The New York press, alerted by their Hollywood colleagues, was certain that marriage was in the air, and Joan and Franchot were trailed day and night—from restaurant to theater, from cocktail lounge to nightclub. On the morning of October 11, they were able to slip away unobserved to New Jersey, where they were quietly married without a single flashbulb in their faces. A week later, they were back in Hollywood—not for Joan's sake, but on account of Franchot's summons from Metro to appear in something called *Exclusive Story.*

For six months, the bride energetically played house—redecorating, repainting, expanding and rearranging rooms at Bristol Avenue and even joining workmen in the most demanding and laborious tasks. There was no immediate film project that she felt was right, but she was receiving thousands of admiring letters every week. Always grateful to her devotees and convinced that she would have no career without them, Joan invited a team of local fans to her home on Saturday afternoons and, assembly-line fashion, they addressed and stamped envelopes while she signed photos and wrote grateful replies to her many admirers. Sixteen-year-old Betty Barker, one of her most loyal fans, became a kind of factotum in Joan's household and, years later, was her full-time Hollywood-based secretary.

While Joan was so occupied, the groom rushed through his roles in four forgettable movies, and by late spring 1936 he was more than ever disenchanted with Hollywood—a sentiment only briefly dissipated when he was nominated by the Academy as best actor for *Mutiny on the Bounty*.[4]

"Togetherness" could have been Joan's motto for her new marriage as she threw herself into a range of activities with Franchot's encouragement and collaboration. They took voice lessons with an opera coach; they recorded duets; they performed one-act plays for friends in a little theater they added to the property; they engaged a physical education trainer for daily workouts; they read aloud to one another—and, as she recalled, "I became a pretty good polo player in order to get over my fear of horses."

Pride of place was given to high culture, as Joan continued to host dinner parties honoring visiting dignitaries, orchestra conductors, musicians, poets and statesmen; in a way, she was taking a page from Constance Bennett and embellishing it. Olivia de Havilland, then at the beginning of a long and distinguished acting career, recalled an evening at the Tones. "Joan Crawford welcomed me and was most encouraging, and she treated me without a trace of condescension or patronizing. She really made me feel like a colleague, and not a neophyte. A few days later, I received a package in the mail. It was a gift from her—a copy of the recently published book by Stanislavksi [*An Actor Prepares*], which she said she was studying and thought that I would find interesting."

Years later, Joan admitted that the master plan during her marriage to

---

4. Clark Gable and Charles Laughton were also nominated as best actor for that film; all three lost to Victor McLaglen's performance in *The Informer*.

Franchot Tone was impossibly idealistic, but at the time she allowed herself to be convinced that together they would be mutually dedicated to a life of shared achievement on-screen and onstage. To this end, she got Metro to cast him in her next project, hoping that his obvious talent would encourage producer Joseph L. Mankiewicz to enlarge Franchot's role once filming began. That never happened.

The picture, made in the spring of 1936, was the ill-fated historical drama *The Gorgeous Hussy,* set during the ascendancy and presidency of Andrew Jackson in the nineteenth century. "I had read the criticisms of me and my movies," Joan recalled later, "and they were discerning. They said that Crawford needs a new deal, and they asked if I was doomed to explore forever the emotional misfortunes of the super-sexed modern young woman. And so, to break away from the pattern, I wanted to do *The Gorgeous Hussy.* Selznick laughed at me. 'You can't do a costume picture. You're too modern.' But I begged and begged and begged, and so they let me do it. I was totally miscast."

Nor was she much helped by the screenplay, which turned a potentially interesting political drama into nothing but another fashion show for Joan (wearing period gowns à la Adrian) as she glides from set to set and man to man—Robert Taylor, Melvyn Douglas and Franchot Tone, whose role remained without color or weight. For better and for worse, it was Joan's picture—she was the title character, Peggy O'Neal Eaton, who was based on a controversial historical lady who made herself important in the lives of great men. But with Hollywood's censors on the prowl, all references to Peggy's bold sexuality had to be erased—and so it remained unclear just why her life was so controversial. Joan never again appeared in a historical costume drama.

The professional situation remained grim with *Love on the Run,* yet another futile attempt at screwball comedy—her fourth in that genre, her third picture with Franchot and her seventh with Clark. By now, Gable had begun a romance with his bride-to-be, Carole Lombard, and Mayer thought it both prudent and bold to cast Gable and Tone once again as rivals for Joan's affections.

The picture makes use of just about every convention established since *It Happened One Night:* the runaway bride, the pursuing reporter and the high-speed chases. But the end result was vacuous and unamusing. Joan played socialite Sally Parker, pursued by two newspaper reporters (Gable and Tone). The trio races across Europe, fleeing from spies and trying to discover who loves whom, but no one cared, and yawns occurred where laughs were expected. Perhaps most regrettable about the failure of *Love on the Run* is the fact that by this time Joan had honed her comedic timing and knew how to play a scene with deadpan gravity. Full of surprise and vitality, her irrepressible performance was not enough to save the picture, for unfortunately, publicity at the time of the movie's release was overwhelmed by the news of Irving Thalberg's sudden death from a heart attack at the age of thirty-seven.

When Douglas Fairbanks Sr. and Mary Pickford were divorced early that year, Irving and Norma Shearer Thalberg assumed a kind of unofficial aristocratic primacy among the Hollywood elite. After her husband's death, Norma at first became merely eccentric—a reaction, most people said, to being widowed with two young children. She went into virtual seclusion for a year, and then she emerged almost a new person, tearing through a series of love affairs that included entanglements with Howard Hughes, James Stewart, George Raft and teenager Mickey Rooney. At the age of forty, in 1942, she completed her last motion picture, married a young ski instructor and retired from Hollywood.

With age, Norma—as she had so long feared—became more and more emotionally unbalanced, insisting that people remember her as she once was and preferring to be addressed as Mrs. Thalberg. Hospitalized after several breakdowns, she attempted suicide at least once and spent the last years of her life mostly demented and bedridden. Norma Shearer died in 1983, at the age of eighty-one; as she had requested, she was buried beside Irving G. Thalberg.

———

AT THE END OF 1936, Joan's accountants reported that her pretax income was $302,307—a sum that made her one of only fifteen Americans who took in more than three hundred thousand dollars that year. She then began filming her scenes in a verbose and lackluster comedy called *The Last of Mrs. Cheyney,* which had been undertaken with high hopes for its success: after all, it had long runs on the stage in London and New York and was a successful Norma Shearer movie in 1929. But Frederick Lonsdale's story of a jewel thief masquerading as a society matron was overwhelmed by huge sets and by wearisome injections of meaningfully moralistic dialogue; not even the skills of debonair costar William Powell could alleviate the tedium.

Making her task even more difficult, Joan miscarried three weeks into filming, at Christmastime—the second or third such incident since her marriage to Franchot. Typically, she blamed herself and her subsequent depression for the failure of the film. "I was having personal problems," she said, "and I let them get in my way. I wanted so to have Franchot's children."

Thus the new year began bleakly, the atmosphere at Bristol Avenue often perilous because of Franchot's dark moods, aggravated by heavy drinking. "I grieved over my losses, and Franchot grieved over his career." Tenaciously, Joan continued to fight for better roles and for her marriage, which was delicately poised between her fragile hopes and his frank resentments.

CHAPTER SEVEN

Joan, Julie, Susan—and God
| 1937–1940 |

*T*HE LAST OF MRS. CHEYNEY was released two weeks after filming concluded, in February 1937. By this time, Joan's name on theater marquees was sufficient to attract crowds, and the picture increased MGM's fortunes once again. Her portrayal of a sophisticated jewel thief—a study in cool poise and comic understatement—was very like that of Marlene Dietrich, who played a similar role in the recently released comedy *Desire*.

According to the market research, women made up the majority of Joan's audience, and when couples or families went to see a Crawford movie, women brought them to the box office. These studies were commissioned by distributors, who quickly reported the results to the studio. Metro knew, therefore, that they had to present their glamorous, fashionably dressed leading lady in as many stunning outfits as could be included in the movie's running time. (That explains the sudden insertions of fashion-show sequences into *Our Blushing Brides, Mannequin* and *The Women*.)

Life took note of all this and more when, in the March 1 issue, its editors proclaimed Joan "the first queen of the movies, [and her] special public is predominantly female, predominantly low-brow." The six-page feature story was titled "Joan Crawford: Mrs. Tone at Home." Accompanied by no fewer than twenty-nine photos, the article accurately noted that she was born on March 23, 1906.

From early June through late October, Joan appeared in two demanding and complicated movies, made back-to-back and almost without interruption— *The Bride Wore Red* and *Mannequin*. These were ambitious productions, the first directed by the formidable Dorothy Arzner (who had completed *The Last of Mrs. Cheyney* after the sudden death of Richard Boleslawski) and the second by Frank Borzage (who returned to direct two of Joan's later features). Franchot costarred in *The Bride Wore Red* and was then busy in non-Crawford pictures.

"We were so busy we never had time [for each other]," Joan said later. When they worked together, she recalled that she "tried very hard to give him more scenes, to build his ego. It just didn't work. It was no wonder that he gradually broke away [and] tried to assert himself," which he did not only through work but also by pursuing a series of love affairs. "One afternoon I dropped by his dressing room to surprise him—and I *did*." As for Franchot, his comments about Joan to reporters were complimentary, but always accompanied by a vaguely insolent subtext:

> *She must get her homework done, her lines learned every day. She has continuous meetings with the producer or the director or somebody else equally important each evening. She has to get up at four-thirty in the morning in order to get to the hairdresser and on to the set. She needs a massage at night before she can sleep for a few hours. She has to eat sparingly and exercise constantly. This goes on and on, and when Saturday night comes, there are other professional duties and priorities—conferences about the next script, talks about dancing lessons, discussions about yoga, tennis and swimming lessons. After all, she's a star.*

Those last three words summarized perfectly the essence of Joan Crawford. "My insecurities made me carry things a little too far—for my own personal comfort and the comfort of the people around me," she said late in life. "I played the star Joan Crawford, not the woman Joan Crawford, to the hilt." Ths is not hard to understand. She labored ceaselessly to eradicate every trace of Lucille Le Sueur, to become the new creature she much preferred and to assume thoroughly the identity of Joan Crawford.

She had been the girl next door in her early years—the girl everybody forgets in real life—and she bought the movie-star image because it seemed to her the ultimate deliverance from her own past. Hence she was always a movie star, even if she went out shopping. A trip to the grocery store (not a frequent chore) was an event precisely because she could be certain of being recognized. And she believed with almost religious fervor that people wanted to see Joan Crawford the star, not the uninteresting and unattractive person she believed herself to be. For Joan, this was neither affectation nor hypocrisy, but rather her conviction that "a star owed the public a continuation of the image that made her a star in the first place." As a star, she never represented the girl next door.

"I felt that I photographed better than I actually looked, so I tried desperately to make sure my make-up and wardrobe lived up to the image on screen." Her audience felt that she represented something like the fulfillment of their dreams and fantasies; the Cinderella tale, after all, never dies—it conforms to an archetypal hope for rescue from a wretched existence. "People liked to read about the way I dressed when I went out. I realized that Mayer was right: I was obliged to be glamorous. If people wanted to see Joan Crawford the star, they were going to see Joan Crawford the star—not a character actress in blue jeans."

In an important way, Joan was very much a transition figure in the history of stardom. Fairbanks and Chaplin, Pickford and Garbo, Novarro and Valentino all lived at a great distance from the public. Dwelling in their fairy-tale castles high up in the Hills of Beverly, they consorted mostly with other Hollywood gods and goddesses, living beyond all mortal contact, or at least with as little contact as possible. They were intermediaries between the real and the imaginary.

Without intending to do so, Joan Crawford effectively changed the notion of stardom. By appearing in public often, by drawing close to her fans, by inviting people to see her in person as they did on-screen, she simultaneously affirmed the glamorous, remote dignity of the star and expressed the fact that it was a reality. Her private life, on the other hand, was hers, and she knew the difference. Impressively generous toward strangers and friends and perpetually demanding of her colleagues, Joan was a jumble of contradictions: regal yet crude, warm but chilly, erotic and puritanical, imposing and vulnerable, ethical and unscrupulous, munificent and egocentric.

She was indeed a woman possessed by a desire to rise above her background and by the need to belong to someone deeply and permanently. But in pursuing the first ambition, she failed in the second. "I've been protected by studio men most of my life, so in some ways, I'm a goddamn image, not a person. I felt an overwhelming obligation to my career, and so I was an actress first and a wife second. I worked almost constantly, and even when I wasn't working, there was that image thing of looking like a star, conducting myself like a star. I just went ahead like a bulldozer. I'm afraid I was a very selfish woman." It is this kind of fundamental honesty that makes the story of her life both compelling and cautionary.

———

THE BRIDE WORE RED, produced that summer of 1937, was based on a play called *The Girl from Trieste,* by Ferenc Molnár. Set in a fanciful Tyrol where dirndls are seen ineptly alongside Adrian's fantastic creations, the movie was obviously made for the sake of the eponymous bugle-beaded gown. Otherwise, the picture was only a spin on the Cinderella tale, once more featuring Joan's agonized emotions and two attractive gentlemen—again, Robert Young and Franchot Tone.

Flaunting a coy sense of indecisiveness and draped in everything from jungle sarongs to proletarian chic to Paris-Hollywood high fashion, Joan the star had been presented to audiences as one who attracted at least two suitors in every story—hence the perpetual triangle.

This was virtually a constant motif in the films of Joan Crawford. She was juggled between John Gilbert and Ernest Torrence in *Twelve Miles Out*, Neil Hamilton and Clark Gable in *Laughing Sinners*, Neil Hamilton and Monroe Owsley in *This Modern Age*, Nils Asther and Robert Montgomery in *Letty Lynton*, Gary Cooper and Robert Young in *Today We Live*, Clark Gable and Franchot Tone in *Dancing Lady*, Edward Arnold and Franchot Tone in *Sadie McKee*, Otto Kruger and Clark Gable in *Chained*, Robert Montgomery and Clark Gable in *Forsaking All Others*, Robert Montgomery and Franchot Tone in *No More Ladies*, Brian Aherne and Fred Keating in *I Live My Life*, Melvyn Douglas and Franchot Tone in *The Gorgeous Hussy*, Clark Gable and Franchot Tone in *Love on the Run*, Robert Montgomery and William Powell in *The Last of Mrs. Cheyney* and Robert Young and Franchot Tone in *The Bride Wore Red*.

Audiences and critics recognized this Crawford tradition, which had become, as she said, "formula stuff," although the familiar structure was not yet exhausted. Yet to come were Alan Curtis and Spencer Tracy in *Mannequin*, Robert Young and Melvyn Douglas in *The Shining Hour* and Henry Fonda and Dana Andrews in *Daisy Kenyon*.

The filming of *The Bride Wore Red* occurred during an anxious period in Joan's life, for she knew her second marriage had by this time irretrievably broken down. As usual, work distracted her—but not from her concerns with the welfare of others. Dickie Moore, a popular child star who was cast in the picture, recalled the day when an electrician fell from the catwalk high above the set and landed not more than two feet from her.

A light fell on top of him, also narrowly missing her. I was whisked away, and production, of course, was halted. The studio ambulance arrived and he was taken immediately to the hospital. Eventually, the scene resumed. I was impressed by Miss Crawford's concern for the man, for his family, for the medical attention he received. She wanted absolute assurances that he was cared for properly, that he remained on salary, and that his family was provided for. She would not resume shooting until those assurances were given, and she called the hospital each day for reports on his condition.

For all the expense and effort that went into making it, *The Bride Wore Red* was a critical and financial catastrophe, and even the fans were dissatisfied: "it was a waste of time for everyone," as Joan said. Critics, weary of the familiar triangular goings-on in a Metro-Crawford picture, agreed—the picture was "a vapid Cinderella pipe dream" whose gowns and sets could not conceal its "underlying shabbiness."

The film's failure was particularly disappointing because buried somewhere in the story's awkwardly paced episodes were provocative, satiric observations on a dying class system. Producer Joseph L. Mankiewicz, whose films were never released without his marked contributions, inserted these into the shooting script. But such points went unobserved, and the negative response to the movie apparently encouraged Mankiewicz in a paradoxical approach to the next project.

On the one hand, he played it safe: *Mannequin* returned Joan to her role as a poor working girl who becomes a rich wife (as in *Possessed, Sadie McKee* and *Chained*)—a formula that was always a surefire Depression-era crowd pleaser. This time, she left a shiftless, opportunistic husband (Alan Curtis) for a generous and adoring tycoon (Spencer Tracy), whom Mankiewicz deliberately cast because Tracy was less "movie-star handsome" than Curtis.

But there was another element in *Mannequin,* and Mankiewicz worked it out in the final script early that autumn, with Joan at his side. This time, in the role of Jessie Cassidy, she is not so much a victim of circumstances as a woman who shapes her destiny by wise choices and a will to work hard: "I'll work in a chorus," she says at one point, echoing her own past in words she added to the script. "I'll work in a laundry!" By matching the character to the actress, and inviting the actress to participate in the creation of the character, Mankiewicz turned *Mannequin* into something more than a return to formula. "I took one look at those poor Delancey Street sets and knew I was back home," Joan recalled. "I *was* Jessie—there was no trick in conveying her."

Jessie appealed to the women of a postflapper era who had learned from the Great Depression not to rely on men for their economic salvation, and Joan's performance was perhaps her most mature thus far. At thirty-one, there was something knowing and wistful about her beauty—something that suggested the confluence of her role and her life. When Jessie is in love, Joan's eyes are not blinded by dreams; when Jessie is outraged by her husband's betrayal, Joan's gaze is not naive but resolute. And Tracy's unaffected performance as the magnate with a conscience broadened the picture's social scope with a pointed political subtext about labor-management conflict and the rights of workingmen.

Joan's only unhappy memory of the production was Tracy. "We whooped it up a little bit off the set," she said, alluding to their brief affair, "but he turned out to be a real bastard. When he drank he was mean, and he drank all through production"—a habit noted by many others throughout Tracy's long career. "He did cute things like stepping on my toes when we were doing a love scene—after he chewed on some garlic. Metro tried to costar us again later, but I begged them to let me off, and they did."

———

JOAN HAD ASKED MAYER to buy the film rights to Keith Winter's play *The Shining Hour,* and she requested Margaret Sullavan and Fay Bainter—two experienced and respected actresses—as her costars. Reminding her that the three women's roles were equal in scope and importance, Mayer tried to dissuade Joan from demanding such stellar coplayers: "Those two talented actresses could steal your picture!" Her reply was immediate: "I'd rather be a supporting player in a good picture than the star of a bad one."

During the coming year, Joan was heard on no fewer than eleven nationwide radio dramas, several of them with Franchot as her costar. In addition, marriage on the rocks or not, they often traveled to New York for Broadway premieres, for Joan was also on the lookout for properties suitable for the movies. While in Manhattan on New Year's Eve, she learned that her father had suffered a stroke at his home in Texas. Declining to attend a party, "she remained in her suite at the Waldorf-Astoria Hotel throughout the night," as the press reported, "and she received calls from relatives." On January 1, 1938, Thomas Le Sueur died at age sixty-nine; there had apparently been no contact between father and daughter, in person or by telephone, since their brief, awkward meeting in 1934.

Back in Brentwood, she routinely assisted, or even dismissed, those servants she regarded as less than fastidious. "The part of me that is 'Craig's Wife' comes out every day," she wrote to a friend in New York on January 25, referring to the character in George Kelly's 1925 play about a woman obsessively concerned with the standards of her home.

Joan's increasing obsession with cleanliness—her mania for an almost impossibly tidy and sanitary existence—was certainly a sign of her interior need to cleanse and purify, as much as it was a sign of her longing to unite her *actual* life with her *ideal* life, to join the reality of the kitchen to the art of her perfect movie-fake kitchen. The laundry assistant was a permanent part of her personality, and something in Joan prevented her from eradicating it.

———

IN MAY 1938, THE *Independent Film Journal,* published by the Independent Theatre Owners Association of America, fired a warning shot at certain complacent Hollywood producers. The results of box-office receipts (not mere popularity polls) revealed that certain names were "poison" for business—among them Fred Astaire, Joan Crawford, Marlene Dietrich, Greta Garbo and Katharine Hepburn. "Practically all the major studios," ran the article, "are burdened with stars receiving tremendous salaries, whose public appeal is negligible." The problem was not the actors, "whose dramatic ability is unquestioned . . . but the fact that their recent offerings have been so disappointing and their box-office draw nil."

This was actually no news at all, and although the denizens of Hollywood affected to be shocked, *shocked,* they had indeed known this for some time. A month earlier, independent producer Samuel Goldwyn had said, "It used to be that one picture of a double feature would be bad. Now you got to expect both of them will be terrible. The American picture industry better do something, and do it soon."

Metro's response to the sight of Joan's name on the "box-office poison" list was immediate. Scripts were to be much improved and productions to be designed more impressively, ran a studio memorandum—which meant more expensively—a situation that prevailed at least until wartime restrictions on movie budgets began in 1942. More to the point, Mayer at once concluded negotiations with Joan's agent for a new contract—$330,000 annually over the next five years. "Box-office poison?" asked Joan rhetorically. "Mr. Mayer always asserted that the studio had built Stage 22, Stage 24 and the Irving Thalberg Building, brick by brick, from the income on my pictures." That was no exaggeration. Indeed, the tight-fisted, cheese-paring Mayer regarded the financial failure of Joan's recent films as but a temporary setback due to the quality of the *films,* not to anything like a lack of talent on her part. Had they seen her as no longer profitable, Metro's executives would not have eagerly acceded to her agent's demands and quickly closed the deal that guaranteed her a record income for five years to come.

The news of her undiminished star power and the continuing executive decisions that dismissed any notion that she was "box-office poison" might have been cause for celebration, but there were too many counterbalances affecting Joan's life in 1938. The most critical reason for her intermittent depression was the failure of her second marriage, a union weakened by their mutual and ongoing infidelities—he with this or that leading lady or aspiring player, she with (among others) Joseph L. Mankiewicz and Spencer Tracy.

"Franchot loved the theater and despised Hollywood," Joan said years later, "and I wasn't as nice to him, or as considerate, as I should have been. I was extremely busy during those years, and I didn't realize that his insecurities and dissatisfactions ran so deeply." Her own dalliances may have been occasioned at least in part by Franchot's alcoholic rages—"physical rows," as she called them. Clarence Brown apparently wanted to knock Franchot out flat when Joan arrived on the set one day with black eyes and a swollen face. She told him that retaliation would only make things worse when she returned home.

Nevertheless, she remembered her second husband as "mature and stimulating. I missed him a lot, for a long, long time. The breakup was another career casualty. If I'd tried a little harder—well, who knows?"

———

FOR JOAN, THE MOST unfortunate and certainly the most enduringly harmful consequence of this time was what she called "the drinking problem that began in my middle years in Hollywood." As witnesses past counting confirmed, Joan's drinking never affected her work: she had too much respect for the business to allow that to happen. "I used to have a few [drinks] before I had to meet the press, but at that time I handled liquor well. We all drank. The film community drinks more than its share—there were parties at home and lunches on and off the set. But I think the problem really began when I had to meet people—it was all because of fright, a type of fright worse than stage fright. Vodka relaxed me, chased away the butterflies, put a certain safe distance between me and everybody else. I didn't cross over the line until much later."

On June 13, Joan told a reporter from the *Los Angeles Herald-Express* that, rumors to the contrary, she and her husband were certainly not going to dissolve their marriage. But on July 20, they announced (via a Metro-Goldwyn-Mayer press release) that they had in fact filed for divorce. "We regret this action, but we feel it is better for us to part." That, of course, was typical lawyer language; in any case, the marriage was finally dissolved the following spring. "I hope we will always be friendly," Joan told Judge Benjamin Scheinman, "but we could not make a success of our marriage. Mr. Tone told me that he was sorry we had married, that marriage was a mistake for him, that he was not the marrying kind and that he wanted his freedom." Wed in October 1935, they had separated in July 1938—a union of less than three years.

———

THE SHINING HOUR WAS finally ready—or at least the script had been approved—for production to begin in August. Robert Young and Melvyn Douglas, playing brothers, joined the cast under Frank Borzage's direction.

This was another muddled romantic triangle (Crawford-Douglas-Young) complicated by the men's jealous sister (Fay Bainter), who certainly seems to have incestuous feelings toward at least one of her brothers. Also on hand is one brother's wife (Margaret Sullavan), a case study in self-sacrificing nobility. Unfortunately, the characters' motivations were blurry, and for all the crisp invective and politely murderous conversations in an elegant country mansion, the movie is oddly uninvolving.

At several important moments, both Joan Crawford and Margaret Sullavan come close to redeeming the picture with their restraint and dignity—but then something absurd occurs in the story, and everyone is left to founder. A singularly wooden performance by Robert Young and an overwrought one by Fay Bainter are at least partly to blame. The picture, which begins with Joan's first long dancing duo in five years, is notable for her insertion of several pieces of her own autobiography, improvised on the spot between takes and placidly accepted by Borzage. "I couldn't go to school much," she says in character. "I was too busy doing shirts in the laundry, and when I finally landed that job in the chorus, it was too late for school."

The experience of working with Margaret Sullavan was, however, extremely important in the development of Joan's emotional life. Maggie, as friends called her, had been briefly married to Henry Fonda and to William Wyler, and in 1936, she had contracted a third marriage, with the theatrical agent and producer Leland Hayward. Their daughter Brooke was born in July 1937, and Maggie often brought the sixteen-month-old baby to the set, where Joan, for one, was thoroughly delighted with the tiny, well-behaved visitor. She helped Maggie with baby chores and looked after Brooke when her mother was called to the set for close-ups. To Joan, Maggie's life seemed complete, more fulfilled than her own. "The baby and I were devoted to each other," Joan recalled, "and I confess I permitted her [to do] what I never permitted a child of my own [to do]—she wrote on my dressing room walls with lipstick."

At the same time, Maggie was again pregnant—a condition in which she took enormous delight, and through which she again sailed without so much as an uncomfortable morning. Children make the world of difference in a woman's life, Maggie told Joan, who had suffered several miscarriages during her marriage to Franchot. Then and there, Joan Crawford resolved to adopt a child. Considering this a quixotic, transient desire, Mayer advised Joan to wait: after all, the notion of a single person adopting a child was all but unknown at the time, and her hope was almost certain to be stymied by custom, prejudice and California law. She took his advice, but not for very long.[1]

In any case, Joan was far too busy to proceed at once with adoption plans. Because of an unfortunate overlapping of production schedules, her work on *The Shining Hour* that autumn coincided with her scenes in a monumentally ill-advised picture, *The Ice Follies of 1939.* Eager to replicate Fox's recent huge success with *One in a Million,* an ice-skating extravaganza starring three-time Olympic medalist Sonja Henie, Mayer and company engaged the same writer and an entire professional company of skaters. The only purpose of the fragile story was to provide a long prelude to a twenty-minute Technicolor skating finale. Joan rehearsed with her skates during late-hour sessions, but she could not manage to remain vertical—hence she never appears skating in the finished picture. That hardly mattered, for her role was that of a former ice queen who turns glamorous actress.

"That movie was trash," said Joan. "Everyone was out of their collective minds when they made this picture. It was a catastrophe, and the public thought so, too. MGM hired the entire company of the International Ice Follies and tossed in an old stage play they had sitting on the shelf called *Excess Baggage,* and Jimmy Stewart, Lew Ayres and I kept trying to figure out where we came in. Advertising art showed me on skates, but I was no skater."

Stewart, appearing with Joan for the second time (after his small role in *The Gorgeous Hussy*), recalled that she was not aloof or temperamental, but full of tremendous vitality and always friendly. "We have both been referred to as perfectionists but being a perfectionist means learning your craft so that

---

1. It has been claimed for many years that Sydney Guilaroff, a confirmed bachelor to his death at ninety, was the first single parent to adopt a child, in 1938. That was true, but the adoption was legalized elsewhere, outside the Golden State.

you can do it and not have the 'acting' show. It means being believable when you're surrounded by machines and cameras and technical men with lights and everything else—that takes learning, and that's when you can understand why Joan Crawford was so good at her job."

———

ACCORDING TO THE CRITICS, the public and everyone involved in Joan's next picture, she was much more than merely good: in *The Women,* she gladly accepted a minor role and performed it to mordant, wicked perfection. Nor did Joan balk at assuming a part in support of her old rival, Norma Shearer: "I'd play Wally Beery's grandmother if it was a good part," she said famously, and she meant it. In fact, she had to fight for the part, which Mayer thought too small and too unsympathetic; she landed the role only after she convinced director George Cukor, who recognized how much she had learned from (and since) *No More Ladies.*

Based on Clare Booth's long-running Broadway play, *The Women* has a sizable all-female cast, each character concerned in some direct or tangential way with the leading lady's unseen and unfaithful husband. As a satire on morals in American urban society and as a commentary on the emotional battering endured by ecstatically masochistic women, the play is entirely of its time and curiously difficult for audiences to enjoy in the twenty-first century. The invective is forced, the noble wife, played by Shearer at her noblest, is almost insupportable, and the constellation of ladies is variously irksome, flighty or downright pathetic. Only the department store salesclerk played by Joan—the husband-stealing, opportunistic foil for all the other ladies—is recognizably human, both venal and single-minded.

Once before, in *Our Blushing Brides,* Joan had played the role of a shopgirl—a job with which Joan Crawford is usually and wrongly associated. *The Women* is under way a half hour before her entrance, but when she is present, she demands the audience's complete attention. Lowering her voice almost below mezzo range, she is the complete schemer, her words marinated in the oil of feminine wiles and egoistic seduction. She is the woman every other woman loves to hate, and whom many men would hate to love. Only very rarely did Joan play a thoroughly rotten character, and perhaps only this time was the role well enough written and the actress prepared to play it without a moment of artifice or mitigation. "I knew that Norma would walk off with the audience sympathy and that Roz [Rosalind] Russell would walk off with the picture, and that I'd be hated. All came true, but I gave a damned good performance and Cukor's direction was superb."

George Cukor had the respect of his entire cast; whatever their offscreen histories, the women received a full education in the craft of movie acting—and none was a more willing learner than Joan, who said that George made her forget her limitations and found subtexts for every line and reasons for every scene. "With George in command," Joan wrote to a friend, "we are being guided every step of the way—he's brilliant! It's long days, but I'm loving every minute of it, so I always feel guilty for complaining that I need more sleep."

"She was serious about improving herself as an actress," according to Cukor. "She played the role with fierce determination, holding back nothing. As the bitchy shop-girl in *The Women,* she knew perfectly well that she would be surrounded by formidable competition from the rest of the all-female cast, many of whom were playing funnier and certainly more sympathetic parts. Yet she made no appeals for audience sympathy: she was not one of those actresses who have to keep popping out from behind their characters, signaling, 'Look—it's sweet, lovable me, just *pretending* to be a tramp.'"

But by all accounts (including Joan's), she did not behave well toward Norma Shearer during the filming. She whispered rude remarks about her within Shearer's hearing; she repeated her own lines in a quick monotone for Shearer's close-ups, while noisily plying her knitting needles off-camera—and she spoke unflatteringly about Norma to anyone who would listen. "Joan did act up on that set," recalled Sydney Guilaroff. "She shouldn't have done that. In my opinion, Joan was too big a star to engage in such antics and jealous actions. It's a pity, because Miss Shearer was really such a lovely person."

———

WITH THE EXCEPTION OF the ice-skating folly, Joan had received very good and often enthusiastic reviews thus far in her career. She received solid endorsement from everyone at Metro, where she was treated as both friend and investment; she was a favorite of critics and audiences; she had learned from directors like Brown and Cukor—and even to her hypercritical gaze, what she saw on the screen gave her fresh confidence in her dramatic abilities.

Now, after her most recent success in *The Women,* she was prepared to depart even more radically from any formula or preceding type of role. Cukor was right: she was serious about improving herself, and improvement meant the welcome challenge of new breadth and depth. Although she longed to work on the theater stage, she also knew that psychologically she could not, for she was terrified of live audiences. She wanted to be a star, she wanted the income, the perquisites, the awards—but, as she said years later, "I wanted only what I could deserve."

For quite some time, Joan Crawford had been one of the Hollywood players who did not simply wait to be handed a role to play in fulfillment of her contract: she actively sought good literary bases, novels and plays that, her experience and intuition told her, would not only be good vehicles for her talents but also right for the movies. She read widely, she spoke with those outside the studio whose opinions she respected—and she often came up with projects that, although the final realizations were disappointing, had been selected with more than prudent caution and limited self-interest in mind. So much had been true of the direct recommendations or indirect pressure she exerted in order to assume her roles in *Rain, Letty Lynton, Today We Live, Sadie McKee* and *Forsaking All Others.* Joan was no scholar, but she recognized the value for the movies of writers like Maugham, Belloc Lowndes, Faulkner, Delmar and Lonsdale.

Thus it happened that she urged Metro to make a movie of Richard Sale's 1936 novel, *Not Too Narrow . . . Not Too Deep,* which was turned over to *Mannequin*'s screenwriter, Lawrence Hazard. In short order, Metro approved what became *Strange Cargo,* which began filming in October. For the eighth time, and again at her request, Joan's leading man was Clark Gable, even though they had to shoot other scenes while he was doing retakes and pickup shots for *Gone With the Wind.*

Regarding her continuing relationship with Clark, Joan was completely realistic. "I don't think Clark would make a good husband—a great lover, yes, and a fine friend, but I imagined him as an unfaithful husband. I didn't think he would be satisfied with only one woman, even me, and he would face endless temptation. I was also certain that he would prefer not having as a wife an actress with a career on par with his—that he would prefer someone who could be happy simply devoting herself entirely to him." That someone turned out to be Carole Lombard, whom Gable married in March 1939, just three weeks after his divorce from Ria Langham and during the production of *Gone With the Wind*.

Joan also petitioned for Frank Borzage, her director on both *Mannequin* and *The Shining Hour,* to return for *Strange Cargo*. Born in Salt Lake City, he was known as a man for whom ethical, moral and spiritual values (but not parochially religious ones) were not just important abstract notions—they also infused and enriched his pictures. He foresaw the horror of Fascism in his pictures *Little Man, What Now?* and *Three Comrades,* and he went immediately from *Strange Cargo* to the intensely moving anti-Nazi drama *The Mortal Storm*. All but forgotten by the general moviegoing public after his death in 1962, Borzage acted in or directed more than two hundred films. Winner of the first Academy Award for directing (the film was the enduring fable *Seventh Heaven*), he was particularly adept at telling, in his own haunting and romantic style, stories about ordinary people facing adversity. No director could have handled *Strange Cargo* with more understanding.

———

THE PICTURE CONCERNS A motley group of Devil's Island prisoners who escape and cut a path to freedom through the jungle and then by a perilous sea journey. Led by a tough rogue named Verne (Gable), the men are joined by the cabaret performer and sometime hooker Julie (Joan) and by a mysterious, mystical figure named Cambreau (Ian Hunter). *Strange Cargo* is simultaneously a suspense yarn, a sea epic and a love story—but most of all it is a meditation on the nature of human solidarity, the possibility of forgiveness and the nature of redemption. This complex of ideas emerges in a film made with tact, restraint and unpretentious depth—a rare combination of qualities in Hollywood at any time.

The impressive and provocative themes coalesce in the character of Cambreau, a role given enormous dignity and quiet credibility by Ian Hunter, cast as an emissary from the world of the spirit who becomes both mystical guide and patient, wise counselor for the ill-fated prisoners. As many critics recognized, he is a Christ-like figure, but without the typically explicit Hollywood brand of saccharine piety routinely associated with that analogy. Compassionate but realistic, gentle and strong, Cambreau brings each of the characters to a recognition of his or her sins and a confrontation with their fears—and each to the point of contrition. In his comforting presence, four of the renegade men die from the rigors of the journey, and at the conclusion, Cambreau—after safely setting Verne and Julie back on land—bids farewell to a helpful fisherman, and walks into the distance. The final shot of the picture shows the fisherman, making the sign of the cross as he gazes after the departing stranger.

For her role as Julie, a wandering crooner and woman of easy virtue who is attracted to Verne, Joan insisted on two things: utterly realistic clothes and a downright haggard, drawn appearance appropriate for a woman struggling to survive in wretched conditions in the jungle and then aboard a sun-baked schooner. To this end, Joan worked with cameraman Robert Planck to achieve a deglamorized look, and she refused even a hint of flattering makeup; gone were the thick eyeliner and the long lashes. In *Strange Cargo,* Joan has the look of an ill and frightened patient, feverish and neurasthenic. And instead of the usual inflated budget for Adrian gowns—her outfits in *The Women* were said to have cost forty thousand dollars—Joan drove to bargain shops in downtown Hollywood, where she and a wardrobe assistant selected three dresses off the rack. The bill was forty dollars.

No one was prepared for Joan's shockingly raw and unalluring appearance on-screen, and to some she was even unrecognizable. But she had wanted to do something completely different—to demonstrate to herself and others that she was a serious actress who had no need of glamorizing techniques to succeed.

She wanted to prove that she was not a fashion plate or a model or someone who had just stepped from the pages of a glossy magazine—and so to hell with the glamour. She achieved her goal, and the picture offers one of her most deeply realized performances.

"We both had good parts," said Joan of her work with Clark. "On the second day of shooting, all of a sudden, he said, 'Joan, whatever you want to do and whatever you want *me* to do, that's the way it'll be. You've become an actress, and I'm still Clark Gable.' I think he underestimated himself, but he was awfully generous with me."

Joan and producer Mankiewicz wanted to do something "good, even fine" (as Mankiewicz said), and this they accomplished, although neither Hollywood nor the American public knew what to do with *Strange Cargo*. The professional dailies saw its virtues: *Film Daily* described the acting as "high-grade—Clark Gable fits his role admirably, Ian Hunter has never done better work, and Joan Crawford gives her best performance to date." *Variety* agreed: "Crawford's role is a departure from those handed to her during the past several years, and her characterization ought to encourage studio execs to cast her talents more properly in the future." Perhaps surprisingly, in light of its usually condescending attitude toward Crawford movies, *Time* considered it "a formula turned into a highly unusual picture, compassionate without becoming mawkish, and with a strange power."

But sadly, box-office receipts merely balanced the movie's budget, and for decades the picture was virtually ignored. Seventy years later, a perceptive Crawford fan Web site reevaluated it: "A rich experience, both cinematically and thematically, *Strange Cargo* is one of the all-time great films. It deserves greater exposure and recognition as a classic film treasure." Created in the tradition of Jerome K. Jerome's early twentieth-century short story and play *The Passing of the Third Floor Back* (and perhaps with Borzage's awareness of the 1935 English film of it), *Strange Cargo* remains one of Joan's most audacious and exceptional accomplishments.

THE FILM WAS COMPLETED with notable alacrity at the end of December, and Joan at once felt vaguely ill. The symptoms were diffuse and therefore difficult to diagnose and treat: general muscular aches and pains, recurring bouts of low-grade fever, coughs and colds. She celebrated Christmas with friends as usual and, although living alone with one or two servants, she sumptuously decorated the house in order to welcome guests during the holidays. But during the first three months of 1940, she was never completely well for more than a day or two. Dr. Branch, who regularly looked after her, recommended as much rest as possible—not a realistic prescription for this patient. Several months passed before her mysterious ailment—very likely due to simple exhaustion—vanished and she felt restored to full health.

Her normal round of activities continued without much interruption. She made several trips to New York, to see plays and to pursue, she hoped, a serious new romantic affair; she dined with Franchot, to assure him of her friendship after the divorce; and she visited Doug and his new wife, the wealthy heiress and divorcee Mary Lee Eppling Hartford. She also read plays old and new, seeking just the right property for Metro to buy—and her list of choices fell not on musicals or frothy comedies but on works of substance. She particularly noted Rachel Crothers's successful 1937 play, *Susan and God,* a serious comedy in which Gertrude Lawrence had starred and which Joan and Franchot had seen during its long run. Perhaps it was no surprise that this work captured her interest: *Strange Cargo* had explicitly treated the theme of the indwelling divine presence in all people, and the Crothers play satirized shallow religious pretense in the person of a wealthy, scatterbrained woman who mistakes fad for faith.

For many years, the tale has been told that Joan took the play to Mayer, who told her that it had already been purchased for Norma Shearer, then being fitted for costumes. Then (so the story continues) Joan took a call from Mayer in late January: Norma had reneged and withdrawn from the picture, explaining that she did not want to play a woman old enough to have a teenage daughter (Shearer was thirty-eight). That development supposedly opened the door for Joan to assume the role she coveted.

But this account is a pleasant fiction that no documentation can support. Norma Shearer had, of course, happily played the mother of a preteen in *The Women,* and a year later, audiences would readily have accepted her as the mother of a teenager without presuming that this meant Norma was aging. The truth is that Norma had read the play and the revised screenplay, and she could not quite fathom (or did not find agreeable) the satire on phony religious sentiment.

———

SUSAN AND GOD REFLECTS indirectly on the nature of an authentic religious conviction—that is, the play affirms faith as mystery and, primarily, a matter of goodwill to others. Rachel Crothers, one of the most important and respected of American playwrights, had seen twenty-eight of her plays staged since 1907, and in *Susan and God* she treated by satiric inversion the oversimplification and dilution of real faith. In the title, Susan's name precedes God's, just as Susan's selfish needs and fashionable self-image blind her to love for others. Religion, for her, is nothing more than a pleasant way of thinking nice things about oneself, of managing the private lives of her friends and driving them almost to madness with her constant prattle. Religion, for Susan and her like, is, in other words, only a pleasant social diversion in which she can still luxuriate in her privileged, upper-class life, all but discounting the demands of her marriage, the needs of her daughter and any claims others might make on her effort, attention or kindness.

Absolutely certain of her own rightness, Susan consorts with a frivolous English aristocrat who has founded the "movement," and she blithely neglects the love of her husband and daughter. Susan's religion, then, is "thrilling and fun," as she announces—and it consists of little more than social-climbing self-righteousness and the singing of feel-good songs mistaken for hymns. But finally, and to her surprise, she discovers that the journey of true faith happens within, and not from public exhibition and contact with polite society.

Susan and God is a play that retains its fierce and timely relevance many decades later, for it punctures every pretense represented by empty, sanctimonious cant. This probably explains why the play has been so seldom performed after revivals in the 1950s, and why the movie of it—remarkably faithful to the theatrical text in every regard—is usually ignored. Critics who wanted to keep their jobs did not defy the injunction against commentary on matters religious except for simple news reporting about this or that personality—in other words, it would have been inadvisable to endorse wholesale the satire so persuasively written by Rachel Crothers. And it is common knowledge that audiences do not want questions raised about comfortable presumptions or facile religious emotions. Better to stay with something "thrilling and fun."

At the same time, the play is nothing like a tract: it is a particular kind of social satire, a high comedy in which the leading actress must be willing to appear monumentally foolish just before a moment of blinding epiphany brings about the beginning of a real conversion. She sees the errors of her ways and the hurt she has caused on the unhappy faces of her family and in the misery she has brought to her friends.

No wonder, then, that Susan's final words in both the play and the movie are so moving: as she tells her husband, "I don't think God is something out there. I think He's here, in us. And I don't believe He helps one bit until we dig and dig and dig to get the rottenness out of us . . . Oh, dear God, don't let me fall down again." And with those words, quietly uttered as she yields to her husband's embrace, the curtain falls on the now truly repentant Susan, who is perhaps at the edge of an authentic new beginning. The recurring theme of *Strange Cargo* had been the indwelling divine presence: "You are the temple of God," as Cambreau reminds his companions when he opens the Scriptures and reads from Saint Paul. Rachel Crothers is concerned, in however different a dramatic style, with nothing less.

Joan's acting was a triumph of improvisation, a virtuoso succession of mockeries, capricious gestures, witty intonations and credible dynamics: she understood Susan keenly and made her restlessly alive. Cukor noted her mysterious anxiety about the role right from the start of production in March, when Joan had an unusually difficult time conforming the role to herself. "Big trouble at first," she admitted. "I simply didn't understand how a woman could give up her husband and her total lifestyle and everything she'd lived for to become a religious nut. I went to George Cukor a little hysterical, [unable to] understand who the hell I was playing and why. In fifteen minutes, George straightened me out. It was a very difficult part, and I owe a lot to [her leading man] Fredric March, who played foil to me very generously."

Chirping gaily until the finale, Joan brilliantly communicated the identity of flighty, insouciant Susan, oblivious to others and fundamentally hypocritical. When a maid brings her breakfast, for example, she demands "quiet time" for prayer before she can accept her coffee and hot muffin. She reclines dramatically on a chaise, crosses her hands over her chest and closes her eyes devoutly, dismissing the maid as she insists she must take her day's instructions from God. But as soon as she is alone, Susan reaches for the muffin, jumps up and starts the day with empty, evangelistic fervor. Evidently God tells Susan to hop to it—to go for the muffin, and never mind the quiet time.

Joan's understanding of Susan's arch moralism and her concomitant fear of being abandoned made the movie's final moment of epiphany credibly affecting. In this regard, *Time,* one of the few periodicals to take the movie seriously, defended the script's lengthy conversations precisely because "it has more to say."

As for Joan: "She found all the comedy in the silly, empty-headed woman who finally, funnily rose to emotional maturity," recalled Cukor. "Whatever she did, Joan did wholeheartedly."

CHAPTER EIGHT

A Trilogy of Transformations
| 1941–1942 |

JOAN KNEW THAT *Susan and God* advanced many of the serious themes
of *Strange Cargo;* she also recognized that the two pictures had suited her
state of mind. With reporters, fans or strangers, she never discussed religion or
the spiritual life: she had neither the vocabulary nor the temperament for such
topics, nor could she abide anything like pious proselytism. Nor did husbands
or lovers ever quote her on the topic. But in letters to friends who were in
emotional crisis or suffering because of illness or the deaths of loved ones, she
was frank in her belief in a spiritual life and in divine providence. And late in
life, she was quite forthright: "I believe in God, but I don't think He cares a
hell of a lot about whether a person is a Catholic, Protestant, Jew or Muslim, as
long as that person has a record rolled up that includes more good marks than
bad ones. I think Roz Russell is the best example of a practicing believer. Her
Catholicism is very strong, but she doesn't impose it on others. I think faith is
wonderful, but when you try to impose it on others, it's irritating and boring.
Have faith, but don't become a hooker about it is all I can say."

There is no doubt that at least from the end of 1939 and throughout 1940,

Joan Crawford was indeed enduring a kind of interior crisis of her own. She certainly would not have called it that, but the words adequately describe her state of mind and heart.

What were the causes of this crisis, manifested in vague physical complaints and constant disaffection? Why, no fewer than four times between January and April 1940, did she telephone to the studio or arrive on the set complaining that she was "sick . . . unable to rehearse . . . unable to make a test . . . and depressed"? These phrases appear frequently on Metro's call sheets and production notes that season, and they were unprecedented in her career.

There were several reasons for this unusual state of affairs, but primary among them was Joan's longing for children. Her friendship with Margaret Sullavan had revived that desire, hitherto frustrated by miscarriages and Franchot's indifference to fatherhood ("I don't think he especially wanted a child," she said). She knew the legal obstacles were formidable, but recently she had spent time talking over the matter with Gloria Swanson, at a party given by Margaret Sullavan and Leland Hayward. "I was amazed," said Swanson, "when I heard that I was Joan Crawford's idol, the woman she wanted to be like. I could not quite imagine a person feeling that way about another person."

At that time, Swanson's career was in sharp decline. Her opulent life was no longer envied, it was resented, and she was out of work and idling in Hollywood. She was about to begin work on a picture that turned out to be her last for a decade, until the temporary comeback in *Sunset Boulevard*. But Gloria had two children and, like Sullavan, she told Joan that motherhood provided great fulfillment in her life. When Gloria mentioned that she had been single when she adopted a son—three months after her divorce from her second husband in 1922—Joan at once resolved on a bold course of action toward the same goal.

But the issue had become more difficult by 1940. Mayer had been correct when he warned of obstacles in the way of realizing the goal of adoptive parenthood. As Joan soon learned, an unmarried man or woman could legally adopt children in only a dozen American states—but such an adoption would not necessarily be recognized in California. Perhaps thinking of her own benighted childhood, and perhaps thinking, too, of the danger of becoming Susan Trexel—living for herself only and without reference to the needs of a child—Joan began to investigate adoption agencies across the country.

Stymied by negative responses for almost a year—but no less determined—she eventually took a route pursued by many wealthy and celebrated people in Hollywood and across the country. With the utmost discretion and acting through private intermediaries, she contacted illegal baby brokers—most of them women who bought (or just as often kidnapped) unwanted or neglected infants and then sold them at a huge profit. Among the most notorious of these flesh peddlers were Bessie Bernard and Georgia Tann. They worked independently, both of them making handsome livings from unwed mothers and from people desperate to provide unwanted children with loving homes and willing to hand over large sums for the privilege. Bernard and Tann were helpful to Joan at different times over the course of eight years. Both were eventually stopped by the law, but the proliferation of baby brokers continued.

———

BETWEEN SPRING 1939 AND June 1940, Joan, sometimes accompanied by someone posing as the potential baby buyer, traveled to New York, New Jersey and—where the trade was most brisk—Miami. "I was told originally of five pregnant girls, their backgrounds and their problems." The story of the fourth moved her, and the mother was right there in Los Angeles. Joan paid for her medical expenses during pregnancy and for the baby's delivery, on June 11, 1939, in Hollywood Presbyterian Hospital. But the course of love did not proceed smoothly, for California law still would not permit a single woman to adopt a child. This had only rarely been permitted, after the papers had been cleared in another state.

Hence (as the production histories stated) Joan's "inabilities to rehearse, her absences due to depressions and illnesses . . . and her general anxieties" during the first months of 1940, while filming *Susan and God,* were due to the fact that she had unwisely brought the baby home with a nursemaid. This, of course, was a dangerous course of action, for the child could summarily be removed by court action, as Joan was informed by Gregson Bautzer, a Los Angeles lawyer to whom she turned for counsel.

A solution was found, although it was not easy to finesse. "I left California with the baby, so that I could adopt her legally elsewhere," Joan later explained. The plan was for her to go to Las Vegas, for Nevada permitted a single person to adopt. First, however, she took the baby to New York during the winter, where friends were solicitous and sympathetic—among them, Helen Hayes and her family, who lived north of Manhattan in a quaint town on the Hudson River.

But there was another reason for her journey to New York—to spend time with a man who had come into her life and had brought her great happiness. The relationship explains her long trips to the East Coast, her subsequent long holidays in Northern California and her concomitant periods of absence from work; she was officially granted no fewer than three prolonged leaves of absence from Metro between the spring of 1939 and the winter of 1942.

Charles McCabe was a wealthy New York businessman whose serious romance with Joan was conducted on both coasts for several years. A public figure, married and with a family, he had to conduct the affair with the utmost discretion, and Joan was completely cooperative. Briefly, it seemed to her as if they would one day marry, but his professional life, religious background and social position restrained him from raising the topic of divorce with his wife, a woman highly placed in New York society and charitable circles. Even when the affair ended, after three years, Joan maintained her silence, referring to McCabe only obliquely in her published memoir, *A Portrait of Joan*. Describing him as "a marvelously mature man, one of the best people I've ever known," she found McCabe not only an appealing and steady companion but also a man who offered the kind of paternal and protective affection she always sought.

And so she had to settle for a relationship she called "long and lovely." He taught her to hunt and fish, and she went on these sporting trips with a group of McCabe's male friends who had his absolute confidence. "I carried my own gun and my own camera," she remembered. "I waded through streams in the vanguard; and at noon when we camped, I helped fix lunch and surprised them with snacks packed away in my knapsack, just in case they didn't catch any fish. [He] introduced me to politics, to banking, big business and public affairs."

Because she "carried her own camera," Joan documented many episodes during this love affair, and she kept the filmed record until her death. Several hours long and covering three years, the film was discovered many years later by her family and was first publicly shown on December 5, 2008, at a Joan Crawford festival at the University of California, Los Angeles. The color footage shows a woman happy and relaxed, enjoying her private life with her lover and (by 1942) two babies. Holding the camera, McCabe focused on Joan strolling in the woods, paddling a canoe, reclining on the grass and taking a sunbath. When she held the camera, she took pictures of a pleasant, smiling man, utterly lacking glamour or movie-star good looks.

But she was ultimately disappointed. "This rewarding experience I wouldn't have missed, but his marital situation could not be altered. In his position, he could not afford the publicity of being associated with *any* woman. I understood. Why risk hurting him? What I'd fought for all my life, this career, this name, made it impossible to be anonymous [forever]." The end of the affair cut deeply. According to her oldest adopted daughter, Joan was always "very sentimental about him. She loved [him]; I knew that by the way she looked when she told me. But she said he was married and would never be able to get a divorce from his wife. She had tears in her eyes when she got to that part of the story."

———

JOAN'S SILENCE ABOUT THE baby girl she wanted to adopt was broken when she first spoke publicly, on May 23, 1940, in a news release she carefully prepared. "Her transcontinental journeys were for the purpose of adopting a baby," the *Los Angeles Times* reported. She did not reply when asked the name of the New York orphanage at which she claimed to have obtained Christina—the name on which she had settled for the baby girl. Although biographers have categorically insisted that Joan returned with the child to Los Angeles at once and celebrated her first birthday there with a lavish party in June, the truth is that Joan and Christina remained in New York (a fact confirmed also by Christina). "Miss Crawford was reluctant to disclose any details," according to the same newspaper report. "She and the baby will remain in New York for a few more days."

The days extended to another eight months, until January 1941. The time was spent with Charles McCabe—in suites at Manhattan hotels, at Pennsylvania resorts and (when his wife was absent) at his country home in Connecticut. Mother and daughter then traveled to Los Angeles via Nevada, where the adoption papers were finalized, thanks to Bautzer's expert strategy, which also facilitated the recognition of the Nevada adoption in the State of California. When mother and child finally arrived home in Brentwood, Christina was nineteen months old; a properly furnished nursery, designed by Billy Haines, awaited her.

Of her early years, Christina wrote, "Mother and I were absolutely inseparable. She took me with her wherever she went. I slept in her dressing rooms and on the studio sound stages. I traveled in the car with her from the time I was only a few months old. She saved every bit of hair cut from my head, every tooth from my mouth. All were carefully sealed in envelopes and labeled in her generous handwriting. There were gifts for which she wrote little notes— 'to my beautiful infant—I love you, my darling, beautiful child.'"

Christina also appreciated the source of Joan's generosity and loving-kindness. She was aware that her mother showered her "with the pent-up outpouring of love and affection that had been stifled in her for so many years . . . I wanted for nothing: toys, clothes and baby jewelry. She was constantly holding me and looking at me . . . [and] whenever she didn't take me to the studio, she would rush home in time to feed me and give me my bath. She would sing lullabies to me and rock me to sleep . . . My adoring, indulgent mother couldn't resist giving me anything I asked from her. In return, she had my total devotion."

AFTER INTERVIEWING DOZENS OF women for the role of nursemaid and nanny, Joan finally settled on two—one of whom moved into the house so that Christina would always have a caregiver when her mother worked late hours or had to travel for location shooting or had evening social engagements away from home. The helpers arrived none too soon, for on January 23, 1941, Joan began work on a difficult and demanding picture in which she rendered one of the most exquisitely realized performances of her career.

Joan had seen Ingrid Bergman in the Swedish film *En kvinnas ansikte* (*A Woman's Face*), directed by Gustaf Molander in 1938. The movie had been released in America in the fall of 1939, precisely when Ingrid arrived in the United States under contract to Selznick and appeared in her first Hollywood movie—a remake of her 1936 Swedish film, *Intermezzo*. "I adore Ingrid and once wrote her a fan letter," said Joan. In fact, the letter was about *A Woman's Face,* which she not only admired but which had deeply moved her and planted the seeds of an idea.

The two actresses met at Selznick's party for the premiere of *Intermezzo,* where Joan was able to turn the conversation to *A Woman's Face*. She wanted to know if Ingrid would be offended if Joan were to ask Mayer (Selznick's father-in-law) to secure the rights for Joan to appear in an American remake of the picture. She knew this might seem impertinent, but there were so few good roles for an actress. Ingrid laughed and dismissed the idea of "offense," saying that, after all, they were there to celebrate a Hollywood remake of a Swedish film for *her*—so why not a Hollywood remake of a Swedish film for *Joan?*

In addition to the fact that the story and the role were enormously compelling, there were other immediate reasons for Joan's attraction to this project. For one thing, Mayer was assigning a significant number of the new and interesting roles to newcomers, among them foreigners like Hedy Lamarr, who turned twenty-six in 1940, and Lana Turner, just nineteen. Greer Garson was two years older than Joan, but Mayer believed that audiences would love Garson's English-rose beauty, her accent and her rare combination of whimsy, charm and moral authority; he was right. And Judy Garland, eighteen, was quickly ascending to stardom after *The Wizard of Oz*. In other words, an entirely new breed of actress was receiving Leo the Lion's share of attention in Culver City.

Another reason for Joan's settling on *A Woman's Face* was—her *face*. She was entering a period of mature, almost statuesque beauty, but she was also afraid of being considered too old to be cast as a leading lady. In 1941 she would turn thirty-five, and well-founded rumors were circulating that both Garbo (thirty-six) and Shearer (thirty-nine) intended to quit the business permanently—primarily over disputes about the quality of their assignments, but also because they knew that leading roles were scarce for "aging women" (which meant actresses past their midthirties).

And so Joan approached her boss. "Poor Mr. Mayer," Joan wrote later, remembering the meeting at which she begged him to make *A Woman's Face* for her. "He had borne with me as the bitch in *The Women*, the bleak-looking woman in *Strange Cargo*, the mother of a subdeb in *Susan and God*, [and] now he balked at me playing a scarred woman who hated the world." But George Cukor rose to her defense and agreed to direct the picture, and while Joan was away from California with Christina, Donald Ogden Stewart completed the screenplay. Ready on her return, the production proceeded smoothly and was completed in two months, at the end of March.[1]

Beginning at a murder trial and continuing in a series of flashbacks, the story moves backward and forward, telling of Anna Holm, a woman with hideous facial scars, the result of a fire set by her drunken father when she was a child. Alienated and embittered, she has grown up shunned, mocked and rejected, and her hatred and contempt for people has turned her to a life of crime. While working as the ringleader of a gang of blackmailers, she meets and falls in love with a handsome, unscrupulous aristocrat (played by Conrad Veidt), who is fearful of losing a vast inheritance to a young nephew.

Anna submits to a dozen painful operations, from which, thanks to a brilliant and caring surgeon (Melvyn Douglas), she emerges a beautiful woman, free of scars and apparently ready for a normal life. She is also secretly attracted

---

1. Stewart worked notably on (among many others) the screenplays for *Dinner at Eight*, *The Barretts of Wimpole Street*, *No More Ladies*, *Holiday*, *Love Affair*, *The Women* and *The Philadelphia Story*.

to the surgeon, but he is married to a scheming, shallow and unfaithful shrew (Osa Massen).

Now that Anna has been rendered physically whole and attractive, what of her inner life, her character? The test of her real recovery comes when the aristocrat, exploiting her emotional vulnerability, coerces Anna into going along with his plan to murder his nephew, thus securing his wealth and, he promises, their future together. But when she goes in disguise as nanny to the boy, she realizes she is not only incapable of murder but also loves the child and his family. When the villain arrives and the murder plot is set in motion, Anna saves the boy and indirectly causes the death of the aristocrat. At the trial that links the story's episodes, Anna has been accused of murder; she is, however, acquitted, and the ending implies that she and the surgeon will begin a new life together.

Makeup artist Jack Dawn created a repellent scar that took hours to apply each day—"from eye to mouth on the right side of my face," as Joan recalled, "a hideous mass of seared tissue" that was clearly seen for the first forty-seven minutes of the picture. Metro, afraid that too many people would wrongly regard A Woman's Face as a horror picture, released no photos or even hints of the character's disfigurement. Cukor's direction was, as usual, expert, and Robert Planck's atmospheric cinematography consisted of shifting pools of key lights and arresting shadows.

Joan delivered a performance of quiet, often chilling intensity. Before the surgery, her Anna is a cauldron of astringent contempt, a woman eager for love yet fearful of trusting anyone; afterward, the character gradually warms and deepens—an acting achievement even more remarkable in light of the discontinuous filming of sequences.

It is difficult to understand why MGM did not put Joan forward for an Oscar nomination that year.[2] Her portrayal was a masterpiece of psycho-

---

2. Joan Fontaine won the Academy Award as Best Actress of 1941, for *Suspicion;* the other nominees were Bette Davis (for *The Little Foxes*), Olivia de Havilland (for *Hold Back the Dawn*), Greer Garson (for *Blossoms in the Dust*) and Barbara Stanwyck (for *Ball of Fire*).

logical realism. She revealed the emotional terrorist lurking in Anna's soul alongside a poignant helplessness. Both victim and victimizer, the scarred woman becomes only gradually a candidate for the human race, and this duality struck audiences as something they could understand in a woman to whom they could relate. She was neither angel nor demon—she was a human being, and Joan neither erased the toughness nor exaggerated Anna's tragic sense of isolation. Joan expressed the conflict raging for ascendancy within Anna and within herself. In the latter case, it was the conflict between the demands of stardom and the desire for a contented private life with husband and children.

"I have nothing but the best to say for *A Woman's Face*," she told an interviewer many years later. "It was a splendid script, and George [Cukor] let me run with it. I finally shocked both the critics and the public into realizing the fact that I really was at heart a dramatic actress. Great thanks to Melvyn Douglas [costarring with Joan for the third time]; I think he is one of the least appreciated actors the screen has ever used. His sense of underplay, subordination, whatever you call it, was always flawless. I say a prayer for Mr. Cukor every time I think of what *A Woman's Face* did for my career. It fortified me with a measure of self-confidence I'd never had."

Cukor's fourth picture with Joan left him with a lifetime of respect for her talents: "She played a disfigured monster of a woman who would not flinch from killing a child, and she did not soften it a bit" until the story developed to the proper point. Cukor was also impressed with her technique. "In the days before zoom lenses and advanced electronics, cameras often had to be mounted on great cumbersome cranes, maneuvered by as many as twelve men, and close-ups might well require all this to be pushed from extreme long shots to within a few inches of an actor's face. Many found it difficult to overcome some understandable nervousness as this juggernaut ground closer and closer. Not Joan Crawford." Nor were the critics unmoved: *The Hollywood Reporter,* for one, called Joan's work "the greatest acting of her career—she is superb."

Cukor was right to stress the significance of Joan's close-up shots, which became an ever more crucial element in the power of her films. The close-up was entirely an American innovation—a camera technique eliminating the distance between actor and audience and so rendering unnecessary the theatrical reliance on gestures and mime. A stage actor (as André Malraux observed) is a little head in a huge hall; a movie actor is a huge head in a little hall. As Joan realized more fully after her Fairbanks father-in-law first mentioned it, the subtlest facial expression—a mere trembling of the lips, fluttering of eyelashes or raising of the brow—became visible and eloquent. She had no need to exaggerate her expressions: the close-up could communicate what she felt.

A Woman's Face might well be regarded as the third picture in a trilogy of transformations. From the tested Julie of *Strange Cargo* to the chastened Susan in *Susan and God* and on through the transformation of Anna Holm, Joan drew on the crises in her own life to present three women. This was certainly not a conscious intention on her part—nor were the films planned as a trilogy— but an actress cannot leave herself at home when she steps onto a soundstage. It was *this* Joan Crawford at *this* time of her life, with *these* experiences and this complex of psychological states that enabled her to draw on deep feelings within herself. In childhood, she knew feelings of abandonment and rejection; early in her career, she felt inferior and unacceptable. The Fairbanks clan had always regarded her as unworthy, and Franchot was a living reminder of the vacuity of her intellectual life and the poverty of her education. The McCabe affair was emotionally fulfilling, but it was doomed to impermanence. Only in refining her talent could she discover any reason to keep fighting for self-respect. That was the one thing she could depend on.

There was another element in this transformation, tentative and inconstant though it certainly was. Perhaps without deliberation but with conscious goodwill, she saw unwanted babies as small mirrors of her early self—children who needed to be "saved" from a childhood like hers.

———

IN EARLY APRIL, SHORTLY after production ended, Joan had a call from a baby broker she had contacted during her 1939 search. One of a booming network of such women, Alice Hough lived in Los Angeles and had heard "through a friend" of Miss Crawford's desire to have a family. Would she be interested in adopting another baby, due to be delivered by a local mother in early June?

Joan did not delay. On June 3, 1941, a boy was born, named Marcus Gary Kullberg. Alice Hough worked fast, and ten days later, Joan collected the illegitimate child at Hough's "fine, palatial residence," as Kullberg saw for himself years later, after researching his ancestry and early childhood. "It was evident Hough was handsomely rewarded for her craft." Joan returned to Brentwood at once with the baby.

But in October, after months of news stories had appeared about Joan's second adoption, Kullberg's mother (as he wrote) "started to feel guilty about giving up her child and decided to pursue my return." A single news release giving his exact birth date, followed by some basic private detective work, led the mother to her baby's new residence. "She wrote letters to Alice Hough and Joan Crawford, demanding my return, threatening suit and negative publicity. I was returned to the Kullberg home in November of 1941."

So it happened that, for five months, Joan had an infant son she had named Christopher Crawford, and then he was gone. "She adored you," wrote Betty Barker, Joan's secretary, years later, "and she was broken-hearted when she had to return you to your natural mother. I remember that she wanted to fight the case, but her lawyers convinced her that she couldn't win. When she lost you, all of us were afraid to mention your name to her for years, as it was a tender subject with her. She would have loved to have known what happened to you."[3]

———

DURING THAT SUMMER WITH Christina, Christopher and often Charles McCabe, Joan performed in one of her least known and most unfortunately neglected movies. *When Ladies Meet* was based on another successful play by Rachel Crothers. Joan read a first draft of the script and petitioned successfully

---

3. After a second, happier adoption, Marcus Gary Kullberg was known for the rest of his life as D. Gary Deatherage.

for the role of Mary Howard, a novelist who attempts to resolve her romantic difficulties through her fiction and the plot of her novel through a resolution of her romantic life. Her costars were Greer Garson, Robert Taylor and Herbert Marshall, and filming began at the end of June and was completed by mid-August. The screenplay finalized by S. K. Lauren and Anita Loos wisely preserved most of the play's sharp dialogue.

The ladies who meet in this shrewd and trenchant tale are the wife of a publisher and the writer who hopes to replace her in his affections. Characters race about, trying to discover who loves whom and why, and the mood is alternately amusing and deadly earnest. At the conclusion, the novelist realizes what a fool she has been, and for the first time the publisher's wife knows that she must rethink her marriage.

When Ladies Meet is the sort of picture that perhaps could not be made many decades later: it is essentially dialogue—briskly comic repartee alternating with wise observations about marriage and the sexes. The venerable tradition of weekend visits to country houses; the concern for moral values in the tangle of romance; the notion of expediency and pride, of fidelity and its opposite—all this is handled in long verbal exchanges, without physical humor, pratfalls, car chases, slapstick or exploding bombs.

During the first half of the twentieth century (and before the ascendancy of Lillian Hellman), Rachel Crothers was the most famous and popular female playwright in America. Her works, which she also directed, appeared at the rate of one a year from 1906 to 1937, and they never failed to find appreciative audiences and adoring critics on Broadway and on tour. *When Ladies Meet* is a classic of high comedy—a genre the author mastered over many years.

High comedy exploits local color and scenery (in this case, expensive and elegant Manhattan penthouses and beautiful country cottages), and it outfits the characters in glamorous finery in order to deal with social pretenses. Represented also in the works of Wilde, Coward, Behrman and Barry, high comedy exploits the traditions of mistaken identities and the revelations of double lives—elements as old as ancient Greek theatre. *When Ladies Meet* uses the refinements of class, education and wit to mock society itself; and in the best tradition of high comedy, it reveals something truthful yet suspect in human nature, something grubby underneath the glamour. This notion is perfectly encapsulated in Joan's acute performance, as her Mary Howard moves from emotional certainty to something like maturity.

All this succeeds as sparkling entertainment, thanks in no small part to the skill of Robert Z. Leonard, who had directed *Dancing Lady* and was working on his 135th picture. Very much an ensemble piece, *When Ladies Meet* remains a rare kind of grown-up comedy. It contains an enormous amount of common sense combined with smooth moviemaking craftsmanship, perfectly timed and subtle performances and a rare knowledge of and faith in human nature. Like *Susan and God,* the original Crothers play won coveted prizes; as a movie, *When Ladies Meet* retains a wise and mature humor that only the most cynical can reject.

———

NOTHING REMOTELY SIMILAR can be said of Joan's next picture, which she undertook voluntarily—even insistently—just after America entered World War II in December. On January 16, 1942, Clark Gable's wife, Carole Lombard, was returning to Los Angeles from a bond-selling tour, exploiting her celebrity on behalf of the war effort. She and her mother were among the passengers in a small aircraft that crashed in Nevada, killing everyone on board. Carole Lombard was thirty-three.

Joan at once contacted Gable; almost wild with grief, he raced to her home, where she provided a refuge from the press. It must be counted to her credit that Joan then approached Louis B. Mayer and asked if he would permit her to assume the role planned for Carole in a film at Columbia Studios. Mayer disliked the idea of loaning out one of his major stars, but Joan's next script was not yet ready, and he stood to make a profit of more than $250,000 on the deal.

Produced from late February to mid-April, *They All Kissed the Bride* reveals why Columbia was, at the time, considered a grade-B studio. Prepared as a screwball comedy just right for Lombard, it was made on the cheap for Crawford, who played a hard-edged business tycoon who at last succumbs to love. The sets were minimized and cheaply dressed due to the imposition of wartime construction costs, and there was no time to revise a script loaded with a tedious series of episodic, predictable and alarmingly unfunny sequences.

Strange Cargo, Susan and God and *A Woman's Face* had convinced Joan that she had an important and ongoing place in movies. Unaccountably, she had a low regard for *When Ladies Meet,* but nothing could have prepared her for the disappointment of *They All Kissed the Bride.* Nevertheless, she turned over her entire salary for the picture ($112,500) to the American Red Cross, which had braved the wintry elements to recover the remains of Carole and her mother. When she learned that her manager had withheld his 10 percent fee and sent on the balance to the Red Cross, she made up the sum and promptly dismissed him.

———

JOAN'S RELATIONSHIP WITH Charles McCabe came to an end that spring. She had found herself too deeply attached to settle for the permanent role of the other woman in a real-life remake of *Back Street,* and when it was clear that they could never have a life together, she had to end the affair. Perhaps contrary to her expectations, she was at once unutterably depressed. She had lost the second adopted baby, and now McCabe's departure left her feeling lonely and useless.

In May, Joan asked the press agent Harry Mines to dine at North Bristol. He asked if he could bring along a friend—a man she had met once, very briefly, when he appeared in a silent bit in *Mannequin.* The extra guest's name was Phillip Terry. Unmarried, temperate and fond of children, he was a tall, handsome, bespectacled actor with considerable technical training but no notable credits.

Born Frederick Kormann, in San Francisco, he had graduated from Stanford University and then studied drama in England before MGM signed him as a contract player and gave him a new name. After his first visit to Joan's home, he was invited often and on his own. He and Joan dined quietly, read scripts and talked about the challenges and rewards of raising children. Phillip's presence, she recalled, was "comfortable and comforting. I wasn't alone. Someone was content just to be with the baby and me. The men who'd attracted me before were passionate, volatile [Fairbanks, Tone, Gable]. The man in New York [McCabe] was a dynamo, but I couldn't have him—and now here was his antithesis, an easy-going, unpretentious man who seemed to adore me, who was calm and absolutely uncomplicated."

Because he maintained an absolute, discreet silence for the rest of his life about his time with Joan Crawford, it is impossible to assess the nature of Phillip's attraction to Joan or the depth of his love for her. He certainly saw her as an exciting, vibrant, influential and talented actress, and her company was never boring. She was also an exceedingly sensual woman, and there was no reason for him to ignore her advances. And advance she did—quickly. Joan considered Phillip primarily as a father for Christina and the children she hoped to adopt in times to come.

On July 21, six weeks after their first evening together, they were married. Admonishing Joan that she was "walking into the sunset with some unknown actor," Mayer huffed and puffed but could not blow down her plan for a domestic life with a man she deemed perfect for the role of doting father. For the present, she got her wish: he was the gentlest of paternal figures, tending to Christina and hoping for work.

The wedding took place during the production of what turned out to be Joan's penultimate movie under her Metro-Goldwyn-Mayer contract; in fact, the picture was one of the reasons the agreement was soon dissolved. *Reunion in France* was the story of a successful French modiste (Joan), highly placed in the millinery business when Hitler marches into Paris. Learning that her lover (Philip Dorn) is collaborating with Nazi officers, she transfers her affections to a downed American pilot working with the Royal Air Force (John Wayne), and she is soon impoverished. But she then discovers that her Frenchman is actually working in the Resistance, and they are happily reunited while the American politely resumes his flying exploits. Thus ends the wartime love triangle.

"It's too bad the Nazis do not really know France," says the hero triumphantly at the fadeout. More to the point, it was too bad Metro did not really know France. The movie reduces the anguish of the Nazi occupation of France to a traditional romance, and on almost every level of cinematic storytelling it can only be regarded as an outline of how not to make a movie and how to miscast an intelligent and popular star.

In the role of a shallow Frenchwoman, Joan was all wrong, and she knew it ("I really wasn't suited to the wartime melodramas they were turning out"). Although her emotions as a war victim are never less than subtle, she was always (and remained here) an American: by no stretch of a viewer's imagination could she be regarded as a native Parisian—especially because she is surrounded by a cast speaking English in heavy German and French accents. Worse, she is shown, scene after scene, in a series of Metro's most stunning gowns and in perfect makeup—hardly appropriate for an unemployed woman in occupied France. Nor was she helped by John Wayne, whose performance was carved out of wood. "Take John out of the saddle and you've got trouble," she muttered years later. The talented Dutch actor Philip Dorn, as the apparent traitor, was cruelly out of place: attractively urbane and properly low-keyed, he endured the fate of many Europeans whom Hollywood imported and then wasted in inferior roles.

"Making it was hell," recalled director Jules Dassin. After reading the screenplay, which had been tortured into submission by a squadron of poorly equipped writers, Dassin asked for a meeting with Mayer and company and outlined his gravest reservations. "But they wanted only to talk about one thing—Joan's clothes and her hats. They wanted to dress her for her fans, and they were going to do just that—and this was talked about for hours." Hence a character stripped of every resource and all dignity never appeared in the movie looking less than wealthy and dazzling.

Joan was tense and annoyed at having to appear in this dreadful concoction—hence her collaboration with the director had none of the easy confidence that had distinguished her performances when she worked with Clarence Brown, George Cukor and Robert Z. Leonard. When Dassin called "Cut!" for the first time and approached her to revise a scene, she turned her back and left the set.

That evening, Mayer fired him, but his unemployment was brief: Joan invited Dassin to dinner at Bristol Avenue and asked if he rated her a poor actress. He protested the opposite, but added that perhaps like any good actor, she could, from time to time, improve a gesture or a line reading during another take. She then instructed him never to call "Cut!" but furtively to draw a finger across his brow, and that would be her signal to stop and *ask* to repeat the shot. Anxiously aware that Metro executives were scrutinizing her every moment in the picture, Joan attempted refuge by playing the diva with her director, an unfortunate pose that she sometimes repeated (to no good effect) in the years to come.

"I think Joan was just about at the end of her rope," recalled Natalie Schafer, who appeared in a small but effective role as the wife of a Nazi officer. "She wasn't brutal or offensive to me or to anyone else, just tightly wound. I think she knew her days were numbered at MGM, [and] she was smarting over the assignments they had given her. *Reunion in France* was not right for her, and she just did not want to be in it. But she remained very professional in spite of all that. That was Joan. Whatever was going on in her mind, you might see glimmers of it in her expression and in her off-camera mood, but she was always about getting the work done and being a pro."

The critics were merciless. *"Reunion in France* is glibly untruthful on serious matters,"* ran a typical notice. "It infers [*sic*] that the French [Resistance] comes from its moneyed society folk and spendthrifts—hardly an ordinary French citizen appears in the film." Making matters worse, both the situations and dialogue seemed to be lifted from a bad Italian opera, as when a dressmaker asks, "How can you expect a woman to cry at the collapse of an empire?" *Time* summarized the entire mess: "Whatever it is, it is not France."

———

PUTTING THIS DISAPPOINTMENT behind her, Joan was grateful for no duties more exacting than household chores and giving parties for friends and her daughter, for which no expense was spared. But she did not separate herself from the world. Before America entered the war, Melvyn Douglas and

Edward G. Robinson had spearheaded a movement in which they asked Congress to end all trade with Germany. Joan was among the first to sign their doomed plea-for-peace document. After Pearl Harbor, she exploited her name by joining a group offering daytime care for children whose mothers worked in airplane and munitions plants. She also raised money for various medical and civilian defense programs.

But Joan was still bound to Metro-Goldwyn-Mayer, and in November she went back to work on yet another movie set in war-torn Europe. This one turned out to be a remarkable and effective entertainment, however. Based on a novel by Helen MacInnes, *Above Suspicion* successfully treated the horror of war and the futility of murderous espionage by satire and allusion. Director Richard Thorpe economically guided Joan, costars Fred MacMurray, Conrad Veidt, Basil Rathbone and a large and capable roster of European actors through the episodes of a literate and witty screenplay.

Much of the success of *Above Suspicion* derived from its frank adherence to a formula already perfected by Alfred Hitchcock in the 1930s, in his successful seriocomic thrillers *The Man Who Knew Too Much, The 39 Steps* and *Secret Agent.* Hitchcock had come to America in 1939, and after completing *Rebecca* had turned out the masterful *Foreign Correspondent,* which is virtually a template for *Above Suspicion.*

All the major Hitchcock elements are here, enclosed within an espionage caper that involves a romantic couple unwittingly drawn into foreign intrigue as they try to uncover a secret in prewar Europe—precisely the situation of *Foreign Correspondent.* In their picaresque journey from England to Germany and the Tyrol, the newlyweds (MacMurray and Crawford) encounter agents and double agents, informers, underground Resistance workers, Nazi troops and unrepentant villains who (as always with Hitchcock) seem like the most civilized and sophisticated members of polite society. At the structural midpoint of the movie is a sequence lifted straight from *The Man Who Knew Too Much*—a symphony concert at which the firing of a bullet is timed to coincide with a *fortissimo* from the orchestra.

The movie pleased critics as *Reunion in France* had not. "The hour and a half pass like twenty minutes in this completely entertaining thriller," read a typical review, "and Joan Crawford is a very convincing heroine."

Above Suspicion certainly seems to be a kind of homage to Hitchcock. The absurd story is spun so deftly that there is time only to enjoy the polished performances and the breakneck pace of the comic action. Although she chafed more than ever under Metro's incautious handling of her career, Joan nevertheless created a portrait of a spritely, loving and confident bride who becomes a resourceful spy. Although she claimed not to have enjoyed the production, this is never apparent. As in *Chained, Love on the Run, Susan and God* and *When Ladies Meet,* Joan's talents extended beyond flaming-youth clichés and romantic melodramas. The dark *film noir* roles and unsympathetic female antagonists were yet to come, but she put her producers and fans on notice that the techniques of first-rate, literate comedy were on her palette, too. Contrary to conventional wisdom, she had an acute sense of comedy and comedy timing. It was unfortunate that these gifts were not exploited more often.

CHAPTER NINE

Oscar

| 1943–1947 |

I IMAGINE YOU'VE heard about our adopting little Phillip Terry II," Joan wrote to a friend in May 1943. "He is just ten months old and has light hair and very blue eyes. He is such a little angel."

Above Suspicion had wrapped in February, and at once she asked for a leave of absence from Metro. This Mayer allowed her, aware that she wanted the time to seek and find a second child for adoption. "I was so pleased with my little girl that, after Christina was a few years old, I knew I wanted to have another child. I didn't want her growing up alone." So it happened that Mr. and Mrs. Terry welcomed a ten-month-old boy into their home in April 1943, and henceforth Christina had a brother they called Phillip Jr., or, more whimsically, Phillip II (after the sixteenth-century Spanish king and emperor).

For the first time in eighteen years—since the winter of 1925—Joan did not receive any calls, memoranda, ideas, suggestions, treatments or screenplays from Metro-Goldwyn-Mayer. She had appeared in more than sixty films, had attained as much privilege and power as any contract worker and was among the most reliable and profitable players on Metro's roster. But the studio never considered her an actress of any stature: she was a star, which is something very different.

Things had changed in Culver City. Garbo and Shearer had slipped into effective retirement, and the attention of the corporate bosses in New York and Culver City was now turned to projects favoring Katharine Hepburn, Judy Garland, Lana Turner, Ava Gardner, Greer Garson, Hedy Lamarr, eleven-year-old Elizabeth Taylor and a three-year-old male dog called Pal, then being groomed for stardom as a female named Lassie.

In such circumstances, what was an actor to do—change careers? retire? Not Joan Crawford. She simply found pastimes until she could resume working, and it was natural for her to pursue challenges or chores she could dispatch with the same urgency and energy she applied to movie acting. Now she was a more attentive mother than ever. She also broadened the scope of her volunteer work; she raised money to open nursery schools for the children of working parents; and she hosted receptions for servicemen on their way to war. When Phillip was not working on a film (invariably in a minor role and for a brief time), he helped her tend their Victory Garden—those rows of fruits and vegetables planted at homes across America to reduce the pressures on a public food supply during World War II.

Because the war meant a shortage of servants, Joan did all the housework: cooking, sewing, decorating, repainting and, with Phillip's help, a fair amount of repairing and rebuilding. Most of all, she had her own intensive method of cleaning, which was a way of putting her seal on something, of exerting control, of making something turn out right. Her methods of housekeeping were excessive and needlessly repeated, but this was a benign compulsion. And so she scrubbed and cleaned and reorganized her closets, and then she cleaned some more, and applied fresh paint to the cupboards. "There were spells between cooking, cleaning, washing and sewing when I never gave movies a second thought!" Joan told columnist Hedda Hopper.

In June, she arranged a lavish party for Christina's fourth birthday, and friends and neighbors were invited to enjoy magicians and clowns, pony rides and a private circus—"a miniature Disneyland before one ever existed for the public," as Christina recalled.

"Joan Crawford's daughter Christina," recalled Brooke Hayward (Margaret Sullavan's daughter), who was a frequent guest, "was the most envied party hostess, because invariably she offered the longest program: not only puppet shows before supper and more and better favors piled up at each place setting, but movies afterward; besides, her wardrobe was the fanciest—layers and layers of petticoats under dotted Swiss organdy, sashed at the waist with plump bows and lace-trimmed at the neck to set off her dainty yellow curls."

But life without gainful employment was ultimately intolerable to Joan, and so she went to Mayer. After two long and intense meetings, she agreed to Mayer's demand that she pay one hundred thousand dollars to MGM to cancel her contract for several more pictures. For the rest of her life, Joan never uttered a word against Mayer—although she confided to friends that she felt shabbily treated during her last few years at the studio. Before and after Louis B. Mayer's death in 1957, she spoke of him only with gratitude and respect, even when it became fashionable and profitable for people to complain of the bad deals they had been dealt, the unjust treatment, the harassments and unfair dismissals. "Mr. Mayer was a beautiful man," she said as late as 1973.

On the morning of Tuesday, June 29, Joan drove to her dressing room at the studio. She packed her belongings carefully, carried them out to her car and then took her vacuum cleaner and scrub brushes inside and thoroughly cleaned the room, the small kitchenette and the private bath. When she departed through the gates of Metro-Goldwyn-Mayer Studios that summer afternoon, no one acknowledged that she had been a star there for eighteen years—and one who had substantially enriched the studio's coffers.

"It was difficult to leave Metro after eighteen years," she wrote to Lotte Palfi Andor, an actress who had appeared with her in *Above Suspicion*. "But when I started to feel too depressed, I suddenly remembered what lousy stories they'd given me, and then I got good and mad and walked out without a tear. The people I hated leaving were my crews—the electricians, makeup people, hairdressers, wardrobe. They really seemed like family to me."

One worker who had been at Metro more than twenty-five years recalled Joan's departure that day. "It was as if we had lost a part of our history," he said. In fact, they had.

———

BUT JOAN'S NEW AGENT, Lew Wasserman, had not been idle. Two days after she left MGM, in a development she had not expected when she went to see Mayer, Joan went on the payroll of Warner Bros. She was to receive a total of five hundred thousand dollars for three pictures, payable over six years at $1,667 per week—the equivalent of twenty-two thousand dollars weekly in 2010 valuation.

She was also granted approval of screenplays and directors for all her forthcoming Warners productions. Most important to her was the concomitant prerogative of contributing to (if not actually controlling) every aspect of production, from script development through art direction and photography to the final editing. As producers and directors were to learn, they ignored her questions and suggestions at their peril, for by this time Joan Crawford knew more about the crafts of moviemaking than many studio personnel.

Still, the prolonged period of professional idleness continued: there was no project at Warners for fourteen months after she signed the contract. But Joan continued with her duties as a star, welcoming to her home the portrait photographer John Engstead, who was preparing a photo-essay for *Harper's Bazaar*. "She came up from working in her garage," Engstead recalled, "her face flushed and with very little makeup."

"Excuse my appearance," Joan said, smiling and breathless. "I've been ironing. It's impossible to get help, so I do my own housework." Engstead felt this was not a complaint but an explanation. Moments later, in a change of wardrobe and freshly made up, she patiently stood for a two-hour session while Engstead painstakingly took his photographs.

Finally, in August 1944, Joan worked for one day on *Hollywood Canteen*, the studio's all-star movie salute to the troops, in which she appeared with the actor and soldier Dane Clark in a ninety-second cameo. "You look like Joan

Crawford!" he tells her on a crowded dance floor. "My husband says the same thing," she replies with a smile before whispering in his ear, "Don't look now, but I *am* Joan Crawford."

The movie title was the name of the club where, during World War II, American and Allied military men and women could, without paying any fee, socialize, eat, drink and dance while on leave or before they were shipped overseas. John Garfield and Bette Davis came up with the idea for the place, and soon Joan joined them and other stars as volunteers. She worked at the Canteen one or two nights a week, serving food, dancing with boys in uniform, autographing postcards for them to send and recording songs for the troops abroad. Like all the actors in *Hollywood Canteen,* Joan contributed her time and appearance without payment.

Some people described this period of professional inactivity as the most serene time of her life, but Joan was not among them: she found it "most difficult—frankly, I was bored, because the actress is half of this woman, and the actress had no outlet." Eventually, she informed Wasserman that she was taking herself off salary at Warners and would not accept her regular weekly paychecks.

"What does she mean—*off salary?*" grumbled Jack Warner when he heard this news. "Nobody's ever asked to be taken off salary! She must *want* something!"

She wanted a good picture, Joan told Warner. "Since I wasn't making one, I didn't feel justified in taking the salary." Soon afterward, one of Warner's producers gave her the screenplay for a domestic comedy called *Never Say Goodbye,* to be directed by Edmund Goulding. She read the script, which concerned a separated couple's resourceful young daughter who contrives to prevent their divorce. Joan promptly pronounced the project unsuitable for any sensible actress. The picture was finally made with Errol Flynn and Eleanor Parker, but without Goulding, who was also cool to the screenplay.

After Joan had rejected several more treatments and screenplays, she was summoned to a brief meeting by Henry Blanke, a producer at the studio. "I'll tell you something, Joan," he said quietly. "It's hard to find a role for you because you keep turning things down. My advice to you is to get a good property and do it. To be honest, no one is waiting for you, and many people have the idea that you're difficult to work with."

The only drama in Joan's life that year took place on December 29. As she was finishing supper with Phillip and the children, they heard the sounds of someone lurking and mumbling outside the house. Rebecca Kullberg, the natural mother of the child who had lived briefly with Joan in 1941, resided in nearby West Los Angeles. That evening, after reading about Joan's adoption of another baby boy, Kullberg—in a state of mental confusion—went to Bristol Avenue to retrieve what she thought was her own kidnapped child (who had, in fact, by this time been adopted by a loving family). She burst into the house and wandered madly about, demanding the immediate return of her son. Joan was frantic to protect the children; Phillip Terry called the police; and Mrs. Kullberg was forcibly removed. Later, after making continued threats to Joan and to the original baby broker, the poor woman was committed to a psychiatric institution. By a strange irony, Joan had just begun work on a film that was oddly appropriate to this absurd and violent domestic melodrama.

———

JAMES M. CAIN'S SPECIAL brand of hardboiled novel had been enormously successful since the 1930s, and two of them—*The Postman Always Rings Twice* and *Double Indemnity*—had already been filmed.[1] Cain published his novel *Mildred Pierce* in 1941, and Warner Bros. quickly purchased the movie rights and commissioned a treatment and then several drafts of a screenplay. At once, the Hollywood censors were strongly dissuasive: "The story contains so many sordid and repellent elements," wrote Joseph Breen, from the Office of the Motion Picture Production Code, "that we feel the finished picture would not

---

1. In 1943, *Postman* was filmed in Italy by Luchino Visconti, as *Ossessione;* it was remade in Hollywood under its original English title in 1945. Billy Wilder's movie of *Double Indemnity* was released in September 1944.

only be highly questionable but would meet with a great deal of difficulty on its release"—by which he meant, "Drop it!"

But a thirty-three-year-old producer named Jerry Wald went ahead, turning the script over to various writers until finally one of them, Ranald Mac-Dougall, handed in a version suitable for filming. Hungarian-born Michael Curtiz, director of a wide variety of movie genres (and a recent Oscar winner for *Casablanca*), signed on in October while the search continued for the right leading lady.

Joan had read the book and told Lew Wasserman that if there was to be a movie of it, this Mildred Pierce was a woman she completely understood. Mildred knew poverty and deprivation, as had Joan. Mildred was ashamed of her early life and family background, as was Joan. Mildred chose men unwisely, and she was prepared to be a slave in order to realize her ambitions. Most of all, she was neurotically and masochistically committed to lavishing every good thing on her daughter and granting her every wish. In the process, Mildred transforms herself from a poor, weary housewife into a wealthy restaurant tycoon—but in the process, she loses two husbands, two daughters and her business.

Because he had heard exaggerated rumors of Crawford's demands at Metro, Curtiz was hesitant when Wald mentioned her name. But when Joan went so far as to say she would submit to a screen test in order to prove her mettle—something an established star was never asked to do—Curtiz had no choice but to direct the test. To his astonishment, he then had to agree that they had found their Mildred. Joan (who wanted to play the role even before reading a screenplay) was the first major player signed for the movie, in October. Jack Carson was engaged shortly thereafter, and Zachary Scott, Eve Arden and Ann Blyth signed contracts in early December 1944.[2]

Location filming and process shots were produced that same month, but

---

2. Contrary to rumor, only Joan was offered the title role; see LaValley, 47. But he is wrong in stating that Scott, Arden and Blyth were not hired until January 1945: the "Daily Production and Progress Report" sheets for *Mildred Pierce* indicate that these players worked as early as December 13, 1944.

there was still nothing remotely resembling a completed script. No fewer than ten writers worked feverishly on as many lengthy treatments and scripts, but there was no "final draft" when shooting began. The screenplay is credited to Ranald MacDougall, who certainly had a major hand in the writing, along with Louise Randall Pierson (one of the many writers not credited).[3] The final product is a masterpiece of improvisation—indeed, a surprising amount of dialogue was extemporized on the set. The picture was scheduled to wrap in February 1945, but it took until May—and fresh pages of script were delivered almost every day during production. *Mildred Pierce* was held back for release until the autumn of 1945, after the end of the war.

———

THE DIRECTOR WAS NOT an easy man. On Joan's first day of filming, Curtiz greeted her by clutching her shoulders and shouting, for everyone to hear, "These damn pads of yours—they are awful! Off with the shoulder pads!" With that, he tore the dress from neck to hemline, only to see that she was wearing no shoulder pads. "Mr. Curtiz," Joan protested, "there *are* no pads—I bought this dress off the rack at Sears yesterday for two dollars and ninety-eight cents!"

She fled in tears from the set to her dressing room, pursued by the assistant director, Frank Heath, who warned that this was Curtiz's usual way of reducing to subservience every actor in his movies. The director had recently terrorized the usually unflappable Rosalind Russell on the set of the comedy *Roughly Speaking*. Russell's costar had been Jack Carson, who also had the important role of Wally Fay in *Mildred Pierce;* no pushover he, Carson supported Heath's description of Curtiz. Joan went back to work.

"When I started the tests for *Mildred Pierce*," Curtiz said in his heavy

---

3. The Warner Bros. script library at the Wisconsin Center for Film and Theater Research contains scripts for *Mildred Pierce* written by Catherine Turney, Margaret Gruen, William Faulkner, Louise Pierson Randall and Ranald MacDougall.

Middle European accent at the end of production, "I heard my star was very deefeecult. So I say, okay, Crawford, Curtiz will be more deefeecult. She took it like a trouper. We have now finished the picture and I see she is one swell actress. We get along fine on the picture. I luff her." With that, Joan stepped forward with a splendidly wrapped gift box for him. Inside was an oversized pair of shoulder pads.

She worked closely and agreeably with her makeup and wardrobe team, selecting simple daytime dresses, designing the upswept contemporary coiffures and picking the appropriate accessories. Gone were the absurdly lengthened eyelashes: only the patrician forehead and the high line of her eyebrow suggested strength.

With her colleagues, Joan was all business; and to some—like sixteen-year-old Ann Blyth—she was actually protective. Warner and Curtiz had not wanted Ann for the role, but Joan was adamant when she saw the girl's test. Her confidence was justified, for the result was Ann's chillingly effective portrayal of the spoiled, cruelly self-centered Veda. "The Joan Crawford I knew," recalled Ann Blyth decades later, "was dedicated and kind. She fought for me to have the part of Veda, and she told the director when she thought I ought to have more close-ups. Nobody I ever worked with enjoyed being a star more than she, but because she was so beautiful, I think people forgot she could act. There was a very deep core of vulnerability in Joan that she usually kept hidden. I saw it, as did others. She was a generous and caring friend to me throughout her life."

From the story conferences on *Mildred Pierce* that began in August 1944 through the final editing almost a year later, Joan had never been so totally involved in a production—nor so worn out by its demands. "The hours are from 5.00 A.M. till 7.30 P.M.," she wrote to a friend that winter. "Then there is the bath—makeup off—dinner—hair to dress and dry—study—to bed, if I'm lucky, by eleven! But it's worth it, as I believe we have a good picture."

———

CAIN'S NOVEL HAD TO undergo radical alteration in its journey to the screen— not only to placate the censors but also to make the role suitable for Crawford.

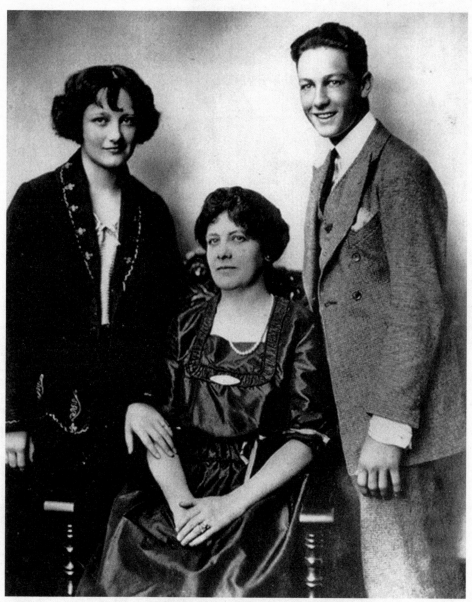

With her mother and brother (1922)

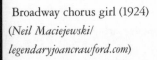
Broadway chorus girl (1924)
(*Neil Maciejewski/*
legendaryjoancrawford.com)

Harry Rapf bestows
the new name (1925)

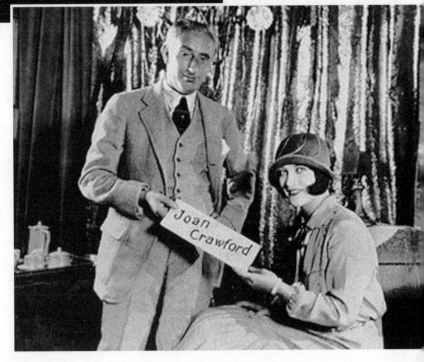

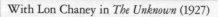

With Lon Chaney in *The Unknown* (1927)

At MGM (1925)

(Neil Maciejewski/legendaryjoancrawford.com)

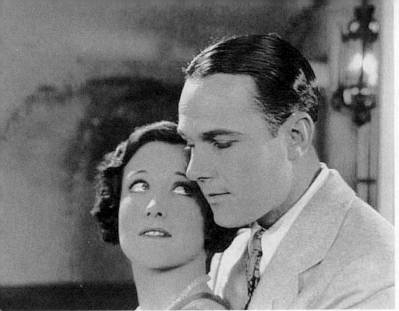

With William
Haines in *Spring
Fever* (1928)

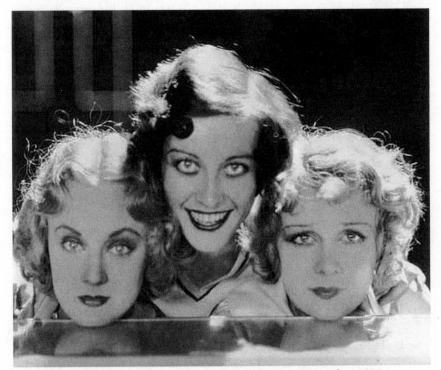

With Dorothy Sebastian and Anita Page in *Our Dancing Daughters* (1928)

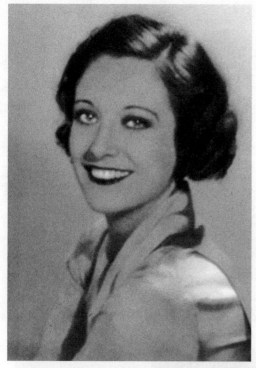

MGM Star (1928)
(*Neil Maciejewski/*
legendaryjoancrawford.com)

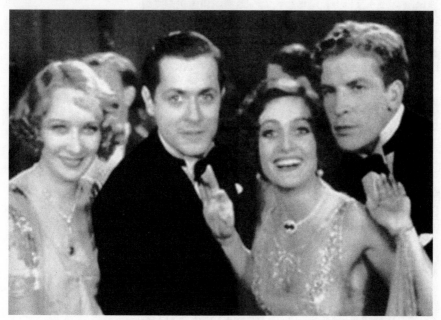

With Gwen Lee, Robert Montgomery and Don Terry in *Untamed* (1929)

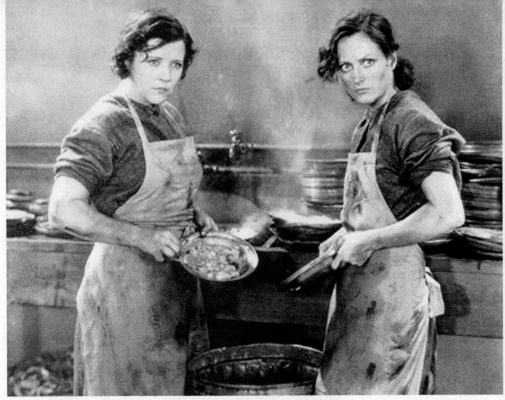

With Marie Prevost in *Paid* (1930)

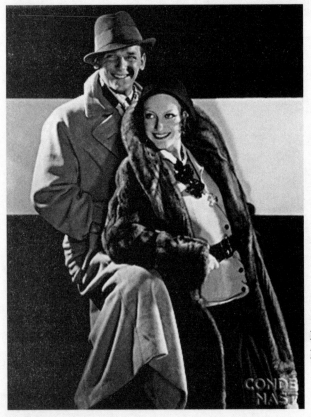

Mr. and Mrs. Douglas
Fairbanks Jr. (1930)

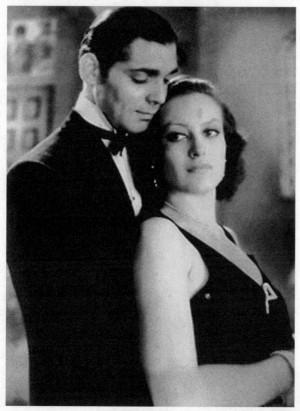

Clarence Brown directs Crawford and Gable in *Possessed* (1931)
(*Neil Maciejewski/legendaryjoancrawford.com*)

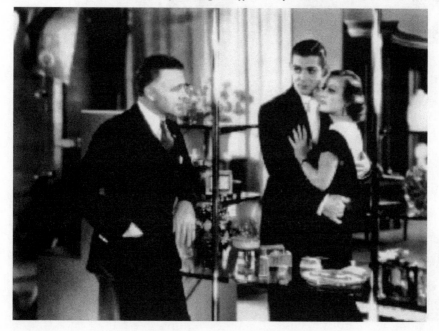

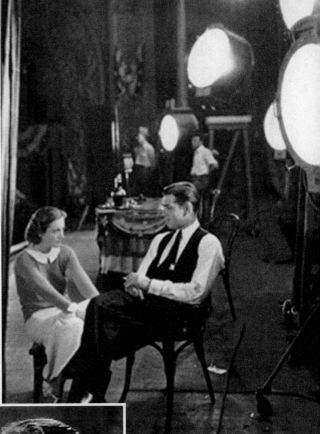

Crawford and Gable at work
(Neil Maciejewski/
legendaryjoancrawford.com)

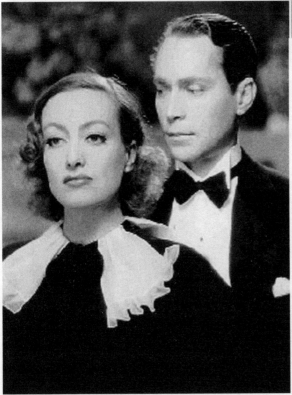

With Franchot Tone in *Sadie
McKee* (1934)
(Neil Maciejewski/
legendaryjoancrawford.com)

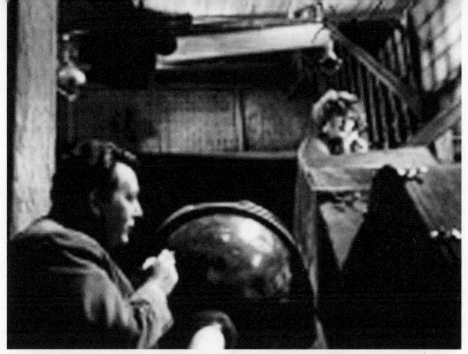

Lewis Milestone directing *Rain* (1932) (*Neil Maciejewski/legendaryjoancrawford.com*)

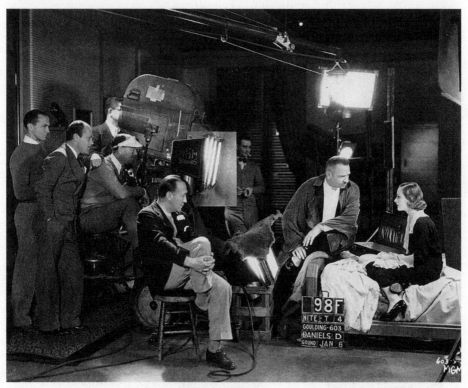

Edmund Goulding directs Wallace Beery and Joan in *Grand Hotel* (1932)

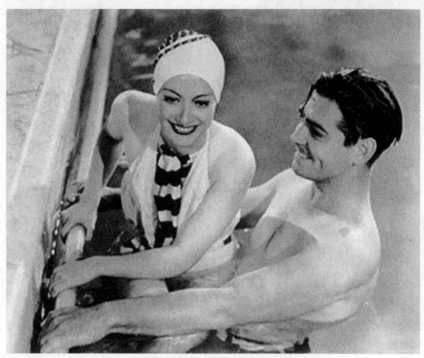

With Gable in *Chained* (1934)

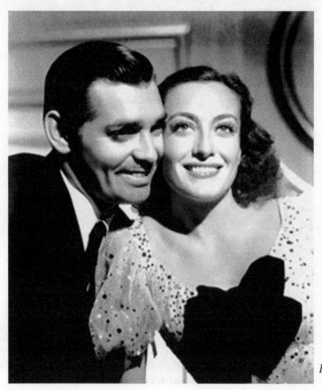

Love on the Run (1936)

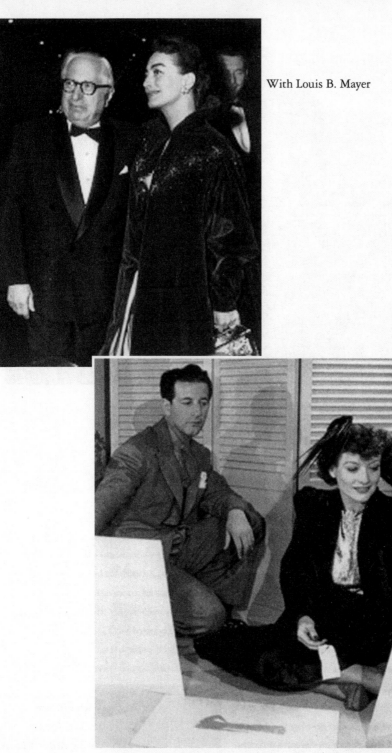

With Louis B. Mayer

With Adrian (1939) (*Neil Maciejewski/legendaryjoancrawford.com*)

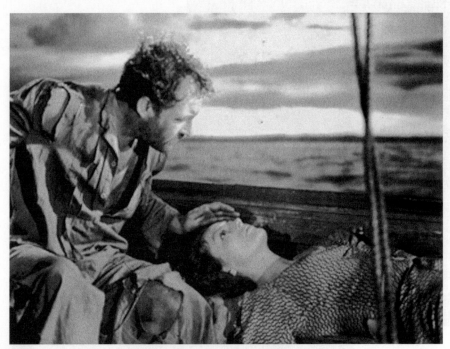

With Ian Hunter in *Strange Cargo* (1940)

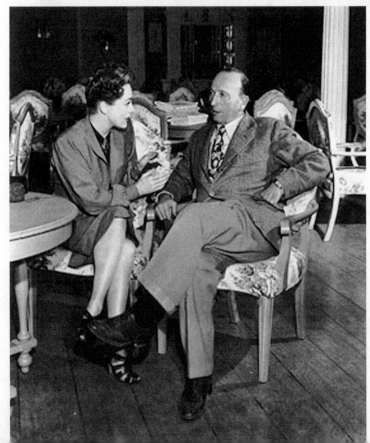

With director
Michael Curtiz
during *Mildred Pierce*

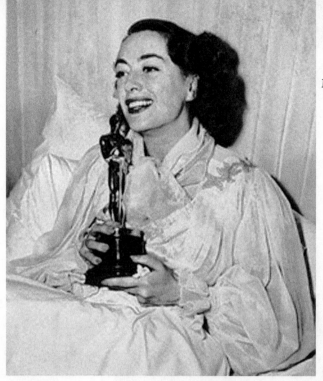

March 7, 1946

With Zachary Scott in *Mildred Pierce* (1945)

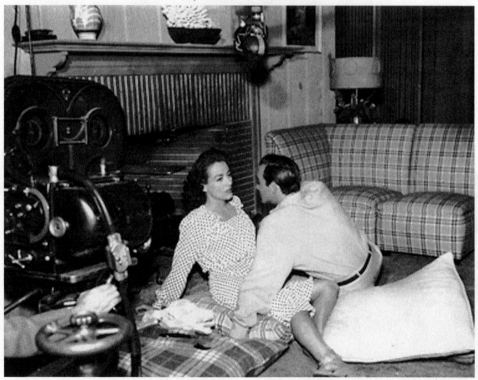

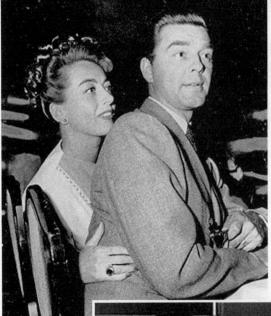

Mr. and Mrs. Phillip Terry (1945)

With director Vincent Sherman (1951)
(*Neil Maciejewski/legendaryjoancrawford.com*)

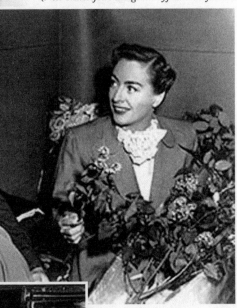

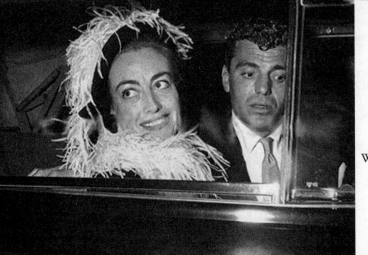

With Greg Bautzer (1948)

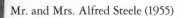

Mr. and Mrs. Alfred Steele (1955)

At Christina Crawford's
marriage to Harvey
Medlinsky (1966)

The Steeles with Senator
John F. Kennedy (1959)

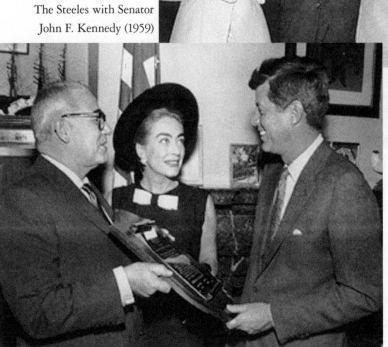

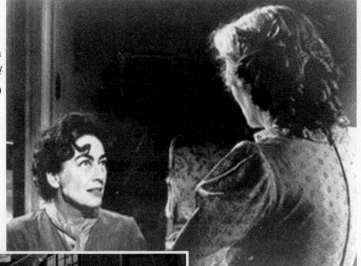

With Bette Davis in
*What Ever Happened
to Baby Jane?* (1962)

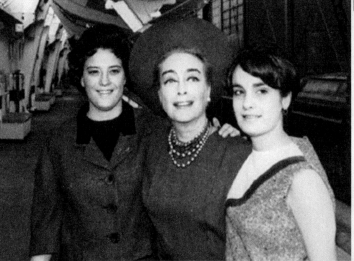

With twins Cindy and
Cathy Crawford in
London (1966)

With Ty Hardin,
Herman Cohen, Judy
Geeson and Diana Dors
during *Berserk* (1967)

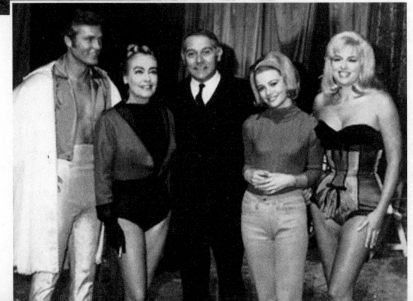

The book's Mildred, after separating from her husband at age twenty-eight, becomes a woman of easy virtue, always ready for casual sex with the wrong men. As Cain wrote: "Romance wasn't quite the word [for it], for of that emotion she felt not the slightest flicker. Whatever it was, it afforded two hours of relief, of forgetfulness." The dominant tone of the book is one of bleakness, of economic and psychological annihilation; long passages describe Mildred's wearying efforts to find work in Los Angeles during the Great Depression, and whole chapters detail women's contempt for men. All this was omitted from the movie.

But the film of *Mildred Pierce*, brilliantly designed and constructed, adds elements nowhere found in the book. Where the novel is a realistic social treatment of people torn by poverty and destroyed by their own obsessions with money and status, the movie adds the framing device of a murder and its resolution, shown in flashback and narrated by the title character. At the conclusion of the picture, the malignant daughter Veda, for whom everything has been foolishly sacrificed, is revealed to have killed her boyfriend—who is also her mother's second husband, the exploitive, shiftless, once wealthy playboy Monty Beragon (played by Zachary Scott). Mildred is left with nothing to show for her extreme sacrifices.

The book and movie share the theme of a mother's unhealthy dependence on her daughter's estimation. As Cain wrote: "It always came back to the same thing. She was afraid of Veda, of her snobbery, her contempt, her unbreakable spirit. And she was afraid of something that seemed always lurking under Veda's bland, phony toniness: a cold, cruel, coarse desire to torture her mother, to humiliate her, above everything, to hurt her."

From first scene to last, Joan brought to life a Mildred unlike any character she had yet attempted. Appearing depressed but insistent, bereft but unyielding, she invested Mildred with impressive shadings of feelings. She knew when she read the novel that however recognizable Mildred was—however realistically presented in her time and place—she was certainly no ordinary woman.

"The character I played was a composite of the characters I'd always played," she said, "and there were a few elements from my own personality and character, too. In a way, I think I was getting ready for *Mildred Pierce* when I was a kid, waiting on tables and cooking. But there was not a single Crawford mannerism in my performance. I sailed into [it] with all the gusto I'd been saving for three years. The role was a delight to me, because it rescued me from what was known at MGM as the Joan Crawford formula. I had become so hidden in clothes and sets that nobody could tell whether I had talent or not."

———

EVEN MAYER AND WARNER may well have doubted that Joan could portray so complex a woman—highly neurotic yet somehow sympathetic, brought to the brink of destruction by her own tenacious obsession. But Joan knew she could, and she knew how to refine a word here or a phrase there to make the point of a scene more precise. When Cain saw the movie, he sent Joan a signed first edition of his novel, inscribed "to Joan Crawford, who brought Mildred to life just as I had always hoped she would be, and who has my lifelong gratitude." That Mildred came so fully alive on-screen was due in large part to Joan's insistence that Curtiz exploit the power of the close-up—not only for herself, but also for other players. Ann Blyth, for one, recalled that the director was favoring Joan too much during their important two-shots. "Michael," Joan said, "you've simply got to have more close-ups of Ann during our scenes together—it's right for the character, and it's right for Ann's career."

Earlier movies about maternal self-sacrifice—Claudette Colbert in *Imitation of Life,* for example, and Barbara Stanwyck in *Stella Dallas*—glowed with sentiment and a warm rush of noble uplift. But Mildred Pierce's fate is disastrously empty, and although the film's final shot shows her leaving police headquarters to find her dull ex-husband waiting, the audience knows that it was he who set in motion the story's tragic downward spiral when he left Mildred and the children for a rich neighbor who subsequently abandoned him.

Joan's portrait of Mildred Pierce was a study in understatement, moderation, control and depth—the triumph of her old adage that in the movies, less is more. When Mildred strikes Veda, the sting is reflected in her own reaction.

When Mildred begs Monty to marry her for the sake of Veda's status, we see the collapse of a struggle for self-worth in a single sidelong glance.

Joan played a character comprehended not primarily through loud words or broad gestures, but rather by rich and subtle expression, by vocal nuance, by wide, unblinking gazes and by a restrained look of incalculable sadness. However much *Mildred Pierce* has of traditional soap opera, it is raised to a higher level of disturbing complexity by Joan's complete mastery of her craft. Most critics dismissed the movie as just another sodden tale of derailed mother love, and praise for Joan came mostly from the trade journals. Many reviewers were unsure how to receive it—the difference from the mold of Crawford characters seemed too vast to gauge, and seldom was a title character so disconcerting. Mildred can be neither endorsed completely nor condemned entirely, and this tension made it difficult for many critics to appreciate it.

All the tortured whorls of the character's confusion are externalized by means of Ernest Haller's angular lighting and nightmarish shadows, by the pools of light that enshroud even as they partially illuminate. Haller's striking cinematography colludes with Anton Grot's disorienting sets for the interiors of the beach house and the mansion—locations that suggest decadence more than luxury. These elements of photography and setting do more than exploit some elements of contemporary *film noir:* they express the dangerous depths of depravity to which Mildred willingly exposes herself and from which she is all but unredeemed. It is she, after all, who has tried to cover for her guilty daughter by implicating Wally Fay (Jack Carson), her lover *manqué* and former business partner. This was indeed no ordinary woman.

With this character and this movie, Joan Crawford commenced what might be called a third act in her motion picture career. From 1925 to 1938, she had represented successively the raging party girl, the sensual but irrepressible working woman, the benighted or isolated victim and the society matron. From 1939 to 1943, she brought a remarkable technical complexity to a wide variety of roles in no fewer than five first-rate films (*Strange Cargo, Susan and God, A Woman's Face, When Ladies Meet* and *Above Suspicion*). But *Mildred Pierce* took her and audiences to a new level, in which she would embrace types often shunned by actors eager to maintain a loving fan base. Henceforth, the women Crawford played would be tougher, more seasoned, more resourceful. This was, of course, no preseason game plan, mapped out as a program from 1945: it became a logical if accidental development she embraced when it occurred.

———

BEFORE THAT YEAR WAS over, Phillip Terry's presence in Joan Crawford's life had ended. "One day he just didn't come home," recalled Christina. "I don't think much was said about it, except that he wouldn't be back. He was just gone." On December 17, 1945, Joan publicly confirmed their separation. Very soon after, Joan legally changed the name of young Phillip Terry Jr. to Christopher Crawford.

After ending the romance with Charles McCabe, Joan had married Phillip Terry because, as she admitted, "I was unutterably lonely. Never marry because of loneliness. I owed him an apology from the start. We just weren't made for each other. I had never really known Phillip and now I realized that I had not really loved him, either." As legal proceedings commenced, Joan learned that her divorce was going to impose considerable penalties, for the settlement awarded Terry a sizable share of her wealth. "I was almost destroyed financially," she said years later. He requested no rights regarding the custody of the children.

Terry had deeply resented the attentions lavished on Joan by the Hollywood lawyer Gregson Bautzer, a notorious playboy involved with many Hollywood women. Fidelity to his several wives or mistresses was not an element in Greg Bautzer's character, and he routinely infuriated women like Lana Turner, Dorothy Lamour, Ginger Rogers, Terry Moore and Jane Wyman by his simultaneous escapades. Over six feet tall, ruggedly handsome and powerful in both presence and career, he had known Joan since her efforts to adopt Christina, and now set up a business meeting at which he at once arranged a date. She agreed to dine with him, and at first there was no more. But soon Greg seemed to be lurking everywhere, and in due course Joan fell into bed, if not into love.

At the same time, as if on cue, Charles McCabe arrived in Los Angeles, as Joan wrote to Genie Chester on March 22, 1946. Their reunion was apparently brief and cordial, although it is impossible to know the exact nature of the Crawford-McCabe relationship by this time; in any case, Joan was sincerely happy when she learned that Charles and his wife were expecting another child.

The formal dissolution of the Terry marriage, effective April 25, 1946, may have legally required absolute and perpetual silence on Phillip's part, for he never publicly uttered a word about Joan for the rest of his long life. He married again, had a disappointing career of no great significance and finally abandoned acting for work as a financial consultant. His last twenty years were blighted by a series of strokes and other grave illnesses, and after years of relative seclusion, he died at the age of eighty-four in 1993, reticent to the end about his years with Joan Crawford.

———

BY THE TIME PHILLIP TERRY left North Bristol Avenue, Joan had already begun work in script sessions and wardrobe fittings for her next Warners picture, a remake of the silent movie *Humoresque*. Based on the Fannie Hurst story about a struggling violinist chafing under the possessive patronage of a wealthy, married, self-destructive and alcoholic socialite, the screenplay by Clifford Odets and Zachary Gold was completed while *Mildred Pierce* was in production; Joan got hold of a copy and pressured the front office for it to be her next role.

Jack Warner and Jerry Wald objected that the part of the highly neurotic and finally suicidal Helen Wright was not sufficiently large or attractive for Joan, but she was insistent. "There may have been scant sympathy for this dipsomaniac married woman," she said, "but it was uncompromisingly dramatic." More to the point, this was the sort of role suitable for a serious actress coming to terms with the fact that she was forty.

Helen Wright was not a character role, but she was certainly an unforgettable woman, and Joan may have foreseen that henceforth she could corner the market on women whose beauty and drive masks dangerous psychoneurotic impulses. Her audience, after all, was still mostly female, and Helen could touch the feelings of women who had married the wrong man and then fallen into a pattern of unrequited love. Sophisticated, rich and important to a young violinist called Paul Boray (John Garfield), this Helen was certainly a soap-opera figure—but a terrifying one, doomed by her possessiveness to lose her life because of her own obsessions. She was irresistible to an actress who wanted a substantial, unforgettable role—not merely one that would win the love of fans and critics.

Humoresque began filming in late December 1945, and with her weekly salary still in place, Joan was able (after taxes and salaries to agents, managers, publicists and a new team of household employees) to bank about $40,000 that year. This was a princely income at a time when the average American salary was $3,150 annually, and when a substantial home could be purchased for $12,500.

The production was interrupted for one day—Thursday, March 7, 1946. At Grauman's Chinese Theatre on Hollywood Boulevard, searchlights were mounted on trucks and beamed into the night sky. For the first time in five years, now that the war was over, celebrities again wore sparkling formal dress to the Academy Awards.

The events of 1945 had been literally cataclysmic. President Franklin D. Roosevelt died in April. The following month, Nazi Germany surrendered to the Allies, and so began the long, slow process of rebuilding Europe. That summer, two atom bombs were dropped on the civilian population of Japan. In San Francisco, the United Nations was founded. But Oscar night 1946 seemed to inaugurate a new period of industry optimism, or at least of adjustment to peacetime.

Decades later, it seemed that the most popular movies of 1945 had indeed withstood the test of time—among them, Alfred Hitchcock's *Spellbound,* Leo McCarey's *The Bells of St. Mary's,* Billy Wilder's *The Lost Weekend* and Michael Curtiz's *Mildred Pierce.* Together, this quartet of films received twenty-two nominations, six of which related to *Mildred Pierce,* in five categories—for best black-and-white cinematography (Ernest Haller), for best screenplay

(Ranald MacDougall), for two candidates as best supporting actress (Ann Blyth and Eve Arden), for best picture and for Joan Crawford as best actress of the year 1945.

Also nominated in Joan's category were actresses with formidable talents: Ingrid Bergman, in *The Bells of St. Mary's;* Greer Garson, in *The Valley of Decision;* Jennifer Jones in *Love Letters;* and Gene Tierney, in *Leave Her to Heaven.* Garson, Bergman and Jones had each taken home an Oscar over the previous three years, but nothing in the rules said they could not step up to the stage again.

As the crowd settled into their seats at Grauman's, it quickly became clear to the audience that Joan Crawford was not present. Word then went around that she was ill at home with influenza.

Over the years, many people asserted that she feigned illness for dramatic effect: if she won (so the argument went), the press would be forced to hurry to her home, where she would hold court in regal, private splendor, sharing the spotlight with no one. And if she did not win, she would not have to affect a gracious smile.

Forever after, Joan insisted that she had indeed been confined to bed with a high fever, and that her physician would not permit her to leave the house. "I was running a temperature of a hundred and four," she said, "and had been suffering with flu for the past week, while filming *Humoresque.* The picture could not be delayed, and flu, coupled with the nervous tension of being eligible for an Oscar, had me shaking with chills and fever."

When it was announced that she had won the best actress Oscar that night, there was a virtual stampede up the aisles of Grauman's. Friends, colleagues, reporters and photographers jumped into their cars and raced west to Brentwood. Photographs taken that evening show Michael Curtiz handing the statuette to Joan in her bed; by this time, she had applied her makeup and brushed her hair, and she seemed well on the way to recovery.

Not long before she died, Joan spoke frankly. "I remember how I felt the night the Awards were presented—hopeful, scared, apprehensive, so afraid I wouldn't remember what I wanted to say, terrified at the thought of looking at those people, almost hoping I wouldn't get it, but wanting it so badly. No wonder I didn't go. I stayed home and fortified myself [with alcohol], probably a little too much, because when the announcement came, and then the press, and sort of a party, I didn't make much sense at all."

———

"IT WAS A GOOD film and I did a good job," she said years later of *Mildred Pierce*, "but I think the Academy voters honored me as much that night for *A Woman's Face* and *Strange Cargo* and maybe *Grand Hotel* as they did for *Mildred Pierce*. Or maybe it was just for staying around so long!"

Joan returned to work two days later with new confidence. She had been in Hollywood for over twenty years but had never been proposed for any accolade. With *Mildred Pierce,* she was raised to the professional pantheon, and she took the award very seriously. Her most important scenes in *Humoresque* were still to be filmed, and she worked with more intensity than ever.

Released in December 1946, the picture remains something of a curiosity. On the one hand, it represents Warner's new approach to prestige postwar moviemaking: it is a serious story of obsession and selfishness that capitalized on the new interest in abnormal psychology that became so popular in Hollywood after the death of Freud in 1939 and in light of the horrors of World War II. (*Spellbound* and *The Snake Pit,* to name just two other movies, also concerned mental illness.)

On the other hand, *Humoresque* is self-consciously artistic with its protracted classical music for violin, orchestra and piano. Thus attempting to be both psychologically provocative and culturally high-toned, the movie seems to collapse under the weight of its own mixed methods. That Joan's performance was not undone by such structural finagling was a testimony to her strength and skills as a maturing actress.

She first appears thirty-three minutes into the picture, drinking excessively, flirting with young men, spotting a fresh victim—the struggling young violinist—and then moving in for the kill. Some viewers have described *Humoresque* simply as the love story of two mismatched souls. But Helen and

Paul feed off their respective selfishness: if she gives in order to own, he takes in order to have. Nor is his mother (acted with proper cunning by Ruth Nelson) the loving, protective person she seems at first blush: she, too, is frighteningly possessive, manipulating her son and his wacky benefactor behind a mask of altruistic devotion. In *Humoresque,* love does not conquer all—or even help anything; facsimiles of love destroy.

Joan was enormously inventive in bringing Helen Wright to life, and she was canny in undertaking so unsympathetic a role. In this regard, it is fascinating to see how she managed her career in the postwar period, finding new roles and fresh depths in herself. Unconcerned about the amiability of the characters, Joan pitched herself into the challenge of turning negative stereotypes into recognizably human (if sometimes grotesque) specimens of humanity.

Mildred Pierce is a highly neurotic masochist with consciously good intentions, but her motives paved a hellish road. She works her way up to financial success, which was just what American women wanted to see after the war, when many of them had worked hard at all kinds of jobs on the home front. But then her ambitions for her daughter lead to the loss of everything. Helen Wright is even more possessive and manipulative than Mildred, and to the point of manic self-destruction. Mildred learns to gulp down a shot of bourbon at noon, but Helen reaches for a decanter of Scotch at breakfast.

About *Humoresque,* Joan was typically forthright: "I have mixed feelings about that one. John Garfield, who really was a brilliant young actor, did a fine job. [Jean] Negulesco directed it with feeling, the right sort of feeling. And most of the time, I thought I was doing well. But when I saw the final print, I cringed. I overacted and overreacted in so many scenes. I don't know. I should have done better." But late in life, she stressed, in letters to friends, how much she "adored making that film with John [Garfield]."

The critics were impressed. "Moviegoers will note that Joan Crawford, once a mere MGM clotheshorse, has made great progress as an actress since her Charleston-dancing-daughter days," ran a typical notice. "She remains a bit handsome and unmussed to be a convincing drunk, but her jittery, unhappy egocentric is just what the script calls for."

———

THE FILM WAS COMPLETED by the end of April, just when Joan was briefly involved with a short, stocky cowboy star named Don Barry, best known as "The Red Ryder" in a series of forgettable Westerns. The affair ended abruptly when Barry presumptuously told a Hollywood theatrical producer that he could deliver Joan Crawford to star in a play. With that, the cowboy was booted out—and Greg Bautzer returned.

The Crawford-Bautzer liaison, which blazed, cooled and then flashed again in a constant, dizzying cycle, lasted from late 1945 until early 1949, while they both pursued numerous other affairs—he with (among others) Ginger Rogers and she with (among others) the fledgling producer Peter Shaw. "Joan Crawford was slightly confused," according to a newspaper column, "when hearing over the air that she was to marry both Greg Bautzer and Peter Shaw. Said Joan, 'Is it a sin for a girl to have fun in this town? I'm not thinking of marrying anybody, and if I do, it'll probably be an unknown.'" (Not long after, Peter Shaw was sprung free of this *ronde*, and from 1949 to his death in 2003, he was very happily married to Angela Lansbury.)

The relationship with Bautzer cannot accurately be called a romance, for it was marked by constant quarrels, "sharp words and nagging" (as she admitted), scenes of jealous recrimination and tempestuous physical attacks—it was, in other words, a foolish liaison between two people who should have known better. During this period, they were, as one reporter noted, "the most photographed film-town couple."

"It disturbed my sense of balance," Joan said later with hilarious understatement. "We didn't have an exclusive arrangement, so I couldn't say to him, 'I'm jealous and I don't want you seeing other women.'" Soon, others witnessed their outbursts, at public receptions, private dinner parties and movie premieres. They were, in other words, quite impossible.

At times, she became his slave. On February 5, 1948, a columnist reported,

"Joan Crawford turned in her old Cadillac and got two new ones—one for herself, another for Greg Bautzer." On July 14, it was reported from coast to coast that "Joan Crawford's flare-up at Greg Bautzer the night of [a party] is the talk of Hollywood. She called him later to stage a reconciliation, but he was in a mood to stick with a tall glass [of whiskey]."

Christina recalled incidents "that scared the daylights out of me. They used to have terrible fights late at night. I was frightened because I hated the screaming and yelling and kicking and pounding." According to Bautzer, things occasionally became dangerous. "I had been in several fights with men," he told an interviewer, "but no man ever put a scar on my face. I've got about four scars on my face that she put there. She should have been a New York Yankees pitcher—she could throw a cocktail glass across a room and hit you right in the face two out of three times." On his side, he landed a few punches that left Joan with blackened eyes and a swollen jaw more than once.

Hollywood gossips knew about the affair and, according to the custom of the time, described it as a "romantic friendship" in which the couple was "dating." When things went along too smoothly and Joan was either too arrogant or too possessive, Greg simply went out on the town with other actresses. If he had his way too often, Joan made certain she was photographed at a restaurant with her old friend Clark Gable; in short order, the faint toll of their imminent wedding bells was heard in the public's fantasies—and Bautzer was again brought to heel. And so it went, repetitious and tedious, until even the principals grew weary. "We always got together again," Joan said, "until we didn't." When *Sturm* finally separated from *Drang,* many in Hollywood breathed more easily.

———

THE TENSION AND VIOLENCE of the Crawford-Bautzer affair was matched decibel for decibel by her next picture. Based on a story by Rita Weiman, *Possessed* (which had no connection to her 1931 movie with the same title) required one of Joan's most intensive efforts. "I worked harder on it than on any other picture," she recalled. "Don't let anyone tell you it's easy to play a madwoman, particularly a psychotic. It was a heavy, heavy picture, not very pleasant, and I was emotionally and physically exhausted when we finished shooting."[4]

Silvia Richards wrote the first draft of the movie—but in an effort to duplicate the success of *Mildred Pierce,* Jerry Wald engaged Ranald MacDougall to do a total rewrite. Filming began in June but was interrupted for six weeks that summer while Joan visited psychiatric wards in Santa Barbara, Santa Monica and Pasadena. Imprudently, she and director Curtis Bernhardt did not ask permission to witness a patient at one clinic undergoing a session of electroconvulsive shock therapy. Warner Bros. later had to pay a substantial sum to the woman, who claimed invasion of privacy.

Considered retrospectively, *Possessed* was like the final installment of a Joan Crawford trilogy that had begun with her portrayals of neurotic Mildred and continued with destructive Helen. In this "heavy picture" (as she called it), Joan was the extreme character of the previous two: lovesick, psychotic Louise Howell, consumed by a lunatic obsession for a man who does not return her brand of possessive love. Here, characters formerly rendered by Ann Blyth and John Garfield were subsumed into one played by Van Heflin.

Louise was perhaps the most difficult role Joan had yet undertaken, for it would have been easy to get her wrong—to play the woman merely as a terrifying psychotic, and so to risk losing her audience. Instead, Joan found the woman beneath the tragedy, and so made Louise comprehensible, if not particularly warm and likable. And yet at odd moments, Bernhardt seems not to have exerted control over his star. Occasionally, Joan is uncharacteristically somewhat over the top, and she reverts too often to silent-movie histrionics—as, for example, when her eyes widen with madness, and when (far too often) she wrings her hands and then runs them through her hair.

---

4. Some accounts wrongly claim that Joan inherited the role in *Possessed* when Bette Davis went on maternity leave before the birth of her daughter Barbara. But this could not have been the case: Joan signed the contract for *Possessed* in March 1946, and Davis's child was not born until May 1947.

Those moments of fake hysteria notwithstanding, she was nominated for a second Academy Award (but lost to Loretta Young, who played a much cozier farmer's daughter).

The picture opens with disjointed shots of a distracted, neurasthenic woman wandering the streets of downtown Los Angeles. Taken to the hospital in a state of catatonic withdrawal, she is treated by doctors—and so begins the story, told in a long flashback, precisely the structural framing device used in *Mildred Pierce* and *Humoresque*. Joan dominates the action, "performing [as critic James Agee wrote] with the passion and intelligence of an actress who is not content with just one Oscar." Indeed, she seemed to *demand* another statuette.

This was a portrait of a woman possessed by a derailed notion of love—something Joan knew not only from her hospital visits and research meetings with psychiatrists that summer, but also from her ongoing relationship with Bautzer, which existed on a level very close to psychosis. The character of Louise Howell and the personality of Joan Crawford were more than uninhibited: they were often on the edge of destruction that year.

Not all troubled women find their way to treatment. Some, like Louise, kill; others, not so far gone, like Joan, merely flirt with the madness of multileveled possession. In considering the fusion of actress and role, it is critical to recall that these were projects and characters Joan Crawford fought to play, and she played them with an almost manic intensity precisely because something of them existed in her. Actors, after all, have no other raw material with which to work than their own experiences, their intuitions and their correspondences with those they wish to represent, however briefly. No wonder *Possessed* was both unpleasant and frightening for its star. No wonder, too, that she required an interval before she felt well enough to begin another movie.

CHAPTER TEN

Children! Children!

| 1947–1951 |

MILDRED PIERCE, HUMORESQUE and *Possessed* were enormously success-ful movies, and this trilogy restored Joan Crawford to secure stardom worldwide. Her agent could therefore renegotiate her Warners contract for $250,000 per picture, for which once again Joan had the right to approve every screenplay, director and leading man. But for her first movie under the new deal, she was loaned out to Twentieth Century-Fox, for Otto Preminger's production of Elizabeth Janeway's fine, best-selling novel *Daisy Kenyon*.

"I seem to be the follow-up girl," she said at a dinner party given by Billy Haines and Jimmy Shields in February 1947. "I'm to make a picture [*Daisy Kenyon*] at 20th that was intended for Gene Tierney, and I'm negotiating with Columbia about doing *No Sad Songs for Me*, which Irene Dunne stepped out of." In reply, another guest at dinner observed aloud that this was a pattern: Joan had followed Lana Turner in Greg Bautzer's affections. Her reply has not been documented.[1]

---

1. Joan did not appear in *No Sad Songs for Me,* which was released in 1950 with Margaret Sullavan in the leading role.

While the screenplay for the Preminger picture went through the usual revisions, Joan again contacted baby brokers. Eager to give more children a home, she was informed that illegitimate twin girls had been born on January 13 in Dyersburg, a small town in western Tennessee. A week later, their mother died of kidney failure, and the babies were deposited in an orphanage known as the Tennessee Children's Home Society, in Memphis. In fact, this place was a notorious cover for the kidnapping and illegal sale of children, an operation under the control of none other than Georgia Tann, Joan's baby broker. In September, the twins were brought to her in Los Angeles after the adoption had already been legalized outside California's jurisdiction. She named the babies Catherine and Cynthia, and they were always called Cathy and Cindy.[2]

Daisy Kenyon was produced that summer of 1947 and released at year's end. Joan worked amiably with costars Dana Andrews and Henry Fonda, and she described director Otto Preminger as "the kindest, sweetest man"—not a typical sentiment about a man with the reputation of reducing actors to tears, nervous collapse and feverish anxiety. None of those involved in the production of *Daisy Kenyon* retained a high regard for it—which is odd, for it not only offers one of Joan's most forthright and warm performances, but also showcases her in a story of striking complexity and maturity, one of her most important and appealing pictures. Joan was fortunate to work with Andrews and Fonda, first-rate actors she specifically requested, both of them remarkable in this movie for giving deeply affecting performances.

Very faithful to the novel, the film tells of Daisy, a commercial artist living in New York's Greenwich Village, an independent woman with a busy career and a complicated love life. A long and frustrating affair with a married lawyer (Andrews) is made even more complicated when she responds to the attentions of an Army veteran (Fonda) haunted by the death of his wife and by his experiences in the war. The structure of the picture, a kind of realist

---

2. In 1991, the twins finally located and met their father.

romance, follows not only the course of her romantic dilemma—which man will claim her in marriage?—but also the challenges facing career women in postwar America. A clever woman who knows how to exploit her feminine wiles, Daisy is neither hypocrite nor femme fatale. Instead of status or wealth, she yearns for love—but not at the price of her career.

Daisy Kenyon presents, with a rare kind of emotional honesty, a trio of credible adults struggling with unhappy situations. After the labyrinthine psychological corridors of the previous three Crawford films, this was a refreshing return to more everyday situations, but it was no less dramatically compelling. Joan employed neither tics nor tricks, and Preminger paced her scenes—composed mostly of intelligent dialogue—with admirable respect for the integrity of the story and the feelings of the characters.[3]

———

THE MOVIE WAS COMPLETED in early autumn 1947—just as the twins were being settled into their new home—and for the next year, Joan did not work on any picture. Although she read scripts and literary properties constantly, most of her energies were now spent attending to the children. She was also trying to sort out her increasingly violent relationship with Greg Bautzer, which did not end until 1949.

By 1948, Christina Crawford was eight years old and quite naturally beginning to assert her own personality. In her late twenties, she began to compile notes for a memoir of her childhood and young adult years. Redrafted, edited and given focus by New York editors, Christina's voluminous but disorganized pages were eventually turned into a book, thanks to the sheer tenacity of the publisher; it was released the year after Joan's death with the title *Mommie Dearest*. In light of what occurred in the children's lives from the late

---

3. Much of the story is set during a New York winter. Preminger had the soundstage kept at a cool temperature so that the actors' breath would realistically be seen in wintry air and they could more comfortably wear heavy clothing for long scenes that were set outdoors. This was Joan's preference in any case: a chilly temperature on the set prevented her makeup from running.

1940s onward, it is worthwhile to consider the contents and claims of this controversial book at this point in an account of Joan's life.

There is a strange and enduring paradox about *Mommie Dearest* and its author—indeed, there seems to be a glaring logical flaw at its center.

Christina Crawford asserted that her life was blighted by Joan's cruelty. But from the age of ten—precisely when she claims the punitive disciplinary acts shifted into full gear—Christina was in fact having considerable success at several schools, where she enjoyed the admiration of her teachers and the friendship of her classmates. From her elementary years through her college education, she achieved high marks and was awarded diplomas and degrees with honors. She worked hard from a very early age, trying to be as successful, in her way, as her mother.

Mommie Dearest, and the grotesque 1981 movie based on it, shaped a lasting but unbalanced view of Joan Crawford that endured for decades after. Downplaying Joan's talents, the collective significance of her movies, and her impact on popular culture, Christina portrayed her mother as a monstrously abusive, alcoholic tyrant. Virtually all other considerations of Joan's life and career were minimized or dismissed. With the passing of years and the accumulated witness of other voices than Christina's, it became clear that *Mommie Dearest* offered at the least an overstated, skewed image of its subject. At its worst, it was a vituperative act of revenge after Joan excised her two oldest children from her will after many years of discord. "When Joan didn't include [Christina] in her will," according to Nolan Miller, one of Joan's couturiers, "Christina wrote the book as a retaliation." He was not alone in this opinion, which was shared by a legion of Joan's friends—and by Joan's adopted twins.[4]

The tone of Christina's book is summed up in her own words: "That evil goddamned BITCH!!!" she wrote. "She's just a mean, rotten bitch to the mar-

---

4. A petty crook from the time of his adolescence, Christopher severed all relations with Joan when he was seventeen. In exchange for his endorsement of Christina's book, he received a financial consideration from her.

row of her bones . . . God, I hated her." Throughout, the text is not remarkable for nuance or understatement.

Christina's reasons for her undiluted antipathy were put forth unambiguously: Joan, she contended, was a fierce disciplinarian who inflicted painful corporal punishment for minor acts of disobedience, withheld meals for venial infractions of household regulations and inflicted horrific penalties during bouts of alcoholic delirium.

Perhaps most notoriously, according to Christina, Joan became psychotic with rage when she went to her daughter's closet and found some of the clothes suspended on wire hangers instead of the upholstered ones mandated to prevent stretch marks on the fabrics. This incident, which inspired the movie's most bizarre and infamous scene, actually reflected a time when Joan *forbade* hangers rather than a time when she nearly killed the child for *using* those hangers. (Christina never wrote that she was beaten *with* wire hangers, but rather that she was beaten *because* she had wire hangers in her closet.)

But the truth of the matter is that the laundry company and the dry cleaners to which Joan entrusted the family's clothes were under strict instructions to return all clothing on the richly covered hangers Joan provided. Could the company have failed once and thus caused Joan's irrational outburst? Possibly—except that the task of returning the clothes to the wardrobes after the deliveries was assigned to the housekeeper. Had this instruction been contravened or omitted, heads (or at least jobs) would have rolled. Hence, the episode of the hangers refers to an injunction from Joan reworked by Christina as an actual event that precipitated a mad scene worthy of Italian opera.

The horror stories accumulate in *Mommie Dearest* almost without interruption. According to Christina, Joan tore to shreds the child's favorite dress after the girl absentmindedly picked at a piece of wallpaper. On one occasion, Joan supposedly tied up Christina in the shower; on another, she locked her in a linen closet. Christina also implied that her mother was constitutionally incapable of seeing anything wrong with this kind of tyrannical behavior, for which Joan never apologized.

Unfortunately, Christina's credibility was not strengthened by the many errors of simple fact that crept into her book—mistakes that could have been corrected before the book was rushed into print. She states, for example, that she was "not yet ten years old"—that is, it was before June 1949—when Yul Brynner came to the house in Brentwood while he was in Hollywood filming his role in *The King and I*. But that movie was produced from early December 1955 to late January 1956. Christina also claims that, in the late 1950s, "no movie star did commercials for television." But beginning in 1954, Ronald Reagan was one of many who did just that—in his case, as pitchman for General Electric, when he pronounced the company motto, "Progress is our most important product"—a magnificent example of high-toned meaninglessness.

THERE ARE ALSO ODD inconsistencies between the horrific discipline and what Christina described elsewhere. "Unexpected moments of real closeness between us always brought tears to her eyes," Christina wrote about her relationship with Joan. And to a journalist, she said, "Mommie was with me constantly. No matter where she went. When she traveled across the country, I went along too. And she read poetry to me in that marvelous voice of hers—the poems of Edna St. Vincent Millay and the sonnets of Shakespeare. When I learned to read, we took turns reciting stanzas. Mother loved poetry and she wanted me to be exposed to it as early as possible." When she spoke of Joan's preoccupation with her career, Christina was, on another occasion, quite understanding: "As I grew older, I saw less and less of Mommie. Not that she didn't try to give us time. The problem was that she didn't have that much [time to give]. You can't build a career like she built and have a great deal of time left over for yourself or anyone else." That was quite a different tone from the one sounded in *Mommie Dearest*.

"We have wonderful memories of holidays and special occasions," Christina said before she wrote her book. "Sometimes, Mommie used to drive Chris and me to a place called Mandeville Canyon, just ten minutes from the house, and we took a picnic lunch big enough for an army. And when Mommie was working, she always managed to meet us for sodas or lunch downtown. When she was terribly busy at the studio, she took me along onto the set, just so I could be near her."

These 1960 recollections bear very little resemblance to the Joan Crawford who shrieks and claws her way through the pages of *Mommie Dearest*. When Joan took all the children for a holiday in Northern California each summer, she often offered Christina, as the oldest, some special private time with her mother. "Mommie and I took long walks along the sea wall [in Carmel, California]. We talked a lot, [and] I know that she was telling me important things, but they escaped me because I was too young."

"I was a strict disciplinarian—perhaps too strict," Joan admitted not long before her death. "I have had problems with Christina and Christopher, yes, but they have things to answer for, too." She acknowledged that perhaps actresses like her "should not have had children, whether we bore them or adopted them." The reason, she believed, was clear: "We didn't have time for children . . . and so being a mother was a lousy idea. You *wanted* to be a mother, but there just wasn't time for it. A part of us [actresses] wanted a real, personal, private life—husband, kiddies, fireplace, the works—but the biggest part of us wanted the career, and that biggest part had to live up to the demands of that career."

Women and their children have often paid an especially high price for fame and its perquisites. On the one hand, women are encouraged to work, to have careers, to pursue success and even, ultimately, to equal the successes of men. On the other hand, they are pilloried when they do so—or they are soundly criticized for being unable to have intense and successful careers *and* to be entirely present to their children (and husbands) as devoted homemakers. Similar charges are not usually leveled against men.

Celebrity is a jealous mistress, and many actors, while seeking reinforcement of their identities, in fact lose them in a lifelong pursuit of public endorsement and approval; the creation and maintenance of an image require more energy and more subterfuge than most people can supply. And the casualties of this eternal quest are often children. As Joan said, perhaps she ought not to have adopted them. "She was not a maternal person," according to

Dorothy Manners, who inherited the Louella Parsons column. "It was not her instinct. Adopting those children was the thing to do. Joan was a kind person, but her blind spot was her children." It seems, then, that there was indeed strict discipline in the Crawford home—but that it was neither as brutal nor as physical as *Mommie Dearest* claims. (By the time Christina was nine, she and Joan fought almost constantly: "I was probably not too pleasant a child," she admitted.)

Joan never offered excuses for disciplining her children, but she did offer explanations, and they provide an understanding of the period from 1948 to 1951. As she often said, she wanted to give her children everything she had been denied: she wanted to erase her own past by raising the children both properly and luxuriously—and with the discipline necessary to prevent them from being spoiled.

It is important to recall that Joan's only frame of reference for motherhood was the experience of her own early years. Anna was a distant, unhappy single parent who preferred Hal to Lucille and never hesitated to slap her daughter's face, and the headmistress at Rockingham was frankly cruel in administering corporal punishment. In other words, Joan had only her own past on which to base decisions about child rearing. And she had to make these decisions as a single parent.

Joan hated her past. But as often happens, she recreated its circumstances in order to reverse it once and for all. It is also worth nothing that, from this time in her life, she very rarely undertook a sympathetic movie role. Unhappy with her past and with what she had become, she would not permit the children to repeat those realities. Just as Joan saw abandoned, unwanted children as mirrors of herself—babies who needed to be "saved"—so there was a dark side to her intentions. Because she saw them as little versions of her earlier self, discipline was a way of negating that person. With goodwill, she adopted children in order to save them from a childhood like her own. But she so resented that childhood that she tried to erase its signs and symbols. The discipline, in other words, was a way of preventing her own children from becoming distorted versions and repetitions of Joan Crawford. But the forms of the discipline were not, it seems almost certainly, the hideously cruel versions set forth in *Mommie Dearest*.

Joan gave her children everything she never had; on the other hand, she feared that they would grow up like other Hollywood children—with too many material things and not enough self-reliance. Some Hollywood children have coped poorly in dealing with the fame of their parents; some have resented their parents' fame and deplored the fact that equal fame was denied them. "Joan never complained about her difficult children," recalled Myrna Loy, who knew the entire family over many decades. "Christina and Christopher made me glad I didn't have children."

Elva Martien, frequently Joan's movie costumer, was also familiar with the Crawford household; she insisted that Joan "loved those children and was really a devoted mother. She felt that her kids, when they grew up and went off on their own, might not be able to afford a grand Hollywood lifestyle. She wanted them to be able to go out and face the real world, and that's what she tried to prepare them for." Director Herbert Kenwith knew Joan over many years and often visited the house. "Joan demanded perfection and could be rigid with her children," he recalled, "but the things Christina alleged just never happened." And Cindy Crawford offered firsthand testimony: "Mommy was a disciplinarian because she wanted us to grow up independently—self-reliant and with good goals. We had a maid and a cook, but we had to make our beds and wash our dishes. She wasn't the kind of person Christina wrote about. She was very caring and loving."

———

WHATEVER THE EXTENT OF Joan's discipline with Christina and Christopher, her tactics had changed by the time the twins were out of infancy. Cathy and Cindy Crawford always insisted that they had a loving home life without any of the harsh treatment Christina described. "I think Christina was jealous," said Cindy Crawford years later. "She wanted to be the one person she couldn't be—Mother. But our mother was very good to us—I think she was good to all four of us, really. She cared for us. We grew up knowing what was right and what was wrong."

"My mother was a very warm person," added Cathy, speaking for both twins. "She was always there when we needed her. She was a working mother, but she always had time for us, and as far as *Mommie Dearest* is concerned, it's a great work of fiction. Christina must have been in another household. She says Joan was rotten, but I say she was a good person. She was tough on us, sure—you'd get a swat once in a while, but there were none of those physical beatings. Christina committed matricide on Mother's image." After working as the first editor of *Mommie Dearest,* Judy Feiffer felt that "Christina had, in a way, tried to be Joan." One might add that when Christina realized that effort was futile, she killed Joan off—in her book.

The twins recalled that indeed Joan was "strict—she believed in discipline," as Cathy recalled, but she insisted that they were "the luckiest [children] in the world—I wouldn't have chosen any other mother, because I had the best one anyone could ever have. She gave me backbone, courage and wonderful memories to last all through my life." According to Betty Barker, who worked for Joan for forty years, Joan was "never out of control. I never saw her do anything wrong with her children—I would swear to that. She deserved a lot better than she got back from the two older children she adopted."

Book reviewers were not impressed by *Mommie Dearest.* "Everything about the book tastes bad," wrote the senior critic for the *New York Times,* "from its whining, self-dramatizing tone to its seizures of preposterous stuffiness." The public, however, grabbed it from bookstore shelves, and within two years it had sold several million copies.

—

PERHAPS FROM SHEER DESPERATION over the problems with Greg Bautzer and her two older children—and impelled by the need for income—Joan returned to work in the autumn of 1948, after more than a year's absence. According to the terms of her contract, Joan was paid only when she actually worked; otherwise, she was formally placed on suspension. She had, therefore, given up a year's salary to be a stay-at-home mother, but this had put her in a precarious financial position.

The project Warner Bros. prepared for her, based on Robert Wilder's novel and play *Flamingo Road,* had been offered to various producers, directors and actors, but it had interested no one. Then, anticipating success if he reteamed Joan with Michael Curtiz and Zachary Scott, producer Jerry Wald swung into action with determination. Unfortunately, he miscalculated. "The script missed," Joan said accurately. "Curtiz missed. I missed. My judgment screwed up completely."

Over the years, many of Joan's fans championed *Flamingo Road,* but it is difficult to endorse their passionate defense of it. Cast as a down-at-the-heels carnival dancer, Joan was forty-two and playing twenty years younger—but there were worse obstacles to its success. The story and screenplay are a tedious muddle about political machinations in a southern backwater. Will Joan save Zachary Scott from the wicked Sydney Greenstreet? Can she stand by politician David Brian as he tries to rise above scandals? Could she transcend dialogue in which "I'm not sure" is her most repeated assertion? Did anyone care? Vaguely resembling the road-company version of a bad Lillian Hellman play, *Flamingo Road* seems to be about political corruption; it is really, however, about Joan's new blond hairdo. But by this time, her name on theater marquees was enough to attract audiences, despite the warnings of reviewers that her role was "utterly nonsensical and undefined," as one of the kinder notices put it.

With that turgid melodrama behind her, Joan very much enjoyed working for one day on a Technicolor picture called *It's a Great Feeling.* With cameo appearances by Gary Cooper, Ronald Reagan, Michael Curtiz, Danny Kaye and a dozen other Warners players, this movie was one of the few successful satires on Hollywood. In a parody of herself, Joan is seen wrapped in furs as she approaches Doris Day, Jack Carson and Dennis Morgan:

JOAN: You two boys ought to be ashamed of yourselves! Just think of what you're doing to that poor innocent little girl!

CARSON: But, Joan—you don't understand!

JOAN: Two grown men, acting like—grown men!

MORGAN: Why, Joan—you don't think Jack and I would take advantage of a situation like this?

JOAN: Are you kidding?

CARSON: Joan, I told you—you don't understand!

JOAN (reciting her speech from *Mildred Pierce*): I've never denied you anything—anything money could buy! But that wasn't enough, was it? All right, things are going to be different now!

DAY: Miss Crawford! They aren't doing anything wrong!

JOAN (continuing the dialogue from *Mildred Pierce*): Get out! Get your things out of here before I throw them into the street and you with them! Get out before I kill you!

She slaps the two leading men, and they ask, "What's that for?"

Joan replies politely, "Oh, I do that in all my pictures!"

And with that, she smiles engagingly, blows them a kiss and rushes off in a haze of mink.

This brief scene was worth several productions like *Flamingo Road,* and critics took notice of Joan's rarely exploited gifts as "an amazingly deft comedienne." As Joan said, "It was the first comedy I'd done in ages"—since *Above Suspicion,* in any case—"and I loved every minute of it. It was marvelous therapy after doing all those heavy parts, one after another, starting with *Mildred Pierce.*"

———

CRAWFORD AND GABLE WERE often seen together during 1949, dining at this restaurant or having drinks at that nightclub—so frequently, in fact, that their wedding plans were all but announced in the papers. Soon afterward, all kinds of interpretations and analyses were attached to their joint appearance at a party also attended by Greg Bautzer. The gossips were further confused when Joan was seen in the company of an executive with the National Dairy Association. Finally, in October, she and Greg were guests at a party hosted by Louis B. Mayer. But when Bautzer took Ginger Rogers for a turn around the dance floor, he wrote his own romantic epitaph: later that night, his long melodramatic intrigue with Joan ended forever.

She was neither unoccupied nor alone for long. That autumn, Joan began work on *The Damned Don't Cry,* a first-rate story of crime and criminal personalities, partly based on the real histories of Virginia Hill, Bugsy Siegel and various mobsters during the 1930s and 1940s. Joan had read widely about these fascinating, terrifying people, and she went to Jerry Wald with the idea for a movie based on a story by Gertrude Walker. Joan also mentioned her choice of director—Vincent Sherman, who had drawn fine performances from Bette Davis in *Old Acquaintance* and *Mr. Skeffington.* From the start of *The Damned Don't Cry,* as Sherman recalled, Joan was involved in every stage of the production; it was she, for example, who suggested to Wald the four leading actors engaged for the movie—Richard Egan, Kent Smith, David Brian and Steve Cochran. No casting agent or studio executive could have improved on her choices. "I had heard so many stories about her," Sherman recalled, "and I thought she'd be very demanding, overpowering and overwhelming. But Joan was very much down to earth, very simple, unpretentious and very smart about filmmaking."

"She phoned me almost every day to discuss some story point," Sherman remembered, "or she would come to the studio to talk about her wardrobe. I found her excellent to work with—intelligent, perceptive, and she presented her thoughts in a way that was never high-handed. I had never worked with an actor who knew so much about filmmaking. She could have been imperious, but she never was. She always asked rather than told, and she listened. She appreciated being part of the process of working on the script, even though she had that power [in her contract]." He recalled daily script conferences, at which Joan was present along with Sherman, Wald and writers Harold Medford and Jerome Weidman—meetings to which she came prepared with detailed notes, questions and valuable ideas.

When filming began, the director had more reasons to praise his leading lady. On the set, she at once understood and appreciated his instructions and suggestions. "If she had an idea, she always presented it in a way that never undermined my authority, which she could have done if she wanted to, with her star power. And that attitude gave me even greater authority with the others on the set."

The Damned Don't Cry begins like a silent movie. A car races through the desert . . . stops . . . a corpse is dragged out . . . and then the body is tossed down a sandy hillside. This provocative sequence is followed by the discovery of the remains—and then, ten minutes into the story, the film's long flashback begins, when a glamorous figure, wrapped in mink, is seen on the run. Everything that follows explains who this woman is and how she came to this point.

Joan was in complete command of her material, inhabiting every fiber of the character who is transformed from a simple innocent to a frightening cauldron of ambition. At first, as the housewife and mother Ethel Whitehead, living on the edge of poverty, she wears no makeup, no eyeliner, no false lashes. Ethel loses her child in an accident, and so has the audience's sympathy. Quitting home and husband, she is defiant: "I'm leaving because I don't have anything to hold me here any longer. I want something more than what I've had out of life—and I'm going to get it!" She sounds very like Marian, her character in the 1931 *Possessed*.

So begins a film created with admirable economy, combining realistic characters with crackling dialogue in a disturbing story that effectively takes several of Joan's characters from the 1930s, moving them not toward triumph but disaster. At first sympathetic and then downright repellent, Ethel eventually becomes a refined but hardboiled moll with the assumed name Lorna Hansen Forbes. She uses and is used by progressively more wealthy and powerful men, each of them more extreme in criminal activities; in this regard, the picture succeeds most of all as a dark moral fable that contradicts every unspoken assumption about American life just after World War II—especially the notion that money and possessions can buy happiness. As Ethel learns, they cannot even rent it.

The movie explores the psychological development of a woman through her relations with no fewer than four men, as she learns how to climb her way up in their world. But because the men are either domineering (her husband), morally compromised (the character played by Kent Smith) or downright criminal (those played by David Brian and Steve Cochran), Ethel is doomed. "I got enough nerve for both of us," she says to one of them; alas, she is tragically right. She becomes tough in a tough society and cultured and sophisticated to no good purpose in a world of wealthy, well-dressed, cultivated crooks. From *The Damned Don't Cry,* there is but a short step to the ethos of the *Godfather* movies.

As Vincent Sherman discovered early in their collaboration, Joan not only wanted the role, she also made it her own, precisely because the character contained something of herself. Putting behind her a life of deprivation and disappointment, Ethel is willing to do anything for status, acceptance and love. "The world isn't for nice guys," as she tells one man who degrades himself for her. "You gotta kick and punch and belt your way up, 'cause nobody's gonna give you a lift." One almost hears Joan Crawford speaking to a studio boss. It was this aggressiveness in the character that Joan wanted most of all to be sharpened in the screenplay, and which Sherman soon saw for himself, up close and personal.

There is something quietly revolutionary about *The Damned Don't Cry,* which implies that women have virtually a constitutional right to walk out on a depressing home and a husband who is a poor provider. The censors were still powerfully active in Hollywood in 1950, when the final release print was submitted for approval, but they apparently blinked, for *The Damned Don't Cry* insisted that a housewife was not doomed to live out her fate at home, no matter how grim the circumstances. Joan never liked this noteworthy picture—"a big mistake" was her description of it—and the critics were not even remotely well inclined toward it. This is difficult to understand, for her achievement here was complex, with a subtle but rich emotional range, and the finished film, provocative and uncompromising, offers one of her strongest performances. If *Mildred Pierce* defines Crawford in the 1940s, the same is true of *The Damned Don't Cry* in the 1950s.

According to Sherman, Joan was "the most cooperative actress I ever worked with—and very knowledgeable about what worked and didn't work for her in the story and in her career. When we were preparing the picture, she looked back over her own life as raw material for the character. She had risen from Broadway chorus girl to silent-movie dancer to wealthy and influential star. Her entire past had been a toughening experience for her, and she used it brilliantly."

———

YEARS LATER, VINCENT SHERMAN discussed in frank detail his love affairs with Bette Davis, Rita Hayworth and Joan Crawford. During the preparation of *The Damned Don't Cry,* he learned that Joan had just ended her tortured relationship with Greg Bautzer—an affair that had left her particularly sad and vulnerable. Sherman, too, was in an anxious state, trying to resolve serious marital problems as his wife, Hedda, grew more impatient with his serial infidelities.

No matter what rumors of Joan's freewheeling sexual life he might have heard before they began work on *Damned,* Sherman was taken off guard when she asked him to watch *Humoresque* with her in a studio screening room. There, as the two sat in the dark, Joan removed her clothes and aggressively initiated a wild afternoon. "Never," he said, "had I encountered such female boldness. I was confronted with a woman who went after what she wanted with a masculine approach to sex." Thus began an intense and passionate liaison that continued for almost two years, during the production of a trio of Crawford movies directed by Vincent Sherman.

And what of his marriage and Joan's attitude toward it? At first, he believed that Joan would be satisfied with a passing affair—that she had staked a claim on her director that would be for her good and the picture's. "She was trying to take control of me and the film," he recalled. But then Joan invited Vincent and Hedda Sherman to dine at North Bristol Avenue. Later that evening, Hedda said to her husband, "She's still a stunning woman, and there's something about her I like and admire. I found her gracious and considerate, and if you look beneath all the Hollywood crap, you can detect a woman who has refused to become a loser, who has pulled herself up from nothing and made something out of her life." Hedda asked straightforwardly if Vincent was having an affair with Joan, and he answered truthfully. "Well," Hedda said, "I guess it's too much to ask of any man that he turn down the opportunity to sleep with Joan Crawford."

"Joan had a constant need for approval and admiration," Sherman said later, "and in this regard, she was like Bette Davis." The need for endorsement, respect and esteem, especially from a talented man like Sherman, was not surprising, but there was another side to Joan's infatuation with her director. "I could sense the heart of an incurable romantic," he said later. "I felt she was much more a romantic than Bette. Joan was still looking for her Prince Charming, and still expecting him to arrive—in a white convertible, if not on a white charger. It was an appealing quality, a kind of naïveté."

A dressing room that was nothing less than a private apartment had been constructed for Joan at the studio, and there she lived from Monday through Friday while appearing in the Sherman pictures. "It was more convenient this way for me to see her at the end of the day," he said; on weekends, she went home to be with the children, who were cared for by housekeepers, nannies and cooks from Monday to Friday.

Eventually, Joan demanded that Vincent divorce Hedda and marry her—a step he had no intention of taking. When he refused, there was a temporary interruption in the affair, and for a while Joan occupied herself, apparently briefly, with another married man—tall, blond David Brian, her costar in *The Damned Don't Cry* and, later, in *This Woman Is Dangerous*.

The first Sherman picture was completed at the end of 1949, and Joan wasted no time in arranging for the second, a remake of a property already twice filmed. For this, Warner acceded to her request that the studio loan her out to Columbia Pictures, which owned motion picture rights to George Kelly's Pulitzer Prize–winning play, *Craig's Wife*. This was something that held a kind of morbid fascination for Joan, and which she recognized as having particular relevance to herself: it was the story of a middle-aged, middle-class woman with a pathological need to maintain a perfect, spotless home and to dominate her husband. This was to be Joan's next film, directed by Vincent Sherman.

She had seen the earlier movie versions (made in 1928 and 1936, with, respectively, Irene Rich and Rosalind Russell), and she knew there was something of Harriet Craig in herself, as she had written to a friend in 1938: "The part of me that is 'Craig's Wife' often comes out, and I wander around my heavenly home [looking for cleaning to do]."

Harriet's arrogance causes her to destroy everything of real value, and finally her perfect home becomes an isolating tomb. Joan may have seen it as a cautionary tale, a warning against some of her most ingrained and potentially destructive habits. If she could not show her less attractive side in real life, she certainly did so by her choice of material and by her deliberate shaping of it before and during production.

In making her final revisions to the screenplay, Joan made certain that some specifically autobiographical elements were inserted: "I've come a long way since working in that laundry," Harriet says. And at the climax of the movie, as Harriet is abandoned in the house she has placed before her husband, Joan herself composed a long speech unlike any other in her career—a description of her childhood that goes a long way toward providing an understanding of both Joan Crawford and Harriet Craig:

> *I wouldn't trust the love of any man after the things I've seen. I learned all about what you men call love the day my father left us. He always pretended to love my mother, and I worshipped him. One day after school, I went to his office. I found him with a woman—a cheap, vulgar blonde. What a sight they were! And I saw him for what he really was—a fat old fool with liquor on his breath. He said he was ashamed and that this event had nothing to do with his love for us. I told him I never wanted to see him again. I hated him and I would always hate him. That night, he didn't come home. He never came home. I watched my mother tramp the streets looking for a job. And at fourteen, I had to quit school and go to work, first in a factory and then in a laundry. We almost starved. So don't talk to me about protection. Don't try to tell me about love.*

Joan agonized when she made changes like these to the script, and they indicate not only that she clearly saw the correspondences between the character and herself, but also that in a way she was expressing a kind of regret.

Movies were her reality, and at this point in her life they were more than ever a means of making things right, of providing a cyclorama against which her past, with all its messy jumble, could be explored, its less attractive elements examined and corrected, if not dismissed. *The Damned Don't Cry* and *Harriet Craig* were quintessentially Joan Crawford projects, and somehow, secretly, she made them confessional pieces. She knew that audiences would have to listen very carefully indeed to hear the force of the subtexts.

The title of Kelly's play entered twentieth-century American English soon after its 1925 Broadway premiere—hence *Craig's wife* meant a woman maniacally devoted to maintaining an ideal household without consideration for relationships. "In many ways, Joan was herself the embodiment of Harriet Craig," according to Sherman, "in her obsessive attitude toward her home; her distrust of men and her desire to control; and her power of manipulation."

"The big house at 426 [North Bristol Avenue] is a kind of symbol to Miss Crawford," wrote a journalist who visited Joan in 1950. "She adores it and shines it personally. Few servants can keep up with her, and she changes them almost as often as she changes her bed linen." And at the studio, a retinue of retainers was in attendance: her secretary, hair stylist, makeup artist, wardrobe supervisor and lighting stand-in. With the perfect house and a platoon of people to look after it and her, she was Harriet Craig the actress.

At first, Sherman refused to direct the picture—and tried to dissuade Joan from acting in it, too, insisting that it was hopelessly dated, impossibly negative and perhaps too revelatory of its star. By way of reply, Joan insisted that there was no other property ready for her, and she needed the income. "But *Harriet Craig* turned out to be an enjoyable and rewarding experience," Sherman added, "and I was glad to have been so wrong. Joan's performance was wonderful. I had thought I knew everything, but I didn't."

Which was exactly Joan's judgment when they came to film a scene she considered false and dishonest. "Somehow, I couldn't follow his direction," she recalled. "I lost my temper, and in front of the entire crew, I cried, 'I just don't know what you want me to do! And I don't think you know, either!'"

"Do it your way, then," muttered Sherman.

She did it her way—and then she summoned the entire crew, more than seventy-five people. "Ladies and gentlemen," she said, "a little while ago, you heard me blow my top at Mr. Sherman, in front of all of you. I would like to apologize. I was wrong. He was right."

In assessing Joan's performance, it must be acknowledged that the play and the movie seem severely dated—hence the title character now seems simply grotesque, without a shred of nuance in her steely exterior. That said, the leading lady in this case may be admired for having faithfully rendered a chilling one-note performance. Harriet Craig is a destructive shrew, a monster to her fingertips, and so she will ever be.

When the picture was finished, in late spring 1950, Sherman and Crawford made the long drive from Los Angeles to Canada's Lake Louise for a private holiday. Hedda Sherman accepted her husband's excuse that this was a business trip for work on their next project at Warners. But there was a gap until that began, and friends and colleagues soon began to notice Joan's excessive drinking. She turned forty-five in 1951, anxious because she had no immediate job and aware that her affair with Vincent Sherman was doomed, like those with Charles McCabe and Greg Bautzer.

———

WITH HER ROLES IN *The Damned Don't Cry* and *Harriet Craig,* Joan began playing mostly unsympathetic characters. It would perhaps be going too far to suggest that she *consciously* chose to play these women precisely because they were aspects of herself—that the roles were Greek masks behind which she hid and through which she conveyed something of her true self. But such a statement may not be going too far: it may be a more or less accurate understanding of a woman who never appeared in public, as she said, unless she looked like Joan Crawford the movie star.

She was never a woman who revealed herself easily. Family, friends, lovers, husbands and colleagues, no matter what the extent of their admiration or intimacy with her, always felt that she withheld something—that there was something restrained in her personality, even when her temper or passion was most evident. Part of the explanation for this fundamental reticence lies in her resentment of her past, of the child and young woman she was—the poor girl from the hardscrabble background, the uneducated daughter of a laundress. She had tried so hard to erase that aspect of herself, and so the commoner she hoped to obliterate had been partly replaced by the aristocrat, which in America meant the movie star, the pop royal. Whereas Clark Gable was called the King of the Movies and John Wayne bore the title of the Duke, Joan Crawford was the quintessential Movie Queen, and so critics and journalists designated her for fifty years.

This complex of ideas suggests another reason for her cool cultivation of the movie-star image. Joan did not like herself, and so she always longed to escape into a role that was both release and relief. Actors, after all, only do professionally what all of us do now and then: we hide behind masks, and for a variety of reasons, we pretend. This is not always sheer hypocrisy—it is self-preservation, and even sometimes a matter of respect for the feelings of others. Joan was first and foremost an actress, and she regarded all potential roles from the obvious vantage point of her craft. How much of a character existed first in herself? With how much could she identify? With every new role, she asked those questions of herself.

———

IN THE WINTER OF 1949, Joan had seen Madeleine Carroll in Fay Kanin's play *Goodbye, My Fancy*, which ran on Broadway for over a year. After her return to Los Angeles, she asked Jack Warner to purchase the film rights, and by January 1951, a screenplay was ready, as were Crawford and Sherman.

Goodbye, My Fancy is a literate political comedy about a character named Agatha Reed, a crusading Washington politician who returns to her New England alma mater to receive an honorary degree. There, she discovers that the professor she had admired, loved and almost married is now the college president—a widower and still the love of her life. But her beloved old school is now run by a board of trustees afraid of her ideas: she is, for example, against war and in favor of open, critical thinking. Also on hand is a photographer from *Life* magazine who had loved and lost Agatha and now sees his second chance. *Goodbye, My Fancy* was therefore another romantic triangle well suited for Crawford—and it also had a liberal social conscience.

Joan's leading men were Frank Lovejoy as the photographer and (in his fourth outing with her), Robert Young as the college president. She asked that the role of Agatha's private secretary and confidante be given to Eve Arden (Mildred Pierce's faithful friend, Ida). With these talents in place, everyone was optimistic about the production. But as filming commenced, studio executives were under considerable pressure from both the Motion Picture Production Code and certain government agencies to change the single element central to Fay Kanin's play.

On Broadway, *Goodbye, My Fancy* had been openly critical of war as a means of settling international disputes. But by the time it was ready to be a movie, the United States was involved in a "police action" that was in fact the Korean War. In 1951, there was no getting around it: the script by Ivan Goff and Ben Roberts had to support or at least not question America's military might. Hence the critical theme of Agatha Reed's antiwar stance had to be cut, and she is merely in favor of some kind of vague academic freedom. This completely bled the life from Kanin's play (and reduced to meaninglessness the university's hysteria over the campus screening of Agatha's unnamed and undescribed documentary film). "*Goodbye, My Fancy* could have been a much more interesting picture," Joan wrote to an interviewer, "but unfortunately the political angle was cut out, and that took the guts right out of it. It got dulled down."[5]

A ho-hum reaction greeted the movie when it was released in May 1951. Almost alone in offering a positive review, *Variety* appreciated Joan's "excellent light touch" after several heavily dramatic roles. But as usual, her own

---

5. The song "I Guess I'll Have to Change My Plan"—one of Joan's favorites—was, at her request, employed for the fifth time in one of her pictures. In *Goodbye, My Fancy,* it is ironic in light of the emasculation of the play.

estimation was frank: she said that she had miscalculated when she thought that *Goodbye, My Fancy* would be a good property for her, and she admitted that either Katharine Hepburn or Rosalind Russell "could have done this sort of sophisticated political comedy better than I did." But given the attenuation of the play when it reached the screen, it may have been impossible for any actress to supply the pungency and substance that had been removed from the text.

Tensions between the star and her director accumulated during the final weeks of filming, especially over Joan's rude treatment of twenty-year-old Janice Rule, cast as Robert Young's daughter. "For some reason, perhaps Janice's youth, Joan took a dislike to her," recalled Sherman, "and whenever I spent an extra moment talking with Janice, Joan became suspicious and jealous, which made it difficult for me and for Janice."

Joan's unpleasant attitude may well have had to do with the fact that she now felt threatened by younger actresses, but this she could not recognize at the time. "I felt that she was unprofessional in her attitude," Joan said of Janice, "and that she regarded movie work as something less than slumming. One day, I told her so. 'Miss Rule,' I said, 'you'd better enjoy making films when you can—I doubt that you'll be with us long.'" But a decade later, Joan saw Janice in another picture called *The Subterraneans* and she was, as she said, "absolutely rapt over the performance of an actress who dances brilliantly and who has a flair for drama and for comedy. The girl was Janice Rule, and I can only add superlatives. Miss Rule: my apologies—I think you're going to be with us a long, long time!"

———

AT THE END OF March, shortly after the movie was completed, the telephone rang late one night at the home of Vincent and Hedda Sherman. He recognized Joan's slurred voice when she whispered, "Goodbye, Vincent." Alarmed, he raced to Brentwood, where he found her incoherent, a bottle of sleeping pills nearby. While Joan's cook prepared a pot of coffee, he dragged her from bed and forced her to walk about until she was more alert. "I begged her to be sensible and to understand that I cared about her, but I could never leave Hedda or my children. I also reminded her that I had told her this when we first met. It was almost five in the morning when I got back home." Soon after, Vincent Sherman gently ended the nearly two-year-long affair when he went off to direct Clark Gable and Ava Gardner in *Lone Star.*

—

"AT THE MOMENT WHEN I needed a blockbuster," Joan recalled, "my next picture could easily have been my swan song. It was the type of improbable corn that had gone out with Adrian's shoulder pads."

She was speaking about *This Woman Is Dangerous,* based on an original story submitted to the studio, which starred Joan as Beth Austin, an ex-con who became the brains behind a gang of thieves and confidence men. "Now don't hurt anyone," she says with maternal solicitude as she passes out the guns. To make matters more complicated, Beth is losing her eyesight. A brilliant surgeon (played by Dennis Morgan) saves her vision and wins her heart, but not before improbable crimes and medical miracles intervene. This may be the only movie in history to feature a character who is a world-renowned eye surgeon so dedicated to healing that he rushes from the city to farm country to operate on a boy kicked by a horse. Not even David Brian, Joan's occasional real-life lover, could do much as her scowling crook of a boyfriend. By all accounts, the not terrifically talented Brian was, offscreen, an expert ballroom dancer and a poet. Perhaps he missed his true calling.

The main problem with this picture was not the tired premise of a bad woman going good: it was the poorly constructed script and an absentminded director named Felix Feist, who seemed to have no idea what to do with the actors from sequence to sequence. For one of the very few times in her career, Joan appeared as if she had sleepwalked her way through the picture, unsure just which scene was which.

"I must have been awfully hungry," Joan said later. "The kids were in school, the house had a mortgage. And so I did this awful picture that had a shoddy story, a cliché script and no direction to speak of. The thing just blundered along. I suppose I could have made it better, but it was one of those times when I was so disgusted with everything that I just shrugged and went along with it. It was the worst picture I ever made."

She was not exaggerating. Howard Thompson, a movie critic for the *New York Times* for over forty years, was known for his pithy, one-line reviews. Of *This Woman Is Dangerous,* he wrote simply, "This picture is trash."

CHAPTER ELEVEN

Carrying a Torch Song

| 1952–1955 |

A MONG PEOPLE WHO acted in movies, it is difficult to name anyone who worked more diligently than Joan Crawford. Had it been an option, she might have become a first-rate director: she knew the technical aspects of all the filmmaking crafts, and she was not shy about telling colleagues what she liked and did not. But there was only a very small number of women behind the camera in Joan's time—Dorothy Arzner and Ida Lupino among the few—and the old boys' club of male directors would have made it excruciatingly difficult for a major female star to join their select group.

Joan had known when it was time for her to depart from Metro-Goldwyn-Mayer. Just so, at the end of 1951, she knew she had to leave Warner Bros. and strike out on her own, for her last five pictures had none of the success of *Mildred Pierce, Humoresque, Possessed* or *Daisy Kenyon.* "Warners was putting me in mediocre things," she wrote to a friend. "I suddenly got into a rut and then asked for my release." As the saying goes in Hollywood, you are only as valuable as your last picture, and her recent quartet had not been good for her. So it was that Joan expressed her desire to be free of studio obligations and join the growing list of freelance movie stars.

As early as 1951, Joan contacted an independent producer named Joseph Kaufman. Kaufmann had coproduced or produced nine pictures of no renown, but he was ready for a step upward, and Joan was about to give it to him—in exchange for executive producer status. She had read a recently published novel by Edna Sherry called *Sudden Fear*, a dark, romantic thriller with surprising twists and turns. As she described it for Kaufman, it could be wonderfully cinematic—much of it silent, she said, with brisk action and a contemporary music score.

From the start, Joan thought of *Sudden Fear* as her film, and with good reason. Joan had engaged as screenwriter the expert Lenore Coffee, who had written the dialogue for the 1931 *Possessed*. Joan hired David Miller, a journeyman director she trusted. Joan suggested the composer Elmer Bernstein as the right one to create a modern, percussive score. Joan arranged for saucy Gloria Grahame to play the role of a tawdry accomplice to murder. Joan insisted on Charles Lang, a master of black-and-white cinematography, who had been nominated eight times for an Oscar in that field. And just before filming began (and after some initial doubts), Joan cast Jack Palance as her leading man. He had taken over Marlon Brando's role in the Broadway production of *A Streetcar Named Desire* and followed that with an impressive performance in Elia Kazan's film *Panic in the Streets*. Joan was not keen on Palance's style and his defense of Stanislavsky's so-called Method acting, but she liked his sexy-sinister look and his insinuating tone of voice.

Joan and her cast and crew were ready for location filming in San Francisco in January 1952, and they all scented the aroma of success. "It's wonderful to be casting myself instead of accepting someone else's idea of who I should play," Joan told a reporter from *Time*—but she revealed nothing of the story. In fact, a curtain of silence descended around *Sudden Fear* all during production, and Edna Sherry's agent and publisher were persuaded to delay the paperback reprint until after the movie was released. Crawford and Kaufman had come up with a budget of $720,000 for the picture—a sum possible only because Joan agreed to forgo a salary and instead took 40 percent of the picture's profits. Within a year of its release, her accounts were enriched by more than a million dollars.

Sudden Fear not only proved Joan right when she insisted she could carry out a producer's duties, it also provided her with a positive version of the badly written role she had played in *This Woman Is Dangerous,* and it justified her insistence that she could find a successful project at this difficult time of her life. As the wealthy and successful playwright Myra Hudson, Joan played a woman who has everything except a husband—until she finds an unlikely candidate in the person of an actor named Lester Blaine (Palance), whom she has fired from the cast of her new play because he did not seem sufficiently romantic to her. She marries him for love, only to discover that he has married her for money—for which he is willing to commit murder with the help of his girlfriend Irene Neves (Grahame).

The picture, independently produced under the Kaufman banner and released by RKO in the summer of 1952, was successful in every way—at the box office, with critics and at Oscar time, when it gathered four nominations. Joan offered a moving, restrained yet powerful performance, completely controlled yet not at all calculated, despite scenes in which she had to express Myra's intense passion for her husband and then her equally intense terror of him. From her portrait of a woman falling unexpectedly in love, to her agonizing discovery of his betrayal, to her steely resolution to rid herself of her self-appointed killers—this was acting of a high caliber, confident but not smug, and entirely worthy of the Oscar and Golden Globe nominations Joan received.[1]

Cast relations during production were less than cordial. After several days in San Francisco, Jack Palance refused to reply to Joan's greeting each morning, and this caused a chilly lack of communication between the two stars. Asked why he was so unfriendly to his leading lady, Palance replied that he thought she was insincere. He disapproved of Joan's assistants and said that he regarded her as an aloof movie queen who treated colleagues condescendingly,

---

1. There were four Oscar nominations for the picture: Joan, for best actress; Charles Lang, for best black-and-white cinematography; Sheila O'Brien, for best costume design; and Jack Palance, for best supporting actor. But none of the nominees took home a statuette. (Shirley Booth won the best actress Academy Award, for her role in *Come Back, Little Sheba.*)

as if they were servants. But he seems to have been remarkably disingenuous. As it happened, he was carrying on an affair with Gloria Grahame during production; she disliked Joan and tried to throw her off whenever possible— hence Palance took Grahame's side. Hollywood history provides a host of such petty animosities and coy tricks. (Years later, Grahame thought better of her behavior toward Joan: she told Herbert Kenwith that Joan had quietly guided much of her performance in *Sudden Fear*.)

"It was one of the most harrowing experiences I've ever had," Joan said of the filming. "I had played a trapped character before, but never like this—I went through nine solid days of hysteria, and the closet scene alone took two-and-a-half days to complete, with one baby spotlight focused on me." She was referring to the long sequence in which Myra sets her plot in motion—all of it filmed without dialogue, like a perfectly composed silent movie-within-a-movie. "Eddie [Edwin Allen, her makeup man] just handed me the lipstick, Elva [Martien, the wardrobe assistant] straightened my hem, so deftly I wasn't aware. While lights are being adjusted, there is usually kidding and lighthearted banter on a movie set, but this time Sylvia [Lamarr, her lighting stand-in] stood mutely in my place until we were ready to shoot; and the electrical crew changed lenses quickly to move in for a close-up or out for a medium shot while the mood was sustained. No one asked these people for silence—we all knew it was just right for the job." Indeed, everything was right about *Sudden Fear,* a hypnotic thriller that over time lost none of its power or appeal.

———

DESPITE HER ENTHUSIASM FOR it, nothing was right about Joan's next picture—*Torch Song,* for which she returned to Metro-Goldwyn-Mayer after a decade's absence. "It was like a homecoming," she said. "I loved doing that film. It gave me a chance to dance again. All the right elements were there. It was a field day for an actress, particularly one who'd reached a certain age. They don't write pictures like this anymore, do they?" To which one can only reply that no, they don't write pictures like this anymore, and we are all grateful. Joan always spoke fondly and highly of *Torch Song,* a picture that even her most ardent fans have rightly judged as a complete failure in every regard.

At the outset, things seemed auspicious. In March 1953 she received a screenplay from Benjamin Thau, Metro's casting director. Based on the story "Why Should I Cry?" the script was about a tyrannical song-and-dance performer who alienates everyone around her until she is suddenly transformed by the love of a blind pianist. As the great writer Ben Hecht said in a different context, this was a lot of hooey. But this was also Hollywood. Metro owned the rights to the story and had failed to realize it as a movie with Lana Turner, Ann Sheridan or Cyd Charisse. Because it was widely known that Miss Crawford was on the lookout for new properties, "Why Should I Cry?" was submitted for her consideration. Perhaps to everyone's surprise, she thought it was brilliant, precisely the sort of project she needed. Negotiations were handled quickly, and the star was to receive $125,000 in eighty-three weekly installments, to lighten the tax burden.

And so, in May, after a lavish Welcome Home celebration at Metro-Goldwyn-Mayer Studios in Culver City, Joan arrived to begin work on a movie for which she was totally unequipped in every regard and that had to be completed in twenty-four days—so crowded was Metro's shooting schedule that year. Charles Walters, a director with choreographic experience, was engaged at Joan's request after she saw his film *Lili,* and a supporting cast was hurriedly assembled. But Walters found Joan extremely nervous and insecure about doing a musical for the first time in twenty years—since *Dancing Lady.*

Becoming more anxious by the day, Joan had a quick facelift and then had the wardrobe department fit her with a so-called torpedo or bullet brassiere, which thrust her breasts threateningly upward and forward. Popularized by stars like Lana Turner and Marilyn Monroe, who were much younger than Crawford, this garment had a pointed, conelike shape, to which sweaters and knit dresses clung, exaggerating whatever nature had provided.

Joan had been photographed in color before 1953, in the final scenes of both *The Hollywood Revue of 1929* and *The Ice Follies of 1939.* But the requirements of Technicolor—combined with a wide-screen process and the excessively lavish production values of MGM in the early 1950s—required meticulous attention to the colors applied to sets, makeup and costumes, and the careful examination of color correction in the lab. No such care attended the preparations, filming or editing of *Torch Song*.

John Michael Hayes had delivered a first draft screenplay that might have worked if he and the studio had had more time for rewrites. But Hayes rushed off to work for Alfred Hitchcock, for whom he wrote four memorable scripts (*Rear Window, To Catch a Thief, The Trouble with Harry* and *The Man Who Knew Too Much*). With Metro's clock ticking, the studio assigned the rewrite to—of all people—none other than Jan Lustig, best known for the failed *Reunion in France*. Disaster was therefore in the cards from day one.

To make everything worse, Joan was given complete freedom, without guidance or supervision, to develop her own makeup (heavy and garish), her own costumes (hilariously overdecorated) and her own hair color (tangerine). The result was quite simply one of the most dreadful motion pictures in history—it could have been a textbook guide for creating the ultimate drag show, except that *Torch Song* seemed to have neither wit nor purpose. Some critics, like the anonymous reviewer of *Time,* sympathized with her: "By reducing a performer of Joan's experience and hard-won skills to the cheesecake class, the picture cheats her of the human qualities she has developed." If she recognized this, she never admitted it.

Joan had turned forty-seven that March, and although she had maintained a lithe and disciplined body, she required long hours of dance lessons and longer hours of exhausting exercise for the rigors of *Torch Song*. This left her with no time for singing lessons and vocal coaching, and so she agreed that India Adams would record her songs for the movie.

Her relations with other cast members duplicated the chilly tone that had prevailed during the filming of *Sudden Fear,* except that now Joan was frightened of losing control over her own performance and letting her male costar walk off with the picture. Hence she was all but downright rude to Michael Wilding. At the time, he was married to Elizabeth Taylor, twenty years his junior, who was also working at Metro and liked to visit her husband at work.

But Joan put a stop to that, insisting that Elizabeth be barred from the set—perhaps also because Taylor required no elaborate foundation garments and no heavy makeup: at twenty-one, she was at her most radiantly beautiful, even without a whisper of rouge or eyeliner. By contrast, nothing about Crawford was right, in or out of *Torch Song* that year. She looked hard, almost grotesque; her eyebrows and lips were colored without restraint and seemed to elongate her thin face; and she comported herself off-camera just like her character on-screen, seeming unhappy with the world and ready to lash out at everyone. In the movie, she had the role of Jenny Stewart, a bitter, hostile, lonely star who abuses everyone who comes close to her; Joan's conduct on the set was not much different.

The role of Jenny, in other words, was a portrait of Joan herself, and she seemed to be aware of this when she said late in life, "One of the scary things is the effects a really heavy or demanding role will have on your personal life. During *The Women,* I'm afraid I was as much of a bitch offscreen as I was on. Elizabeth Taylor said that she actually became Martha [in *Who's Afraid of Virginia Woolf?*] in private life, with rather disastrous consequences. I can understand that. I always wondered how Charlton Heston acted offscreen while he was playing Moses."

Like very many politicians, salesmen, teachers and preachers, Joan had to be "on"—she had to be aware of her image and of what was expected of her. Charles Walters recalled that Joan insisted on being seen by the fans who crowded around her dressing bungalow each day, and when she departed from Metro and headed for home every Friday evening, she ordered that the interior lights of the studio limousine be switched on, so that she could be seen inside the car, waving warmly at her admirers. This, after all, was the way of royals when they traveled in closed carriages outside their palaces.

Joan was pursuing a new way of life that almost became disastrous: she was now living full-time, Monday through Friday, in her elaborate studio dressing room, which was contained within one of the soundstages. "This is a pattern I've followed ever since [*Torch Song*] when making a picture," she said later. The reason she gave for this new way of living was that she had been, up to this point, "bringing my worries home, and it was better to leave the twins to their busy days at school."[2]

By living at the studio, "when we stopped shooting, I could see the rushes, go back to my dressing room, talk over the next day's scenes with [the director] and the cast. We ate peanut butter sandwiches, had a drink and talked. After the others leave, I'm locked in that dressing room at night with my script, getting ready for the next day. Sometimes I go over to the empty set and walk it, rehearsing."

But this extreme degree of dedication had obvious perils, for a kind of possession mania was overtaking Joan Crawford.

In *Sudden Fear,* she portrayed a woman terrorized by a husband with murder on his mind. In *Torch Song,* she portrayed a bitter, lonely and hostile star who used and mistreated others. Joan may have assumed this role precisely because it was an accurate portrait of herself—of the woman she could acknowledge and deal with only through role-playing, the woman she could present to the world and then discard, as if by a kind of magic. But by choosing the roles and then living them out in an increasingly distant existence, sealed off from emotional connections to others, Joan was allowing herself no other frame of reference for real life. The characters partly became her.

That summer of 1953, after *Torch Song* was completed, she sent Christina back to the Chadwick School after a two-week holiday at home. "It was a miserable time," according to Joan. "Christina teased her young brother unmercifully, and they both began picking on the twins. I felt the best solution was to send Christina back to school early." With no classes in session and the dormitories closed for the summer holiday, Christina lived with Mr. and Mrs. Chadwick and was paid a monthly salary for helping with chores. The money was in fact provided by Joan herself, who considered it "excellent training for her to earn money by doing housework."

Soon Christopher was living there year-round, too. "My brother and I

---

2. By 1953, Christina and Christopher were boarding at the Chadwick School, where eventually the twins would join them.

both lived at the Chadwick School and didn't go home very often," according to Christina. "We didn't get into the trouble that usually followed one of those weekends at home, so it wasn't such a bad trade-off." Cathy and Cindy came to the same school in 1955, and they had happy memories of their time there, of Joan's regular visits to them all and of holidays in Brentwood.

Living the roles she was playing and socializing only with the cast and crew, Joan in effect *became* the characters in her films. Her dedication to her work, in other words, possessed her to the exclusion of recognizable reality. This helps to explain why she refused to go out in public unless, as she said, she looked like Joan Crawford the movie star: no other character existed.

This complicated and essentially tragic confusion of realms was aggravated by her growing dependence on alcohol, which made her more and more reclusive and prevented any kind of healthy self-awareness. Alone in the dark, she counted on her private stores of vodka to offer an escape from loneliness. But the more she drank, the more ill she felt the following morning and the more time was required to put her right. And the more ill she felt, the more dyspeptically she behaved with directors, cast and crew. This sad cycle deepened and darkened, and for a time there seemed no escape.

———

JUST BEFORE STARTING HER next picture, Joan made her television debut in a half-hour filmed drama called "Because I Love Him," a story that slipped on its own soap-opera suds. Over the next twenty years, she was seen in no fewer than seventeen productions.[3]

Her subsequent feature, *Johnny Guitar,* pleased no one except European New Wave filmmakers. "I should have had my head examined for doing it," Joan grumbled, adding that there was "no excuse for a picture being this

---

3. As of 2010, the Paley Center for Media (formerly the Museum of Television and Radio, with branches in New York and Los Angeles) listed in its archives three extant television dramas starring Joan Crawford: "Rebel Range," an episode of *Zane Grey Theatre* (December 3, 1959); "The Five Daughters Affair," a two-part installment of *The Man From U.N.C.L.E* (March 31 and April 7, 1967); and "Eyes," from *Night Gallery* (November 7, 1969).

bad or for me, for making it." But just as she had overrated *Torch Song,* Joan underrated *Johnny Guitar,* which has many merits, despite a trouble-plagued production, a cast of generally ornery actors and a script that taxed everyone in the production company. Filming began in October 1953 and was completed at the end of December.

As location filming proceeded in Arizona, Joan decided to bring ten-year-old Christopher along for several weeks. Aware that life was often awkward and uncongenial for him in an all-female household, she offered the boy a holiday riding ponies and horses with authentic cowboys at ranches near the movie sites. According to Christina, her brother enjoyed himself enormously and was befriended by sixteen-year-old Tony Ray, the director's son. This was a rare happy interlude during Christopher's years with Joan, for the boy managed to be in trouble from an early age. He had the habit of running away from home, and several times he was found living on the Santa Monica pier or camping out with older friends. Unfortunately, the more he misbehaved, and the more she tried to pressure him into good deportment, the more rebellious he became.

Nicholas Ray set out to direct an unorthodox Western, and he certainly succeeded. Many scenes were photographed in the Arizona desert, and the picture bluntly presented gender reversals, as gritty women (Joan and the formidable actress Mercedes McCambridge) tough it out with gentler male characters (Sterling Hayden, Ben Cooper and Scott Brady). Ray was a fascinatingly perverse filmmaker, and with *Johnny Guitar* he continued a career-long preference for long dialogue scenes, infrequent action sequences and monologues like operatic arias—not the stuff of American Western movies, even though Republic Pictures, the home of that genre, financed the movie.

The screenplay, by Philip Yordan and Ben Maddow (based on a novel written for Crawford by Roy Chanslor), was a pretext for a tale of frustrated sexual relationships, all of which—because of censorship—had to be implied rather than explored. Joan played the role of Vienna, who owns a gambling casino on the outskirts of a nameless town and supports the arrival of a new railroad line. But she runs into trouble with local ranchers, who are unaccountably subservient to a hard-hitting, hot-headed gunslinger named Emma (McCambridge)—a woman with a keen hostility to men.

Vienna, who has no such hang-ups and has distributed her favors liberally, is pleased but nervous when her former lover returns—a transformed outlaw named Johnny Logan, who has hung up his holster, taken up music and now calls himself Johnny Guitar (Hayden). Like all the men in the movie, he is, let it be noted, very much an ancillary character in a story that might have been about a pair of female boxers; but in that case, of course, *Johnny Guitar* would not have its perverse charms. All sorts of romantic and business complications ensue before Vienna kills the villainous Emma and gets to kiss her gentle Johnny Guitar at the fadeout.

Some of the movie's defenders have reached perhaps too high in their efforts to praise the picture: it has been analyzed almost beyond recognition as an expressionist allegory, a commentary on the political witch hunts of its day or an elegy for rural America. But like all academic exercises, these strained explanations are unnecessary and may even deflect attention from the movie's real merits. *Johnny Guitar* may perhaps best be appreciated as an adult Western, noteworthy for presenting characters who declaim and reflect more than they converse—hence the arbitrary dramatic structure and the arrangement of monologues as virtually operatic arias, dialogues as duets and, at the right moments, trios, quartets and quintets.

Joan's low estimation of the picture may have been based on two unfortunate facts. First, very little was asked of her in the role of Vienna: any actress who could brandish a pistol and scowl darkly could have played the role, and this time her contract did not allow her to demand script revisions.

The second troubling aspect was even more critical. "On *Johnny Guitar*," Joan recalled, "we had in the cast an actress who hadn't worked in ten years, an excellent actress but a rabble-rouser. She was perfectly cast as such in the picture, but she played her part offstage as well. Her delight was to create friction. The picture became a nightmare. She would finish a scene, walk to the phone on the set and call one of the columnists to report my 'incivilities.'" Joan never mentioned the name of the actress, but there was only one other woman in the cast—Mercedes McCambridge.

Joan was inaccurate in describing McCambridge as one "who hadn't worked in ten years," for McCambridge, in the previous four years, had appeared in no fewer than five features and five television dramas. But she was in life what she was in the picture—a rowdy, deeply disturbed and highly strung woman who had become an untamable alcoholic. Joan was jealous of McCambridge's more flamboyant role and annoyed that Ray favored this difficult actress with the picture's few close-ups—especially during a bizarre scene in which Emma sets fire to Vienna's saloon and, with an expression of psychotic glee, watches it collapse in flames.

"Unfortunately," recalled cast member Ben Cooper, "McCambridge's alcoholism affected her behavior and created problems for all of us." Joan reacted poorly to these antics, which she considered shockingly unprofessional. Late one evening, she tore McCambridge's costumes to shreds and had them strewn over the Arizona highway—which was also not very professional conduct. "As a human being, Miss Crawford is a very great actress," said Nicholas Ray with undisguised sarcasm.

Everyone on the production was fairly miserable, and the finished film displeased critics and baffled audiences. But a half century after the picture's release, the National Film Preservation Board voted to add *Johnny Guitar* to the United States Film Registry, judging it "culturally, historically, or esthetically important." Whether it deserves that sort of encomium may be endlessly debated, but there is no doubt that *Johnny Guitar* extended the wild frontiers of the Western genre to include unusually well-bred cowboys with obvious psychosexual peculiarities.

As for Joan's career, at this point she must be credited with doing what she promised—something completely different, whenever she could. Recently, she had portrayed a gun moll, a member of Congress, a wealthy playwright and an embittered theatrical performer. To these she had now added the role of gun-totin' Western saloonkeeper. The only thing lacking, it may have seemed, was for Joan Crawford to play a monster from outer space.

—

THAT AUTUMN OF 1954, Joan continued to live in even greater isolation during the filming of Joseph Pevney's melodrama *Female on the Beach,* produced at

Universal Studios. "The only thing wrong with it was lack of credibility," she said—but that absence destroyed the story of a wealthy widow (Joan) stricken with love for a handsome young gigolo (Jeff Chandler) who may or may not have killed the previous occupant of Joan's beach house. Decades later, audiences often howl with laughter when the murderer is finally revealed to be the real estate agent who wanted the gigolo all to herself and who literally made a killing at her job.

But there was a great deal more wrong with the movie than a mere lack of credibility. The dialogue, for example, was a succession of terrible lines, as Joan had to say meaningless things like "The past is buried under a lot of dead years." The real problem, however, was her performance, a self-contained parody of previous Joan Crawford roles. Curiously, and with her own approval, she was photographed hard after being made up hard; she spoke hard; and she plodded her way through the turgid melodramatics as if she, too, found them incredible.

There seems to have been a complex of reasons for this nearly somnolent and surprisingly confused performance. For one thing, Joan had recently extricated herself from a brief liaison with Milton Rackmil, president of Universal. For another, she briefly resumed an earlier affair with costar Jeff Chandler, the studio's most popular star, who was married and the father of two young children. Neither of these entanglements could be called fulfilling romances.

Still another cause of confusion was the present state of her career—without a home studio or a clear way to her professional future. It is not true (as some have claimed) that she was offered only negative or downright repellent characters: on the contrary, there were discussions about her playing more sympathetic roles, which eventually went to Katharine Hepburn, Shirley Booth, Susan Hayward and Deborah Kerr. But at least twice, Joan sabotaged her own best interests when she insisted on her choice of cameraman and wardrobe designer. In fact, she chose off-putting, difficult or negative characters like Lynn Markham in *Female on the Beach* because—intentionally or not—she wanted to present an aspect of herself that audiences would reject.

There was more to Joan Crawford, she seemed to say, and not all of her was admirable or worthy of imitation.

Only this kind of dark motivation, her desire to continue a series of virtually penitential performances, can explain her almost frantic eagerness to purchase the rights to *The Queen Bee,* a novel by Edna Lee, with whom she corresponded directly. The character of Eva Phillips was, as the novelist wrote to Joan on September 12, 1954, a woman of "calculating, greedy destructiveness" whose ruthless manipulation destroys everyone who comes into her orbit. Eva Phillips made *Torch Song*'s Jenny Stewart seem like Florence Nightingale.

Queen Bee, which lost the definite article as it moved from page to screen, was made to order for Joan at this time in her life. She paid Edna Lee fifteen thousand dollars for the movie rights, which she then sold to Columbia Pictures on several conditions: Jerry Wald was to produce; Ranald MacDougall was to be both writer and director; for her cameraman, she chose Charles Lang, who had done her bidding on *Sudden Fear* and *Female on the Beach;* and she had contractual approval on her costume, hair and makeup designers. These negotiations were finalized at the end of October 1954, just when she was seen in her second television drama, as a woman on *The Road to Edinburgh* who offers a ride to a man who fixes her flat tire and who may or may not be a killer.

Joan's schedule called for her to complete *Female on the Beach* in February 1955 and to follow that at once with *Queen Bee.* Betsy Palmer, also in the cast of *Queen Bee,* recalled that the erotic high jinks of Joan Crawford and her costar John Ireland often led to their late and disheveled arrival on the set. In his unpublished autobiography, Ireland detailed the brief affair, their "repeated dinners at Frascati's Restaurant . . . and whatever else we repeated never seemed repetitious, it was always like a first time. She was exotic beyond the meaning of the word."

On New Year's Eve, in her dressing room on the Universal soundstage, Joan was reading her script and sipping a drink when a call was patched through from home. On the line was Earl Blackwell, a celebrity promoter who preferred to be known as a society impresario; he was calling from Las Vegas with a group of friends at his side to extend greetings to Joan. The revelers included

Alfred and Lillian Steele, whom Joan had met a few times at New York parties and charity events. Joan told the Steeles that she hoped they would soon visit her in Los Angeles. And that, she thought, was the end of that.

Queen Bee was completed in late April 1955. "I had a chance to play the total bitch, a worse bitch than I had played in *The Women*—and for a solid ninety minutes, too. I ended up hating myself, honestly feeling that in my death scene I was getting precisely what I deserved." Audiences found the southern gothic hysterics impossible to like, but her fans found it impossible to avoid—it was rather like a roadside accident that demands horrified attention. Joan played the part of Eva Phillips as written—"with such silky villainy that we long to see her dispatched," as one critic wrote. "When she is killed at the end, as she should be, it is a genuine pleasure and relief."

———

SOON THERE WAS A regular visitor to the set of *Queen Bee,* and before long, the cast sensed that love was blossoming in the star's dressing room. The gentleman was not John Ireland.

Alfred Nu Steele, who visited without his wife, was five years older than Joan.[4] Born on April 24, 1901, in Nashville, Tennessee, he was a graduate of Chicago's Northwestern University, where he played football. Steele began his career in the advertising department of the *Chicago Tribune* and then worked in advertising for Standard Oil and the Columbia Broadcasting System. With the D'Arcy Advertising Agency, he managed the Coca-Cola account, which subsequently hired him as marketing director. In 1949 Pepsi-Cola took him on, and by 1950 he was their chief executive officer and chairman of the board; he was made a president in 1951.

Regarded as gregarious, ambitious and socially agreeable, Steele compensated for merely average looks with above-average charm. Rugged but stylish, he had learned a great deal from his world travels for Pepsi, and he was in

---

4. According to biographer Bob Thomas, Steele's father assigned the middle name in honor of the national Sigma Nu fraternity, to which Edgar Steele had been devoted.

demand as an amusing raconteur. He also loved being the star at an event and was fascinated by celebrities. At fifty-four, he was full of energy and plans: he loved his job and lived for it, as Joan soon realized. During his first visit, they dined together on three successive evenings. Money seemed of little concern to him; indeed, some colleagues considered his methods rather too "flashy," and his private financial dealings, according to one investigative reporter, "were not [in the language of the day] always according to Hoyle"—which meant there were often questions about both his debt level and his timely payment of personal invoices.

Steele had already put in motion a variety of measures to improve the fortunes of Pepsi-Cola. He reorganized the management, launched a new advertising campaign and authorized a change in the formula of the drink to make it less sweet. On taking charge, he also concentrated on reviving the morale of Pepsi-Cola's independent workers. Usually local businessmen, the bottlers had been prone to selling out because of dissatisfaction with stagnating sales in the late 1940s. As business improved in the 1950s, Steele still regarded them as problems, because, in his opinion, they were inclined to become complacent and lazy in good times. Accordingly, Steele bought the franchises of several bottlers who were not getting good results in major markets, and he assumed operation of these territories directly. Soon, Pepsi-Cola was its own bottler in over twenty major American markets and in a growing number of Third World countries.

Joan quickly learned a great deal about the man and his business, and she found everything fascinating. Through mutual friends, she had heard rumors that Alfred's second marriage was soon to be dissolved, which he confirmed a few weeks later, when he returned to Los Angeles. By this time, the divorce of the Steeles was in progress. (His first wife was Marjorie Garvey, the mother of his daughter, Sally; his second marriage, to Lillian Nelson, produced a son named Alfred Nelson Steele.)

Things happened with extraordinary speed after Alfred announced to Joan that he was going to marry her. "There was never a question in his mind or mine that I was going to be his wife. The chemistry was right—and beyond chemistry, a breathtaking premonition of new horizons." *Premonition* may not have been the word she meant to use, but there it was—a warning, conjoined to the excitement of anticipating "new horizons."

Alfred Steele took pride in being a man who took charge, however occasionally unpopular his corporate pronouncements or business decisions might be. On his side, he was certainly attracted to this passionate and energetic movie star, but he also must have appreciated the value of marrying one of the world's most celebrated and glamorous women. They agreed that she would not have to abandon her acting career unless and until she wished to do so— but meanwhile, as she said, she could certainly help to market and endorse Pepsi-Cola.

For her part, Joan found the idea of becoming Mrs. Alfred Steele surprisingly appealing. There had been no absence of lovers since her divorce from Philip Terry in 1946, but none of them had been serious prospects for marriage. "I was unutterably lonely," she told a friend, an admission that goes a long way toward explaining the procession of sexual partners. "I was unfulfilled. I am a woman with a woman's need—a husband."

By the end of 1954, Christina was defiant and Christopher was frighteningly out of control. Would they not benefit from the presence of a strong, loving man with two children who clearly adored him? Joan's four children liked Steele, and Christina, especially, formed a good relationship with the man she henceforth called her father. "The first meeting was strange and awkward," Christina told a reporter. "Yet I had the immediate feeling that he was tremendously kind. I have never felt such warmth, strength and understanding in any person. He was my idea of what a father should be."

Gloria Swanson may well have come to Joan's mind once again: she, too, had mostly abandoned acting for a new career as a successful business entrepreneur. Joan did not think of herself in that capacity yet, but she soon began to ask questions about the basics of marketing and corporate strategies. In addition, Alfred Steele was evidently a man of considerable wealth, and Joan was now living from season to season with fewer offers of movie jobs and more expenses for the growing children. There was no reason for them not to marry.

This they did two weeks ahead of the planned date. While dining in Beverly Hills on the evening of May 9, 1955, Alfred suggested that they advance the occasion and leave at once for Las Vegas in the Pepsi-Cola corporate airplane. Protesting that she had not been in a plane since the bumpy ride from Catalina after filming *Rain* in 1932, Joan insisted she would not travel except by train or car. Nonsense, said Steele: she would have nothing to fear so long as he was with her. And with that, he poured her a stiff drink, took her by the arm and rushed her to the waiting airplane. At two o'clock on the morning of May 10, 1955, at the Flamingo Hotel, Las Vegas Municipal Judge Ben Mendoza pronounced them man and wife. Three of Alfred's friends witnessed the event.

The newlyweds departed at the end of June from New York on the SS *United States* for a European honeymoon. "We were madly in love," Joan recalled, "but we were also a strong, mature man and woman, each used to his own way and not about to relinquish it. Alfred had evidently been warned by countless associates that a movie star is self-centered and just naturally annihilates men—that he'd have to subdue me and show me from the beginning who was boss. This I was not prepared for. He'd been a persuasive wooer and a passionate bridegroom, and now I met a streak of bull-headed obstinacy that frightened me. I had longed all my life for a strong lover, but I wouldn't be bullied." The trip was fine, but she was glad to return home—and to work. "I had a lot of suffering to do in my next picture," she said. "But it was easy. In real life, I was suffering over the uneasiness of my marriage."

CHAPTER TWELVE

Some of the Best of Everything
| 1955–1962 |

I T WAS SHEER hell," Joan Crawford said later, speaking frankly about the first year of her marriage to Alfred Steele. "But that was only because we were getting used to each other's lives, making adjustments. Alfred lived at a very fast pace, keeping appointments on the split second. Sometimes I couldn't keep up, and it embarrassed me. But I did what I could," and in fact the occasional dissensions were outnumbered by the long periods of mutual, intense happiness. "We were very much in love. Everybody warned him it wouldn't last—'You're marrying one tough broad!'—but he knew my toughness was an act." Part of that toughness came from Joan's compulsive need to maintain her image as a star, which she now had to transform and reinvent as the full-time wife of a business executive.

There was no question about where the newlyweds would live. Joan soon sold her home in Los Angeles and moved into his New York residence, at 36 Sutton Place South. The address, on a quiet, tree-lined block near the East River, was impressive—but the dimensions of the two-bedroom apartment were not, and soon the Steeles required a larger space for business entertaining and larger rooms for Joan's wardrobe. In 1956 Alfred bought an eighteen-room duplex penthouse at 2 East Seventieth Street, at Fifth Avenue; most of the rooms overlooked Central Park. They decided to turn the residence into eight enormous rooms, and that required considerable architectural renovation and, with the help of William Haines, complete redecoration.

The purchase and reconstruction required an outlay of over one million dollars, a sum that Steele borrowed from the Pepsi-Cola Company. During the two years of renovations, the couple lived alternately at Sutton Place South and, when entertaining, in suites at the Hampshire House hotel. Oblivious to costs, Alfred Steele spent money extravagantly—in fact, with a kind of wild abandon.

Joan, who had recently been paid about fifty thousand dollars per picture, had heavy school expenses for the children and was in the 90 percent tax bracket; she had, therefore, no vast sums to bring to her marriage. Nevertheless, she turned over to Alfred the proceeds from the sale of 426 North Bristol Avenue, and something else that he considered just as valuable as money: her drawing power as an international celebrity. Unlike Joan's previous three husbands, he was not an actor—hence there was no competition, no contest of professional wills, and no concern about uncertain salaries or suspensions. From the start, Alfred impressed Joan as very much his own man, with a secure self-awareness and proud accomplishments in a business of which she knew nothing. But there was an important place for her in his world—not only as the celebrity on his arm as they traveled the globe, but also as a woman with remarkable energy who quickly became the best exponent of public relations in the history of Pepsi-Cola. Joan knew how to meet people, how to handle crowds, how to be endlessly gracious with strangers and how to field questions from reporters.

She also knew how to dress, how to comport herself in strange or difficult situations and how to put people at ease. From 1955, wherever they traveled, crowds turned out to see Joan Crawford, the wife of Alfred Steele; all over the world, Pepsi executives, factory workers and truck drivers brought their wives to conventions and bottling-plant openings, vying for the chance to meet her, to shake her hand and to obtain her autograph. All this, of course, was marvelous publicity for Pepsi-Cola, which was now identified with glamour.

At home, Alfred often asked Joan, on short notice, to host a reception for Pepsi executives, and he presumed (rightly) that she would somehow provide food and drinks for ten or twenty men, most of them as eager to meet the movie star as to discuss business with her husband. "He wasn't as handsome as Doug or Clark or Franchot or Phillip," Joan said years later, "but Alfred had a virility, a sense of assurance, that made him the center of attraction in any room. Women were crazy about him and men liked him. He made everyone feel at ease. I didn't mind going into semi-retirement as an actress, because life with Alfred was so fulfilling. We traveled a great deal, and we established wonderful relationships with the children."

Steele not only took pride in his glamorous wife, he exploited her movie-star image for the good of business, and she loved every minute of it. Thus her movie career declined even as she had an ongoing real-life role as the wife of a highly placed American executive. If her life had been planned like a traditional drama, this would have marked the beginning of the third act.

But it was not a third act without tensions. According to her children and her publicist John Springer, Joan and Alfred had regular disagreements that sometimes escalated into shouting matches. Because he was aware of Joan's sexual history, Alfred nursed a latent but constant suspicion about her intention and ability to be a faithful wife—a doubt he frequently expressed to her in the course of this or that altercation. There was no reason for his distrust of her, for now she had no lovers, but that did not allay his anxieties.

———

BUSINESSMAN'S WIFE OR NOT, Joan still had to fulfill a three-picture deal with Columbia that had begun with the unsavory histrionics of *Queen Bee*. After the Steeles returned from their European honeymoon in midsummer, she hurried to Los Angeles to appear in Robert Aldrich's film of *Autumn Leaves,* which was produced from late August through November 1955.

At first glance, this seemed to be just another soap opera on the rocks, with a twist. In Los Angeles, a lonely middle-aged spinster named Millie Wetherby (Joan) types manuscripts for a living; her only friend is her wisecracking land-lady (Ruth Donnelly). One night at a diner, Millie meets Burt Hanson (Cliff Robertson), a soft-spoken romantic half her age who pursues her with touch-ing sincerity. After considerable hesitation, she finally agrees to marry him. At first, this is bliss unspeakable, and the couple even gets to repeat the most famous scene in Columbia's *From Here to Eternity,* as they embrace on the sand while waves crash over them.

In the bittersweet by and by, Millie learns that her darling is a liar, a kleptomaniac and a schizophrenic who was pitched over the edge when he dis-covered his first wife in bed with his father. The violence continues when Burt beats Millie and then attacks her with her typewriter. Reluctantly, she realizes she must commit him to a psychiatric institution, with full knowledge that, as she cries to a doctor, "if he's cured, he may not need me any more!"

But her doubts have not taken Hollywood into account. Burt undergoes electroshock therapy (twice detailed in close-ups by the director, who had a fondness for things gruesome) and receives intravenous infusions of some milky miracle drug (also shown twice). Millie anxiously paces her kitchen at home, and Burt is at last cured and ready for release. She goes to meet him at the hospital. Will he still adore her? Will they revive the ardor of their pas-sionate December-May marriage? Veteran moviegoers may well guess.

Because the performances by Crawford and Robertson were pitched so perfectly—because the hysterics were kept to a minimum and the menace neatly tuned—*Autumn Leaves* turned out better than it might have in other hands. Perhaps because Alfred Steele had recently dispersed the clouds of her own real-life loneliness, Joan knew how to portray a woman existing in a gray haze of solitude. Her transformation by love never seems incredible, her rapture is poignant and her heartache credibly rendered without exaggerated facial reactions. She was more than competently accompanied by Cliff Robertson in his first important movie role. His performance was notable for understate-ment and for finding the proper balance between terrifying a loved one with lunatic rages and evoking her compassion by his dependence and anguish.

Joan's estimation of the movie was on target: "This was one of my very favorite pictures. It was, I think, the best film of its type ever made—the older woman with a younger lover. The loneliness and desperation of her situation came through with no need for melodrama or overacting—in fact, I played it down. And Cliff Robertson was stunning; very few actors could have brought that kind of credibility to such a demanding part. His mad scenes can't be topped. Good story, believable characters, good script, good acting—consequently, a good film."

Film critics were in her corner. As one wrote, *Autumn Leaves* was best seen as "a mature study of loneliness and mental distress, and the strength of Miss Crawford's performance is that it is natural and controlled. A lesser actress would bring more than a touch of ham to such a juicy role."[1]

Director Aldrich did not find his star an easy colleague. "I admired her," he said, "but I could not get her to [appear like] a drab, ageing woman, and that threw off the balance of the picture." A week before filming began, Joan wanted to bring in Ranald MacDougall for rewrites, but this request Aldrich denied. She then rang the director at home, at two o'clock in the morning of the first day's filming, to announce that she would not appear on the set without "her" writer. In that case, Aldrich replied, they would not make the picture. "The writer didn't show up, but she did, and we proceeded. I really think that's the only way you can deal with Miss Crawford."

Joan refused to speak with him during the first week of production: the first assistant was called on to relay directions to her, and she replied through him to the director. "Then one day," as Aldrich recalled, "she was doing a scene terribly effectively. I was really touched, and when she looked up after finishing it, I tried not to be obvious in wiping away a tear. That broke the ice, and from then on, we were good friends for a long time."

---

1. The original title of the film was *The Way We Are* until Columbia decided to cash in on the popularity of Nat King Cole's recording of the song "Autumn Leaves." Movie rights to it were hastily purchased, and Cole's recording was added to the credits of the film, which was then rechristened. This was a brave and socially responsible decision on the studio's part, for earlier that same year, Nat King Cole had barely escaped death at the hands of racist mobs, just after singing "Autumn Leaves" in segregated Birmingham, Alabama.

Aldrich was right to be disappointed when Joan refused to appear "drab and ageing," for with her own glamorous makeup and the stylish costumes designed by Jean Louis, it is not easy to accept her as a somewhat frigid spinster, living a lower-middle-class existence. Her hair is too perfect, her clothes too attractive—and most regrettably, her lipstick and eyebrows are grotesquely exaggerated.[2] For Joan Crawford, her cosmetics were not negotiable: as in years past, she again regarded the thickly arched eyebrows and over-the-lip gloss as an infallible sign of female desirability, and no director could shake her from that imprudent conviction. In this regard, she began to substitute the intransigent behavior of a diva for that of the agreeable professional. "I think she felt fraudulent," said Cliff Robertson in defense of his leading lady, "precisely because she had crossed the railroad tracks—had come up from nothing—and that therefore she felt she wasn't the real thing because she was just 'acting.' But Joan was the real thing."

In the last years of her career, it is often difficult to find one's way toward an appreciation of Joan's performances: her appearance is something to get beyond, before the quality of the acting can be assessed. Alas, performers of drag quickly got to work and offered depressingly accurate parodies.

———

AS SOON AS *AUTUMN LEAVES* was finished, Joan helped her children pack their trunks and valises, for they were to join her and Alfred on a long winter holiday in Europe. As they prepared to depart, Joan gave Christina her first passport and her birth certificate, "with all the pertinent data on her birth date and the names of her original father and mother." On December 8, they all left by train for New York, and eight days later, the entire family boarded the *Queen Mary* for a memorably happy time in France, Switzerland and Italy. They returned in February 1956.

At this time, sixteen-year-old Christina told her mother that she wanted

2. Crawford's films of the 1950s seem to have been the collective source for Faye Dunaway's caricature of Joan in the 1981 film of *Mommie Dearest*.

to be an actress. Joan used her influence (and Alfred's) to open doors that allowed her to see both the glamorous and arduous sides of the business. "She will be able to study all the things I never had time for," Joan said.

First, she introduced Christina to Broadway producer Kermit Bloomgarden, whose many successes included three plays by Arthur Miller. She then arranged for Christina to meet seventeen-year-old Susan Strasberg, then starring on Broadway in *The Diary of Anne Frank.* She took Christina to an exercise class with drama coach Claudia Frank. They went backstage to visit Margaret Sullavan, who was appearing in *Janus,* and they audited classes at the American Academy of Dramatic Arts. "If you ever decide to make this your life," Joan told Christina, "I want you to know it won't be easy. It has to be your own choice, and I'll never push you. But if you do it, I want you to do it well."

Joan urged her daughter to study drama formally at a university, but after a year, Christina abandoned her studies at Carnegie Tech and took a small apartment in Manhattan. Joan expressed her "displeasure" at this turn of events, "but once she'd made those decisions, my attitude was that if she wanted to tackle the adult world, more power to her." Thus began a long period of estrangement between mother and daughter that matched the emotional distance between mother and son. At the same time, Joan explained the very different rapport she had with Cathy and Cindy: "Unlike Christina and Christopher, the twins don't resent my life."

"I want to try to be an actress," Christina told a reporter in 1956, "and I'll work hard." But as so often in that profession, success was elusive, and she worked only sporadically. Of the roles she had, Christina admitted that they were not large, "and yet after each day I found myself too exhausted to eat. It was much easier after that to understand what it must have been like for Mother all those years ago." Between 1961 and 1972, Christina appeared in a few regional theatre productions, three films and six television shows.

"I began to have a fuller understanding of the process of [Mother's] early years, when she, too, was a struggling actress," Christina wrote years later. "Those were the years that I now knew were filled with pain, frustration and perhaps even humiliation. I wrote her letters about my feelings, about the experience of setting foot on a soundstage myself for the first time, to perform rather than just to visit her. I'd felt her presence everywhere."

Joan responded, referring to one of Christina's recent screen tests:

> *Christina dear, I saw your test, and I thought you were just*
> *lovely. I am glad you had the loving care of {producer} Jerry Wald,*
> *{cinematographer} Bill Mellor, {publicists} Perry Lieber and Don Prince,*
> *and {screenwriter} Philip Dunne. I am sure you will have great success, and*
> *nobody wishes it for you more than your*
>
>

Mommie.
>

But Christina's acting ambitions were never fulfilled: "I continued to get a few acting jobs in Hollywood, but without much success. Finally, I just gave up . . . I disappeared. My life was in a shambles . . . my personal stability turned out to be mere quicksand, and for a while all I could do was try to put myself back together." Later, she tried writing.

———

THAT SPRING OF 1956, Joan was fitted for costumes for her third and final picture for Columbia—this one to be made in England and directed by David Miller, who had done so well on *Sudden Fear.* "This was my last really top picture," she later said, discussing *The Story of Esther Costello,* which was filmed from August to December. The press, noting her twenty-eight pieces of luggage, forty-eight costumes, a trunk full of furs and her millionaire husband, duly covered her arrival in England.

Based on a 1953 novel by Nicholas Monsarrat, Esther's story was alternately heartwarming and provocative. Injured in a childhood accident, she is left in a state of nervous shock that has deprived her of hearing, speech and sight. A wealthy American named Margaret Landi (Joan) finds the teenage Esther (Heather Sears) living in appalling poverty in rural Ireland and brings her back to the United States, where she learns Braille and other means of communication.

Soon, Margaret's estranged husband, Carlo (Rossano Brazzi), pops up like the proverbial bad penny and recognizes an opportunity for easy money. He and a team of unscrupulous publicists force Margaret and Esther to travel on a worldwide fund-raising tour to help disadvantaged children, while Carlo embezzles much of the proceeds. But theft is not his worst vice: this Latin lover is a notorious womanizer, and one night he goes so far as to rape young Esther. The shock restores her senses, and Margaret brings the story to a conclusion by causing the deaths of Carlo and herself. Esther is now free to fall into the waiting arms of a handsome reporter who has been covering her case.[3] (It seems regrettable, not to say incredible, that something so appalling as a rape immediately restores the girl's sight, hearing and speech.)

The Story of Esther Costello offered a pair of unusual performances—by twenty-one-year-old Heather Sears, entirely convincing as a girl deprived of her senses; and by Joan, who conveyed maternal love, womanly passion and moral outrage with the most economical dramatic technique. She and Sears also spent months learning sign language. "It was one hell of a demanding role," Joan recalled, "and I played it in my own pitch, the way I thought it should be played, and I was right. The complexities of the part were staggering . . . [and I] have nothing but very fond memories of it—plus the usual nagging question, why the hell didn't more pictures like this come along? Why did I [subsequently] get stuck in freak shows?" The answer had to do with the limited possibilities for leading ladies of a certain age and the increasing scarcity of literate screenplays.

"Joan Crawford is a star whose thirty-year career has recently bogged down in bad pictures," wrote the reviewer for *Time*. "But she can still turn in a creditable performance—and what's more, is still pretty darn good-looking,

---

3. It is often claimed that Monsarrat's novel and Joan's film took their cues from the story of Helen Keller and Annie Sullivan Macy, particularly as dramatized in William Gibson's *The Miracle Worker*. But *The Miracle Worker* was a 1957 television drama before Gibson revised it for Broadway in 1959 and for Hollywood in 1961. Monsarrat's novel preceded both of these and is primarily concerned with exposing the fund-raising racket.

too." Alas, this was, as Joan said, her last really good movie, and there was a two-year interval between the release of this picture and her next.

———

FOR MOST OF 1957, Mr. and Mrs. Alfred Steele were on the road for Pepsi-Cola, traveling across the United States, Canada, Great Britain, Europe and Africa. At each stop, Joan delighted the public as if the event were a movie premiere: she accepted bouquets of flowers, gave a carefully prepared little speech, signed autographs and posed for photographs. The questions put to her by waiting reporters were vetted in advance; her hair, makeup and wardrobe were always perfect for the location; her jewels sparkled; and she never failed to smile cooperatively for every cameraman. "We found that there was a certain mystique in having Joan Crawford coming along," she said later. "People, especially the salesmen, were impressed, and that was important to Alfred and to the company."

Her schedule for that year listed over 175 interviews for newspapers and magazines and 160 for radio and television. In addition, there were diplomatic receptions, dinners for businessmen and dignitaries and side trips to places of cultural importance. Joan was indeed a movie queen, and her world travels were planned very much like those of visiting royals. The work was hard and the hours long, but Joan Crawford Steele unfailingly transformed mere duties into glamorous occasions. "It seemed natural to me to be part of the company's executive staff. I liked the product, Alfred's way of doing business, and the other executives and sales and promotion people I met. I could communicate fairly well with their wives and with important customers, here and abroad. I've often thought that if I hadn't gone into films so early in life, I'd have found some role in business—I took to it so naturally."

On their return in early 1958, the duplex on Fifth Avenue was at last ready for occupancy, and they moved from Sutton Place South to 2 East Seventieth Street. The new apartment was almost entirely white, with low sofas and tables, and side chairs in pale green and yellow. The master suite had a large fountain, enormous walk-in closets and one of the apartment's two wood-burning fireplaces. Throughout, there was white carpeting, kept pristine by Joan's insistence that all visitors remove their shoes at the door.

Not long after the final pieces of furniture were in place, Joan began rehearsals for a half-hour television drama called "Strange Witness," an episode of the *General Electric Theater*, broadcast on March 23 and repeated throughout the year. The producers cast her as a middle-aged woman, married to a much older man and enjoying the company of a young lover. To free them both and gain the older man's fortune, the young man kills the husband. Perhaps not to the television audience's surprise, the crime does not pay.[4]

It did not in life, either. The previous year, Christopher had run away from a school he had chosen in Arizona. Now, at fifteen, his troubles with the law worsened. On May 10, he ran away from the home of Dr. Earl Loomis, a Long Island psychiatrist with whose family he had agreed to live. The following day, Christopher was charged with malicious mischief after "borrowing" a car and speeding recklessly through the town of Greenport, breaking store windows and streetlights with an air rifle and wounding a teenage pedestrian before police tracked him down. At Joan and Alfred's request, a judge then ordered that Christopher be sent to a school for delinquent and disturbed adolescents.

At seventeen, he was arrested for car theft and was sentenced to a correctional institution. By the age of nineteen, he was working as a lifeguard in Florida, where he married a waitress, fathered three children—and (in his own words) "had no idea" where the family was after he obtained a hasty divorce. He then married a second time and returned to Long Island. He never held down any job for very long, and his second wife worked as an office clerk to support him and their daughter. Christopher Crawford died at the age of sixty-three, on September 22, 2006. "My son was one of the few problems in

---

4. In January 1959, Joan appeared in another television drama ("And One Was Loyal"); and in December, she donned Western garb for the "Rebel Range" episode of *Zane Grey Theatre*—a program for which she filmed another segment, called "One Must Die," in January 1961. Also in 1961, she appeared in something called "The Foxes."

this world that I couldn't solve," Joan said. "Alfred started out thinking I had been too strict a disciplinarian with him, but he ended up thinking I hadn't been half strict enough."

In August 1958, while the Steeles were taking a brief holiday in Bermuda, Anna Le Sueur died in Los Angeles; she was seventy-four and succumbed following a series of strokes. Joan and Alfred hurried to California for her mother's funeral and burial at Forest Lawn Memorial Park on Monday, August 18. Joan wept bitterly—"for the utter waste," as she told a friend, "and for what might have been between us, more than for anything else. My mother wanted what I could do for her, but I don't think she ever really wanted to be part of my life. I know everyone thought it was the other way around, but I honestly tried."

———

THE LOSSES IN HER life reached critical mass during the night of April 18–19, 1959, when Alfred Steele died suddenly of a massive heart attack in their new apartment. He was five days short of his fifty-eighth birthday, and their fourth wedding anniversary would have been marked the following month. Joan had noticed over the previous few days that he seemed unusually tired—"subdued as I had never seen him"—even to the point of profound exhaustion.

With Douglas Fairbanks Jr., as Joan said, she had tried too hard to make the marriage work. With Franchot Tone and Phillip Terry, on the other hand, she admitted that she had not tried hard enough. "I needn't have let my career dominate me as much as I did. I was an established star—I didn't have to work as hard as I did, and I needn't have spent so much time on the image thing." But with Alfred, "I didn't have to try anything at all—everything worked out all by itself, as though it was meant to be. Every minute with him I was *alive*. For the first time in my life, I was really *alive*." In 1963 Joan told a writer, "I know how lucky I was for the four years of my marriage to Alfred. Not many women have been that lucky. I remember only the beauties of our marriage, and not the sadness of his departing." Douglas, Franchot and Phillip were the first three to put through condolence telephone calls.

Two days after Alfred's death and the day before the funeral at Saint Thomas Episcopal Church on Fifth Avenue, Joan received a condolence call from Herbert L. Barnet, the new chief executive officer of Pepsi-Cola. He arrived at the apartment not only to offer the company's sympathy but also to inform her that—"if you would kindly accept it"—the executive directors had unanimously voted to appoint her to the board of Pepsi-Cola. She accepted on the spot.

Joan's appointment was, as Barnet told the press, "not merely a sentimental gesture to the memory of Alfred Steele, but a hard-headed business judgment which makes possible the continuing utilization by Pepsi-Cola of Miss Crawford's intimate knowledge and rare skills in promotion and public relations, which she has so superbly demonstrated to our benefit for the last four years." For her ongoing service, Joan was to receive sixty thousand dollars annually to cover her travel, secretarial and personal expenses while representing Pepsi. "I plan to be a working member of the Board," she told a reporter, "to carry on where we left off and to keep the company growing."

ANOTHER CALL SOON CAME—from Jerry Wald, the producer of six earlier Joan Crawford pictures. He had gone over from Warner Bros. to Twentieth Century-Fox and was about to begin a new picture to be directed by Jean Negulesco, who had worked so well with Joan on *Humoresque*. There was a small but effective supporting role for Joan in a picture called *The Best of Everything,* and Wald offered her sixty-five thousand dollars for a few days' work. "I thought that coming out to Hollywood and working would take her mind off her troubles and be good therapy for her," Wald told a reporter. As he and Barnet demonstrated beyond dispute, Joan had friends and admirers who were willing to back up their good faith and their good sense with good money.

The two offers could not have come at a better time, for within weeks of Alfred's death, Joan was informed by lawyers that his estate was, to put it bluntly, in one big, chaotic mess. She had understandably but wrongly presumed that shrewd financial management was part of his keen business sense and that she would have no worries in the event of his death.

But she had woefully miscalculated. During the four years of the marriage, Alfred had borrowed huge sums from Pepsi-Cola to pay for their lavish lifestyle. And after the purchase, renovation and redecoration of the duplex, he had nothing to leave but debts, including an enormous tax burden Joan was now obliged to pay. To make matters worse, the proceeds that Joan had given him from the sale of her Brentwood home (purchased by Donald O'Connor) had somehow vanished.

Joan's longtime publicist, John Springer, was a kind and perceptive man, and he knew the situation intimately.

"No matter what others might say, Joan and Alfred had a good marriage," Springer said in 1991. "I don't think it was the kind of grand passion she had earlier with Doug or Clark or Franchot, but he was a good companion to her, and when he died, she was really broken up. They both spent a lot of money buying presents for one another and for the children, taking vacations and redoing the whole apartment. Of course it also cost much more to renovate than they had planned, and then he did something I thought was very foolish—he borrowed money from Pepsi against his future salary, and that had to be repaid. But even after she learned about her terrible financial status, she never had a bad word to say about Alfred."

The estate of Alfred Steele was still in probate seven years after his death, and as detailed investigations continued, the situation seemed increasingly bizarre. Besides Joan's income from her sale of the Brentwood house in 1957, he had accepted her salaries from her television work and the cash from life insurance policies she redeemed.

And so Joan sat down and planned a schedule of repayments for all the money her husband had borrowed from Pepsi-Cola as well as the tax debt claimed by the government. Because the sums far exceeded $1 million, she had another reason to continue working, both on the board of directors and in Hollywood. "What I would have done without Pepsi-Cola, I do not know. I just wanted to work and work, to be so tired that when I fell into bed, I couldn't think—and I could just sleep." Joan bore her sorrow alone; she never assumed the role of a grieving widow, and she never asked for sympathy. She simply went back to work. "I have turned to work again and again over the years as an antidote to the pains of life. Work is the best alleviator of sorrow I know, and once again, it is standing me in good stead. So I will work—and cry on my own time."

———

ON JUNE 1, JOAN arrived on Stage 15 at Twentieth Century-Fox Studios in Los Angeles to begin filming her supporting role in *The Best of Everything*—her return to movie work after a four-year interval. Based on a best-selling novel by Rona Jaffe that Wald had essentially commissioned, the picture was planned as a breathless tale of three young women—played in the movie by Hope Lange, Diane Baker and Suzy Parker—who come from the provinces to New York looking for love, money, success or what-you-will while they work at a Manhattan publishing company. All three actresses were under contract to Fox: Lange had just come from *Peyton Place;* Baker was critically acclaimed for her role as Anne's older sister in *The Diary of Anne Frank;* and Parker had launched an acting career after several years as one of America's first supermodels.

Joan's role was that of Amanda Farrow, a foul-tempered middle-aged editor who has sacrificed personal happiness for professional glory and so creates misery for everyone around her; she was, in other words, Jenny Stewart from *Torch Song,* transplanted from the theater to an office. But like that role, it was dreadfully underwritten: without enough backstory to make the character credible or even comprehensible, Amanda is just another spiteful, unpleasant shrew.

When Joan arrived at Fox, it was clear that widowhood had not softened her. A limousine transported her to the studio, where she swept in, accompanied as always by her hairdresser, makeup artist, wardrobe mistress, secretary and stand-in. Cast and crew had been instructed not to address her until she greeted them first, and they had been warned that Miss Crawford asked for the air-conditioning to be set six degrees lower than what was customary.

"That was my first experience of star power," recalled Diane Baker. "She had to have the set almost freezing, and many people caught colds. We tried to figure out why she demanded this, and someone came up with the answer—it had to do with her makeup."

Each of the three leading ladies was young enough to be Joan's daughter: Lange was twenty-eight, Parker twenty-seven and Baker twenty-one, and they were, at first, duly awestruck, but that helped their scenes with the formidable character Joan portrayed. "I was fortunate that there was this tension with her," Lange recalled. "Our scenes were built with tension, and there it was, even before the camera rolled. It had to have been tough for her, to have these three young upstarts—and there she was, in a nonstarring role."

For one awkward scene, Crawford and Lange (as Joan's secretary) were standing near a door as Joan finished a speech and left the room.

"Would you mind letting me close the door after you go out of it?" asked Lange as they rehearsed.

"No, you can't," was Joan's reply. "It's *my* line. It's *my* exit. *I* close the door."

"But I don't know what to do with my hands," replied Hope Lange.

"Why not *find* something to do with your hands?" Joan said with scarcely concealed condescension.

Moments later, she elaborated her impatience for the benefit of a visiting reporter. "These young people spend so much time trying to think themselves into their roles that there's nothing one can play to, nothing one can react against. They're so wishy-washy."

Diane Baker understood Joan most accurately and compassionately. "She had just lost Alfred Steele, and there were moments when she was having a very difficult time. I saw that she was very vulnerable and that she was just about holding it all together. I saw her several times, sitting by herself before a take and crying her eyes out. I brought her a box of tissue and gave her a sign that indicated, 'You're going to be fine!' and that meant a lot to her." For the rest of her few days at Fox, Joan took Diane under her wing as a protégée—and later, asked her to costar in two more Crawford pictures.

"The movie was supposed to showcase a whole bunch of up-and-coming

Fox actors," Joan remembered. "The youngsters did all right, but I sort of walked off with the film. Perhaps it was the part, but I think it was a matter of experience, knowing how to make the most of every scene I had." But the truth was otherwise. Joan did not "walk off" with the film: indeed, she seemed awkward and uncomfortable for most of her screen time. That was at least partly the fault of a screenplay that left her role vague and undefined and her character capricious (as when she has a sudden "conversion" and becomes a darling at the last moment).

But she had not lost her ability or her insistence on making things right for the sake of the production. In one scene, she was to take a phone call from her lover, calling to cancel a date. But when she received the pages of Edith Sommer's dialogue the day before filming, Joan felt the sequence would play badly. At eleven o'clock that night, she rang Jerry Wald: "This scene doesn't seem right to me," she said.

"What's the matter with it?"

"It's flat—it's one-dimensional."

"Can you fix it?"

"I think so."

Joan redrafted the scene, politely asked Sommer's reaction (which was most enthusiastic) and the Crawford version became one of the picture's best sequences. Complimented by her costar Brian Aherne, Joan dismissed the praise: "Oh, Edie did the writing," she said.

But her increased consumption of vodka during production did not help, as she admitted: "After Alfred died, I was really alone, and the vodka controlled me. It dulled the morning, the afternoon and the night." When a writer from *Life* asked why she drove herself so relentlessly—returning to work in a movie just six weeks after Steele's death—she was forthright: "I don't kid myself. I do it to keep from being lonely." But her anxieties, her haughty attitude with the neophytes and her insistence on special treatment caused problems—even with Jean Negulesco, who had returned to direct a second Crawford picture. This time, however, his experience was thornier than it had been during *Humoresque*. "It's difficult to get what you want out of her, because she has such definite ideas," he said at the time. The result, by the end of her work on *The Best of Everything,* was a deeper disconnection from her colleagues, hence a greater loneliness.

For much of the next year, Joan was the international public relations ambassador for Pepsi-Cola, a job in which she logged more than 125,000 miles worldwide and never canceled a meeting or missed a travel connection. The company's employees and executives all over Europe, the Middle East and Africa were astonished at her energy, and they reported to the New York office that her visits improved company morale as well as business.

———

DURING THE 1950S, JOAN had kept in touch with Clark Gable, with whom she then had a solid platonic friendship. Congratulations and presents were exchanged when she married in May 1955, and two months later, when he took his fifth wife, actress Kay Williams. Then, in the autumn of 1960, while he was working with Marilyn Monroe and Montgomery Clift in the Nevada desert—appearing in John Huston's film of Arthur Miller's *The Misfits*—Clark learned that he was going to be a father for the first time. The movie wrapped on November 4, and Clark immediately returned to Los Angeles to be with his pregnant wife. Twelve days later, he dropped dead from a heart attack; he was fifty-nine years old. Joan went at once to offer help and sympathy to Kay, with whom she maintained a close friendship forever after.

———

A REPORTER FROM *REDBOOK* magazine interviewed Joan that year and then tracked down Christina. The result, published in June 1960, was "The Revolt of Joan Crawford's Daughter," which told the public about the long and painful history of relations between the two women—due mostly, the author implied, to the overbearing manipulation of the mother. With that, Joan shifted into high gear and decided to put together some kind of memoir, if not a full-scale autobiography. With the help of a writer named Jane Kesner Ardmore, she began sifting through her correspondence files and scrapbooks. In the summer of 1962, Doubleday published *A Portrait of Joan*—a book remarkable for its brevity, its profusion of factual errors (names, dates and events are incorrectly stated on many pages) and most of all for its sanitized summary of her life. It was, nevertheless, respectfully reviewed, and, thanks to the undiminished number of her fans, the book sold well.

But Joan's financial status remained uneven and, except for her Pepsi-Cola salary, unpredictable. A year after Alfred's death, and after complicated financial investigations, a sum of $607,128 was found in liquid assets. But taxes took $126,000, and Joan rightly claimed $100,000 that she had loaned Alfred in 1957. The balance of more than $380,000 was held in escrow by Pepsi-Cola by virtue of a corporate lawsuit that challenged the legality of Alfred's stock options. Hence the entire estate was and remained fundamentally devoid of assets. (This did not, however, prevent Alfred's second wife and their son from making claims of $28,000 in unpaid "allowances.") In 1961 the estate was declared insolvent and therefore unable to meet its bills and back taxes—an action Joan's attorneys initiated when it was clear that her income was far exceeded by expenses and the high cost of living at 2 East Seventieth Street.

But financial help for Joan was on the way. First, she was paid fifty thousand dollars for a few days of work on a desperately hysterical picture called *The Caretakers,* in which she portrayed Lucretia Terry, head nurse at a mental hospital. Resentful of new methods introduced by a young doctor (played by Robert Stack), she insists that only the use of "intelligent force" can enable nurses to protect themselves against violent psychotics. This she demonstrates as she leads a judo class, which gave Joan the opportunity to demonstrate that, at fifty-six, she could still wear leotards handsomely and not cause observers to run for shock therapy. The movie, marinated in early 1960s psychobabble, reduced Joan's role to little more than nine minutes of screen time—hence her character has but one dimension in a picture whose message was clear: young is good, old is bad.

After completing this job in June 1962, Joan assumed a role that virtually defined the last stage of her career.

During the first half of 1961, Robert Aldrich had been successively in

Mexico, Morocco and Rome, filming a sand-and-sandal epic with the titil-lating title *Sodom and Gomorrah*. His secretary, on the lookout for prospective Aldrich productions, sent him a copy of a recently published novel by Henry Farrell called *What Ever Happened to Baby Jane?*[5] This was the gothic tale of two sisters—quintessential Hollywood monsters who grew up living together in a decaying Hollywood mansion and cherishing an undying hatred for one another. Crammed with the usual elements of the suspense-horror genre—family secrets, resentments, deception, torture and madness—the novel was violent enough for Aldrich's taste, although he realized that some things would have to be toned down for the movies.

"I sent the novel to Joan Crawford," recalled Aldrich, who had main-tained good relations with Joan after their reconciliation on the set of *Autumn Leaves*. "For several years, she had urged me to find a suitable story to team her with Bette Davis." Joan's prompt and enthusiastic response to Aldrich in the autumn of 1961 enabled him to arrange financing, but on a modest scale.

"I was lonely," Joan said toward the end of her life, "worse than lonely, bored out of my skull, and I needed the money. Alfred had left me with noth-ing. Less than nothing."

"I offered each actress a percentage of the picture plus some salary," Aldrich continued. "Joan accepted, but Bette's agents held out for more than I could pay." Joan accepted a salary of thirty thousand dollars plus 15 percent of the net profits, while Bette took a higher salary and a lower share of the income—and, in the end, received much less than Joan's $1,400,000.

Although they were not well acquainted, Joan's eagerness to work with Davis is easy to understand. "Kate Hepburn and Bette Davis top my list of those I admire," she said years later, "because they're so vastly talented and strong-willed and indestructible. Bette can be such a bitch, but she's so dedicated and honest." And whether they acknowledged the facts or not, the

5. Farrell also wrote *Whatever Happened to Cousin Charlotte?* which was the basis for the movie *Hush . . . Hush, Sweet Charlotte; What's the Matter with Helen?;* and *How Awful About Allan.* No one ever mistook a Farrell title for the work of another novelist.

women had similar backgrounds. Both had fathers who deserted the families, and both wanted a father figure who could be a lover; "they were sisters under the skin," as Vincent Sherman said, although he felt that "Bette was seeking a father-figure she could emasculate, while Joan was still a romantic, waiting for Prince Charming to arrive in a white convertible." He could have added other parallels: Joan and Bette each had four husbands and lost one in death; they both supported their mothers and a sibling (Joan's brother, Bette's sister); both adopted children; and both had daughters who later wrote books claiming they had fearsome childhood years.

From the start, Joan wanted to play the quieter, more sympathetic role of wheelchair-bound Blanche Hudson, dependent on her increasingly deranged sister, Jane, who taunts and then tortures her—until Blanche is finally forced, at death's door, to reveal surprising secrets of their past. Additionally, Joan recognized that the more flamboyant role of Baby Jane Hudson was perfect for Davis. Joan turned fifty-six in 1962, and Bette was fifty-four but looked much older. Both women had spent years under bright studio lights and both were smokers, but Bette's skin had aged badly; in addition, the grotesque clown-white makeup she designed for the role finally turned her into an ancient fiend. Joan, on the other hand, abandoned her glamour makeup, donned a matron's wig and looked like a sad and weary invalid who years earlier must have been a great beauty.

Budgeted for a tight, six-week production schedule, *What Ever Happened to Baby Jane?* began filming in Los Angeles on July 23, 1962. With the discipline of two expert and tireless leading ladies, it was completed on September 12. "It was made on such a low budget," Joan recalled, "that we had to shoot it quickly and improvise interiors and even exteriors. I felt as though we were filming a newsreel, not a movie." Less than two months later, the picture was released and became one of the biggest commercial hits of the decade. "I can hardly believe I've been making pictures for close to forty years," Joan wrote to a friend. "I still love it. Not many people can say that about a job they've had for that long, right?"

During filming and throughout the promotion of the picture, Aldrich and his partners had no objection to the grindings of an ugly rumor mill. Stories were deliberately circulated—and readily believed—that Crawford and Davis were mortal enemies, locked in a constant battle of wills for supremacy on the set and superiority over each other. According to the gossips, whose accounts were later vastly inflated in books, the actresses came to blows several times and had to be separated like prize-fighters who were landing punches and causing each other wounds, stitches and scars. This made for newsworthy publicity, but it bore no resemblance to the truth. It was painful enough for Joan to act scenes in which Bette served meals of cooked canary and dead rat.

In fact, the entire production, as taxing as it was, began and ended well. As Aldrich recalled, "Bette and Joan voluntarily came in to the studio and devoted a Sunday to rehearsing physically difficult scenes to prevent our running over schedule."

Also in the cast was a lumbering twenty-four-year-old actor named Victor Buono, who had worked in television for three years and was now cast in his first feature, as a repellent opportunist. As Aldrich recalled, Joan knew the picture was very important for Buono's career. Hence, although she had concluded her scenes for the day and was ready to leave the studio, she got back into her full makeup and costume for the reverse angles of Buono's encounter with Joan as Blanche. "Even though she wasn't being photographed," Aldrich recalled, "she felt he mightn't have the experience to react and speak lines to a roll of blankets on a hospital bed." At the end of that day, Buono's scenes looked perfect, and later he told everyone how grateful he was to Joan Crawford for her extra efforts on his behalf.

She also took a wheelchair home and practiced with it. "I had to learn how to get myself in and out of bed, from and into the wheelchair. I learned from a young paraplegic who taught me how to hoist my body into the bed first and then lift each leg, and how to fall out of the chair—straight forward, and then roll over." Her homework paid off in the performance—a portrait of fear, resentment and guilt, especially effective in the final moments when she lies dying at the ocean, a tragic female on the beach, whispering the truth at last to her mad sister.

What Ever Happened to Baby Jane? required more than merely a competent costar, however, and Joan's recommendation of Bette Davis was inspired. The movie, she told Aldrich, would stand or fall on the talents of the actress playing the title character—a role that permitted (indeed, required) the excesses Davis typically brought to her roles. Like Joan, Bette's great moments in the picture were often silent—the wide-eyed glance, the perfectly timed pause, and the slight change of expression that revealed depths of unspoken feelings and a life crushed by pain and guilt. There remains something ineffably touching about Davis's performance, especially in her scenes with Victor Buono as a potential musical collaborator who, she wrongly presumes, also offers friendship.

As it was, the two legends of the screen, as they were stereotypically termed even during their lifetimes, raised a Grand Guignol thriller to another level—a story of tragic betrayal and of penitential lives. "Oh, Blanche," says Jane gently at the end when she learns the truth, "all this time we could have been friends." The final scene, when remorse is overwhelmed by madness and the possibility of life is all but extinguished, is more poignant than frightening. Decades later, *What Ever Happened to Baby Jane?* seems more suitable for a compassionate audience than one ready to laugh.

———

NEVER, ACCORDING TO ANY reliable account, did either Joan or Bette claim there was trouble between them, and writers who protested otherwise have no firsthand sources. On the contrary, as Joan wrote to a friend on August 25, "Bette Davis is a joy to work with—very professional and completely dedicated to her work. She and I get to the studio every morning, a half-hour before our calls, just longing to get in front of that camera. She is really a dear human being, with a divine sense of humor."

Years later, little had changed in her memory of that movie: "We didn't feud the way the publicity people wanted us to. We weren't friends—we have different temperaments and worked together for only a few weeks—but she is a fascinating actress. We got along, and when the picture was finished, I went back to New York and Bette went back to Connecticut. Our paths didn't cross again. I really can't say anything against Bette. Everyone involved with *Baby Jane* was so professional and so dedicated that what could have turned out to have been a tired, forgettable little low-budget picture turned out to be a good one."

Bette Davis was adamant about the situation. "Will it be disappointing if I say that we got along well?" she asked columnist Hedda Hopper, who was trying to elicit details about bad feelings and tart exchanges at the end of filming. "Of course there's not a prayer that [the press] will admit everything is friendly between us—the reverse makes for a better story." More than twenty years later, Bette told Barbara Walters, "In three weeks of filming together, nothing bad happened between us. Three months might have been different, but the three weeks went just fine." Joan later admitted that she was "tense and nervous and desperately unhappy at the time, [but] that was part of the character I played, so probably no one on the set or in the audience noticed."

When Bette was nominated for a best actress Oscar and Joan was ignored, she bore no resentment. "Months before the awards, I predicted that Bette would be nominated and would win. She was nominated, but she didn't win, and that I'm truly sorry for." As required, Joan spoke enthusiastically about the movie on national television—on October 1, during the premiere broadcast of the *Tonight Show Starring Johnny Carson*.

But at the end of filming, she had been completely exhausted—not primarily from the physical demands of acting and certainly not from any hostility with Bette Davis. Instead, she found terribly depressing the movie's accumulation of horrors, the repressions, the hatred, torture and bitterness; the redeeming poignancy of the picture, after all, was subsequently created in the editing room. "Bob Aldrich loves evil things, horrendous things, vile things," Joan said in 1973. "It can take an awful lot out of you if you have to face those things every day."

CHAPTER THIRTEEN

"Miss Crawford Is a Star!"
| 1962–1970 |

J UST AS JOAN was completing her scenes in *What Ever Happened to Baby Jane?* at the Raleigh Studios on Melrose Avenue, Christina walked onto a soundstage at Metro-Goldwyn-Mayer Studios in Culver City. Scheduled for a brief appearance in the *Dr. Kildare* television series, she was approached by a technician who had been at Metro for more than thirty years and who remembered Joan's ascent to stardom in silent pictures.

"I want to make it on my own," Christina told journalist James Bacon later that day. "I seldom see my mother, but that doesn't mean I don't love her or respect her—I do, tremendously." Asked if the reports of family feuds were accurate, Christina emphatically denied them: "We have had crises, as all daughters do with their mothers—but mine have been complicated because I have decided to make it in my mother's own profession. But there is no feud. I have great love and admiration for my mother, both as a mother and as a great talent. I hope I can achieve even a fraction of what she has in this business."

Christina further documented their good relationship when she wrote about her first marriage, to director Harvey Medlinsky, in May 1966. "My mother was genuinely delighted," she wrote in *Mommie Dearest.* "Mother and I were in daily contact. Mother was superb. She managed every last detail of the event"—the wedding, Christina's dress, the announcements and the reception at the 21 Club in New York. Joan's lavish wedding presents included a pearl necklace she had received from Alfred; later, Joan also gave Christina a gold watch.

After the honeymoon, when the groom had to travel on business, Christina recalled:

> *I was not the least bit lonely {because} I visited Mother nearly every other day, basking in our mutual homecoming and enjoying every minute of it. I had a new apartment to settle, a new life to manage, letters to write, and my mother's love. I spent many evenings at Mother's apartment. For the first time, I felt really comfortable with her. She seemed to feel the same and went out of her way to plan fun things for us to do together. I was almost automatically included in her social events, met the majority of her New York friends and business associates and spent quiet evenings with her just watching television and talking. There were still some days when she was in a bad mood and she drank quite a bit, but her fits of anger were never directed at me.*

Christina wrote at length about the "real understanding and genuine friendship" she enjoyed with Joan. "She trusted me and looked to me for my opinion." Such was their relationship in the 1960s.

———

AS JOAN MADE HER way through 1963, her travel schedule might have wearied a woman half her age, but there she was—greeting this mayor or that foreign dignitary on behalf of Pepsi-Cola; signing copies of *A Portrait of Joan* at a bookstore; opening a new Pepsi bottling plant; appearing on a television drama or talk show; promoting a movie; filling a slot on a quiz or game show. In the early 1960s, she was being introduced as "the legendary Joan Crawford," which annoyed her. Still in her fifties and very much a working woman, she thought the description was more appropriate for someone dead—or at least of very advanced years and long retired. She wore the latest styles, pushed her hair into fashionable hats, put on oversized sunglasses and otherwise did what she could to be of her time. But she was not of her time, and soon she realized that could be a blessing, too, despite her irritation over the rudeness of the culture.

During that decade, there was a long necrology of those with whom Joan had worked, and their deaths always prompted letters to their relatives and kind words to the press; indeed, she was very much touched by the deaths of Margaret Sullavan, Jeff Chandler, Gail Russell, Clara Blandick, Ramon Novarro, Steve Cochran and Albert Dekker. Some of them were younger than she, and to friends like Myrna Loy and Billy Haines she expressed astonishment at the passing of people she thought were, like herself, in their prime.

Her brother was among them. In May, Harold Hayes Le Sueur died in Los Angeles of a ruptured appendix. He was fifty-nine and had for a long time been living in virtual obscurity. Joan had continued to send money over the decades. He never had a career, had not remarried since his second divorce in 1934 and must have suffered enormously from his many years of alcohol and drug addiction—although he had apparently made impressive steps toward recovery in his last years.

At the time of his death, Hal was supplementing Joan's checks by working as a clerk at one shabby downtown motel and answering the telephone at night at another, where he lived alone. His last known public statement about Joan was made in 1954: "For personal reasons, I must refrain from saying why I never see my sister." She did not attend his funeral, which coincided with her visit to the White House as chair of the Stars for Mental Health campaign; she was part of a small delegation meeting with President Kennedy. That November, she was at a Pepsi function in Dallas when Kennedy was assassinated in that city.

BABY JANE WAS STILL drawing crowds during the summer of 1963, and more thoughtful reviews were being published. "A second viewing of Joan Crawford's performance reveals what hitherto I have not believed," wrote Arthur B. Clark in the prestigious journal *Films in Review,* "namely, that she *is* an actress and not merely a beautifully bone-structured personality."

The trade paper *Motion Picture Herald* agreed: "Miss Crawford plays beautifully and nobly." No less a high-toned magazine than the *Saturday Review* was rhapsodic: "A superb showcase for the time-ripened talents of two of Hollywood's most accomplished actresses, Bette Davis and Joan Crawford. Scenes that in lesser hands would verge on the ludicrous simply crackle with tension."

Variety wrote perhaps most lavishly of all. "Miss Crawford gives a quiet, remarkably fine interpretation of the crippled Blanche. Confined to a wheelchair and bed throughout the entire picture, she has to act from the inside and has her best scenes (because she wisely underplays with Davis) with a maid and those she plays alone. In one superb bit, Miss Crawford, reacting to herself on television, makes her face fairly glow with the remembrance of fame past. Her performance is a genuine heartbreaker."

The good notices and continuing media appearances on behalf of *Baby Jane* brought to Joan's door the director William Castle, the self-described "B-movie mogul," who had a script called *Strait-Jacket*—the story, he said, of a woman in her fifties. Joan at once interrupted: "If I do it, she'll be in her forties." Okay, Castle continued, this is a story about a woman in her forties named Lucy Harbin, who is committed to a lunatic asylum after taking up an ax and giving however many whacks were necessary to kill her faithless husband and his girlfriend, whom she found together in bed.

Released after twenty years, Lucy tries to establish ties with her now adult daughter, Carol, who had apparently witnessed the double murder as a child. Soon Lucy's erratic behavior and a few more unexplained decapitations at the family farm indicate that she may have been prematurely sprung from confinement. But no, it turns out that her daughter is the real ax-wielder and has recently taken to dressing up like Mother. This is all easily explained: Robert Bloch wrote the screenplay, just after the success of his earlier novel, *Psycho*— and Alfred Hitchcock's film of it.

As Joan read the script, she saw holes larger than those in Swiss cheese, and so she invited Castle and two of his financiers to lunch. "She was one of the most dynamic women I ever met," Castle recalled. "She knew what she wanted and always got it—including script, cast and cameraman approval." As Joan doled out generous portions of homemade quiche and tall glasses of cold Pepsi, she said sweetly, "*Strait-Jacket* will have to be completely rewritten as a vehicle for me, or I will not accept the role." It was, and she did—for a guarantee of fifty thousand dollars and no more than two and a half weeks of work at Columbia Studios in Los Angeles that August. But *Strait-Jacket* was no better after the rewrites: as one wit suggested, it might have been subtitled *What Ever Happened to Baby Monster?*

"Among the new players in Hollywood," said Joan at the end of filming, "Diane Baker is really outstanding. Although we had very few scenes together in *The Best of Everything,* I was greatly impressed by Diane at that time. Now, after working with her throughout *Strait-Jacket,* I'm firmly convinced that she has impact, she projects, and she is a pro. This girl's got it." In fact, Joan asked for Diane to play the complex role of daughter Carol.

"She was the boss in every way on that picture," Diane recalled. "She saw to it that the set was kept very cold, for the sake of her makeup, and she placed bottles and cans of Pepsi-Cola everywhere she could in the movie's scenes." Joan was also protective of Diane and considerate of her future, and that was one reason she had an assistant on the set taking instant Polaroid snapshots. "If she thought there was something wrong with the way I looked or if the makeup wasn't right," Diane added, "she would show these shots to wardrobe people and say, 'You have to fix this!' "

In the finished film, it's clear that Joan's high estimation was well in order: Diane Baker's performance is entirely credible, at first touching and tentative, then anxious and finally terrifying. It was no surprise to anyone that she went immediately from the shrill pyrotechnics of *Strait-Jacket* to something of greater depth, as Sean Connery's jealous sister-in-law in Hitchcock's *Marnie.*

Joan's achievement in the picture may fairly be described as an A-plus performance in a B-minus picture. The plot twists were created so swiftly that Castle and company obviously paid little attention to character consistency, and audiences over the years continued to ask why Lucy was doing this just after that. But in her scenes as a woman of fifty-something (to which she finally agreed), Joan looks and acts the part of someone who has been unjustly locked away for twenty years—there is something sad, gray and broken about her. Then, at the daughter's insistence, Lucy dresses as she did long ago, and somehow Joan managed to look appropriate in a black wig and a tight dress, shimmying and flirting outrageously with all the trappings of a young tart. It was, as so many attested, impossible for Joan Crawford not to give every bit of her careful preparation, high energy and utmost gravity to a production, no matter how dreadful the role or how disappointing the story and screenplay.

But she was not only a gifted actress—she was also the complete star, and she insisted that this image be acknowledged and presented in every film. In the last sequence of *Strait-Jacket,* Lucy unmasks her daughter, who then goes ragingly insane, kicking up a wild rumpus and screaming that she loves and hates her mother—no, that she hates her and loves her, and, by the way, that she loves her and hates her.

The script and camera setups rightly called for the scene to conclude on Diane Baker's carefully rehearsed and emotionally effective mad scene. But Joan went to William Castle: "We'll end on *me,* Bill, because the picture should conclude with my reaction to what my daughter shouts—'I hate you, I love you, I hate you, I love you.'" Diane understood the reason for this ill-reasoned request (which of course Castle had to grant), and she spoke compassionately about it: "Crawford was so needy that she had to have the last word, her face in the last shot [before the explanatory epilogue with Leif Erickson, as Lucy's brother]. But I suppose this was true not just of Joan Crawford. Any actor or actress who had control of a movie would want the same thing."

———

"ALL THE PICTURES I did after *Baby Jane* were terrible," Joan admitted not long before she died. "I made them because I needed the money or because I was bored, or both. I hope they are never heard of again." She might have added that she was not offered alternatives.[1] Rather than the roles that came to her at the end of her career, it was high time for an actress of her experience and talent to be given more than merely banal and inept screenplays with roles unworthy of her range. "It's too bad that in this business they don't appreciate that someone can be older and know even more than they did when they were young," Betsy Palmer said of Joan. "But you're supposed to look pretty all the way to the grave!"

Joan was, after all, among the very few senior actresses who could effectively portray lovesick, neurotic, weary women—and do so without resorting to overacting. Emotionally vulnerable mothers were as available on her palette as beleaguered or chilling antiheroines; she had shown for forty years that she had access to a deep wellspring of interior possibilities.

Bette Davis and Katharine Hepburn (to name only two of Joan's generation) were actresses with admirable skills and keen intelligence, but sometimes they could be seen *acting,* and just as often their performances were diminished by a convenient and easily recognized set of tics and mannerisms. But Joan Crawford was rare among her peers. She very infrequently made a false move in any scene in any picture: virtually everything she did on-screen was *right* for the moment—she *was* her technique. Colleagues may have found her increasingly difficult, even imperious—but no one ever turned down the chance to work in one of her pictures. She behaved like a star, but she was a great deal more. With the passing of decades and the unfortunate image created by *Mommie Dearest,* it became unfashionable to suggest that Joan Crawford was, in simple fact, one of the few truly great actresses in the history of American film.

———

1. In this regard, it would have been interesting to see Joan Crawford as Mrs. Robinson in *The Graduate,* which was produced when she was sixty-one. Thirty-five-year-old Anne Bancroft memorably created the role, playing a woman who is forty-something.

IN JANUARY 1964, JOAN began a nationwide tour to promote the release of *Strait-Jacket*. Before she left New York, she met with representatives of Columbia Pictures and of Pepsi-Cola, and over the course of several hours they composed a detailed list of requirements for her journey to promote both the movie and the soft drink. She certainly did not anticipate that somehow *Life* would obtain a copy of the document distributed to every publicist in every city. Aware that it provided a window into the will and whim of a quintessential movie star, the editors of that magazine decided to publish it in their edition of February 21. Their readers reacted gleefully.

> The following hotel accommodations are to be prepared. The top suite (including three bedrooms) in the hotels indicated. This should be the best suite available. A single room for Mr. [Bob] Kelly [publicist for Pepsi-Cola] is to be reserved nearby on the same floor. NOTE: The three-bedroom suite is for Miss Crawford and Miss Brinke [Anna Maria Brinke, Joan's housekeeper and maid, whom she frequently took with her on travels; she called her "Mamacita," although Brinke was German]. The single is not to be part of the suite; it is not one of the three bedrooms in the suite but it is to be ready.
>
> NOTE: A special press conference room or suite should be promoted [i.e., obtained free of charge] from the hotel. Press conferences described below are not to be held in the Crawford suite. Press suite to be the size of a normal hotel luncheon room.
>
> NOTE: The two pilots of the Pepsi-Cola plane will have to have a single room each in the hotel.
>
> The following special arrangements are required at each hotel. Use this checklist very carefully: there may be no deviations.
>
> 1. A uniformed security officer is to be assigned to the door of the hotel suite 24 hours a day. You are not to use a city policeman and you are not to use the hotel detective. This security officer should be hired from Pinkerton or some similar organization.
> 2. The following items are to be in the suite prior to Joan Crawford's arrival:

    i) Cracked ice in buckets—several buckets

    ii) Lunch and dinner menus

   iii) Pen and pencils and pads of paper

   iv) Professional-size hair dryer

    v) Steam iron and board

   vi) One carton of King Sano cigarettes

  vii) One bowl of peppermint Life Savers

 viii) Red and yellow roses

   ix) Case of Pepsi-Cola, ginger ale, soda

3. There is to be a maid on hand in the suite when Miss Crawford arrives at the hotel. She is to stand by until Miss Crawford dismisses her.

4. The following liquor is to be in the suite when Miss Crawford arrives:

    i) Two fifths of 100-proof Smirnoff vodka. Note: this is not 80 proof and it is only Smirnoff

   ii) One fifth Old Forester bourbon

  iii) One fifth Chivas Regal Scotch

   iv) One fifth Beefeater gin

    v) Two bottles Moet & Chandon champagne (Type: Dom Perignon).

The detailed instructions . . . are to tell you how far you may go. They are very explicit for the precise purpose that we do not want money spent over and above that required for the details included.

NO CASH ADVANCES ARE AUTHORIZED WITHOUT PRIOR APPROVAL.

NO "PAID-OUTS" EXCEPT AS INDICATED ABOVE ARE AUTHORIZED. NOTE: IN MOST CITIES IT WILL BE POSSIBLE TO "WORK A DEAL" FOR HOTEL ACCOMMODATIONS REQUIRED—IT WILL BE TO YOUR CREDIT IF YOU CAN!

IMPORTANT: WATCH THE COSTS OF THIS TOUR. NEITHER MISS CRAWFORD NOR THIS OFFICE WILL APPRECIATE YOUR THROWING MONEY AWAY. YOU ARE ACCOUNTABLE FOR EVERY CENT YOU SPEND—WATCH IT—AND SUBSTANTIATE IT!

There is a specific way of handling Miss Crawford's schedule in each market. The following detailed outline will provide you with all of the information you require to execute this schedule to the complete satisfaction of everyone. Any proposed deviation from this routine must be cleared first. Assume nothing, take nothing for granted.

1. Miss Crawford will not go to any radio, television studios or newspaper offices. Don't suggest it, don't request it.
2. Plan a print media (e.g., newspapers and magazines) press conference for 10 A.M. Miss Crawford will sit on a couch in front of a coffee table with chairs arranged in a half-moon around the couch and table.
3. Arrange radio interviews for 10:30 or 11:00, depending on the number of reporters at the press conference. These radio interviews are to be set in the same suite (not Miss Crawford's). Arrange for a number of card tables with two chairs each for various places in the suite, and Miss Crawford will go from one to the other for exclusive radio interviews.
4. Television should be arranged for the same suite. They can be set up for 11:00 A.M. depending on the number of radio shows. Television lights and cameras can be set up back at the couch while Miss Crawford is doing her radio interviews from card table to card table.
5. EXCLUSIVES: When it is absolutely necessary, and when the person involved is of truly top stature, Miss Crawford will give an exclusive [interview].

It is extremely important that you arrange events at the hotel exactly as outlined above.

Miss Crawford will be met in an air-conditioned, chauffeur-driven, newly cleaned Cadillac limousine. Instruct your chauffeurs that they are not to smoke and that they may not at any time drive in excess of 40 miles an hour with Miss Crawford in the car.

Miss Crawford will be carrying a minimum of 15 pieces of luggage. Along with the limousine you will meet Miss Crawford's plane with a closed van for the luggage. Have with you a luggage handler who can accompany the van back to the hotel. It will be his task to take an inventory of the luggage as it comes off the plane and into the van, and as it is being brought into Miss Crawford's suite. There will be a few small items which will go with Miss Crawford in the limousine. Mr. Kelly will supervise this particular part of the operation. Luggage trucks to follow limousine and remain within sight of the limousine.

Every precaution should be taken to assure that none of the luggage is misplaced. Fifteen pieces is the estimated minimum. There may be considerably more and it will be possible for confusion to result. Anticipate this problem and be absolutely certain that a careful inventory of all luggage is maintained at all times during the arrival and departure.

Miss Crawford is a star in every sense of the word; and everyone knows she is a star. Miss Crawford will not appreciate your throwing away money on empty gestures. YOU DO NOT HAVE TO MAKE EMPTY GESTURES TO PROVE TO MISS CRAWFORD OR ANYONE ELSE THAT SHE IS A STAR OF THE FIRST MAGNITUDE.

JOAN'S TRAVELS CONCLUDED IN early June, when she arrived in Baton Rouge, Louisiana, to play a role in yet another gothic horror movie, again with Bette Davis and again under the direction of Robert Aldrich ("who loves vile things"). *Hush . . . Hush, Sweet Charlotte,* as the oddly punctuated title ran, was in production for ten days when an accident occurred. At the end of the day's work at a mansion outside town, Joan was resting in her trailer when she awoke to see that it was dark—and that everyone in the company had left the location. Because of a mix-up in communications, she had not been informed that the cast and crew had packed up and left Louisiana. She made her own travel arrangements and, on arriving in Los Angeles, she felt ill.

Proceeding directly to Cedars-Sinai Medical Center, she had her agent inform Aldrich that she had gone down with a respiratory infection and was unable to work. The schedule was rearranged to accommodate her, and she returned to work on July 20, obviously frail. Over the next several weeks, she was often absent—a situation unprecedented in her entire career. After several meetings with Joan, Aldrich made it clear to her that if the company could no longer rely on her, the film would have to be canceled and a small fortune would be lost. With that, she withdrew from *Hush . . . Hush, Sweet Charlotte* and was replaced by Olivia de Havilland, who stepped in as a favor to her old friend Bette Davis and who greatly improved the script's problems with the character in question. The scenes Joan had completed in Louisiana had to be refilmed, and replicas of buildings were reconstructed on the Fox lot.

She was not disappointed at this outcome. The production had become unlike anything Joan had known—more violently repellent, with more of the "horrendous and evil things" (butchered limbs, for example) that she so hated in an Aldrich movie. In addition, the script had been all but abandoned in favor of wholesale improvisation, and this offended her professional sensibility. Adding to her displeasure was the prospect of continuing to work with Bette Davis, who was a "silent" producer on *Charlotte* and who had behaved, during its Louisiana filming, as if it were her picture. Hence, although Joan certainly had physical ailments, she was also weary of the entire distasteful production; taken collectively, these conditions provided a convenient way for her to quit the movie.

By the end of August, she was pleased to be elsewhere—on the Universal lot, working for a third time with Diane Baker on the pilot for a television series that was eventually canceled. Joan played the title character, Della, a wealthy woman who seems to be holding her daughter captive on a vast estate. Years later, this one-hour episode was sent out in a limited theatrical release as *Fatal Confinement,* but it never found many admirers.

FROM 1965 THROUGH 1971, Joan could be seen on local and national television talk shows, as well as quiz and game shows, with astonishing frequency. She also made media appeals on behalf of several charities and accepted invitations from hosts like Bob Hope, Jerry Lewis and Lucille Ball to join their comedy shows. But she was always a star and she wanted to work in films— and she needed the higher income Hollywood could offer. Thus she agreed to a trio of pictures that were to be her last, and they could not have been less fortunate choices: William Castle's *I Saw What You Did,* produced in early 1965; and *Berserk* and *Trog,* filmed in England in 1967 and 1969.[2] Later, she virtually disowned these movies and refused to discuss them with interviewers; her contempt for them was widely shared by audiences.

In the Castle production, Joan briefly shrieked her way through a story about teenagers who make prank telephone calls; she also pursues a married neighbor, played by John Ireland, until her passion for him is killed—as is she, by a lethal thrust of his kitchen knife. Ireland, now a friend and no longer a lover, recalled Joan's displeasure at the rudeness of the new breed of crew members. When an assistant director wanted the two leading actors brought onto the set, for example, he simply shouted, "Okay, bring 'em on!"

Joan stopped everyone cold. "Young man," she said in her most imperious tone and at full volume for all to hear, "I don't know who the hell *'em* is on this set, but let me tell you something. This is Mr. Ireland and I am Miss Crawford. I suggest you learn your craft and manners on some other set, not mine." Considering both the material offered and the new (but not improved) conditions of filmmaking, it is easy to understand why *I Saw What You Did* was Joan's last American feature film.

Before departing for London to film the hapless *Berserk,* Joan finally had to accept that she could no longer afford to live in the huge duplex on Fifth Avenue. She sold it, taking a loss on the combined purchase and renovation price, and bought a less expensive nine-room apartment on the twenty-second floor of Imperial House, located at 150 East Sixty-ninth Street. This residence, facing north and south, provided spectacular views of the Manhattan skyline; she furnished it with an eye on her budget and (because Billy Haines was ill in Los Angeles) with the help of a New York decorator named Carleton Varney.

At their first meeting, Joan asked Varney to use items she already owned. Together, they achieved a clean, functional look for the apartment by stain-

---

2 *Berserk* is very often referred to as *Berserk!* (even on the home videocassette box)—but the film's title design contains no such punctuation.

ing lighter tables to a dark teak hue and, according to the fashion of the time, painting all the walls white to set off the green and yellow sofas and accent pieces. A lime-green Parsons table served as Joan's desk, and in a corner of the bedroom stood a pedestal with the bronze bust of her that Yucca Salamunich made in 1941 and gave her during the filming of *A Woman's Face*. (Joan used the bust in *Strait-Jacket*, where it was featured as the work of the character played by Diane Baker.)

The new apartment was far more comfortable and casual than any previous Crawford residence. Plastic covers were used to protect the furniture from her dogs, but, as friends recalled, they were not used all the time. And because she now preferred polished parquet floors without carpeting, it was unnecessary for guests to remove their shoes.

"I was the cosmetician and she was the director," Varney recalled in 2002. "She blocked out the floor with tape in each empty room and walked around as if she was playing scenes, to sense the way a room was going to work. She enjoyed being neat, clean and tidy, even to the point of covering all her chairs and sofas with plastic." He also remembered that Joan was "a terribly generous person. She never failed to send a thank-you note, or to call when you were ill."

When she was at home, Joan maintained a rigorous schedule, dictating letters to her secretary, answering fan mail, supervising tasks assigned to her housekeeper but doing most of the housework herself. "I'm up early most mornings," she told a reporter in 1969, "doing the chores, driving everyone crazy even though I have help. I like to do things for myself—scrubbing floors, ironing my own things, vacuuming . . ." And if she was away from home on location for a picture, the procedure was very much the same. Arriving for an interview at the suite arranged for her at the Grosvenor House, London, writer Alexander Walker found her wearing a cloth robe and a towel on her head: she ironed her clothes throughout their conversation, for that evening she expected a delegation from a Pepsi-Cola bottling plant in Lebanon.

BERSERK WAS IN EVERY way a horror—the production values, the script and the cheapjack plot about gruesome murders in a circus managed by Joan, in the role of circus owner, manager and ringmistress Monica Rivers. As if producer Herman Cohen had modeled his picture on *Strait-Jacket,* the villain turns out to be Monica's daughter, Angela (played by Judy Geeson).

"When Joan arrived," recalled producer Herman Cohen, "she had four cases of hundred-proof vodka with her, because that strength is unavailable in England. In spite of her sipping the vodka, she was very professional during *Berserk,* and she never took a drink unless I okayed it. She always knew her lines and she was always on time—in fact, she came in very early in the morning to cook breakfast for anyone who had an early call. She was strong-willed and tough—but tough as she was, she could be reduced to tears at the drop of a hat, and there were scenes in our movie when she had to do just that."

The emotion was real. "Joan was a very lonely lady," Cohen continued, recalling that she frequently rang him in the middle of the night to discuss a script point. "She did that because she was lonely, staying up at night, sipping her vodka, going over her lines for the next day."

Judy Geeson agreed: "Joan Crawford said she was lonely, and I could see and feel that she was. She wasn't easy, but I think *Berserk* was hard on her precisely because it *was* a B-movie. And there was something very likable about her—after all, when people show their vulnerabilities, it's hard not to forgive them for other things." Michael Gough, cast in the role of Joan's business manager and sometime lover, located some of her loneliness in the fact that Joan said she felt cast aside in America—relegated to the dustbin in her senior years.

"She wears her loneliness like a badge," observed the writer Roderick Mann, who interviewed her while he was in London that season, and when the subject surfaced, Joan was forthright. "I don't know anyone who isn't lonely. I didn't have much chance to be lonely during my marriage to Alfred, but I've been pretty darned lonely since then. You just learn to live with it. You don't dwell on it. You read a good book—about other lonely people. I've never had an ounce of self-pity in my life, and I'm not about to start now."

Back in New York in early 1968, Joan resumed her travels for Pepsi-Cola and made no fewer than thirteen television appearances during the first nine months of the year. During one of her trips, she learned that Franchot Tone, then sixty-three, was suffering with lung cancer. He had married and divorced three more wives since the years with Joan, and now he was alone. At once she canceled an important business meeting and rushed to his summer cottage in Canada, where he was resting after completing his last movie role. She brought in food, cleaned the place thoroughly and departed only when she was assured that medical help was nearby. Months later, when Franchot was mortally ill and unable to cook or care for himself at his Manhattan residence, Joan often brought him to her apartment for dinner. John Springer recalled visits to Imperial House when he saw Joan caring for Franchot, several days at a time and at her own expense; by this time, he had lost his fortune through unwise investments, alimony suits and foolish extravagances. When Franchot died on September 18 that year, she saw that his requests were honored for cremation and for the scattering of his ashes over the Canadian lake near his cottage.

———

THAT SAME MONTH, JOAN and Christina volunteered to donate time working for Jerry Lewis's charity telethon, raising money to fight muscular dystrophy. Photographs of mother and daughter working together show two adults fielding telephone calls and, during an interval, laughing together and evidently enjoying one another's company. Some have claimed that Joan was not sober that evening, especially during her recital of a poem and her brief conversation with Lewis, and that may have been true. But her stumbling speech may in fact have been caused by her lifelong stage fright and incurable anxiety when speaking before a live audience.

A few weeks later, Christina required emergency surgery in New York, where she was working under contract to CBS, playing a twenty-four-year-old housewife on the daily afternoon soap opera *The Secret Storm*. Her sudden illness caused a major problem for the network—how to provide an immediate replacement for a twenty-nine-year-old actress on short notice. Joan, then sixty-two, leaped to the rescue, and in two days, she taped four brief appearances, to be broadcast that October. "I didn't want them to give the role to someone else," she told a reporter. On the telephone to Christina, she said, "I'll never be as good as you in the role, but I'll keep the spot warm for you." From her hospital bed, Christina expressed her gratitude: she thought it was "fantastic that she would care that much."

But the outcome was disastrous. This time, there was no doubt about Joan's insobriety: she had poured herself too much hundred-proof false courage before each taping, and so she was seen and heard slurring her speech and all but ruining the episodes. Embarrassed at that time, Christina recalled the experience years later. Joan, she wrote, "was beginning to relive her life through me . . . she needed the youth and vitality of my life. In that context, it is not so impossible to understand how she could even consider playing a woman more than thirty years younger than herself. The boundaries of where she left off and I began had become so enmeshed in the projections and imaginings of our lifelong relationship that there were times when we were one and the same person." Unfortunately, Christina's published memoir of her mommie dearest is not always so perceptive.

——

IN THE SUMMER OF 1969, Joan returned to London for her second film with Herman Cohen. "I refuse to apologize for this movie," she said about *Trog* when it was finished in September. "One never intentionally makes a bad picture. Besides, I like to work. Inactivity is one of the great indignities of life. Through inactivity, people lose their self-respect, their dignity. The need to work is always here, bugging me. In this case, I had never played a scientist or a doctor, so I thought this would be fun to do." It was not.

In *Trog,* Joan played Dr. Brockton, an anthropologist in charge of an English research center. After a prehistoric cave dweller is discovered alive and very much kicking in the English countryside, Dr. Brockton tries to study and even to educate this troglodyte. Growling and mindlessly killing like Frankenstein's monster, he is incapable of speech and badly in need of complete facial reconstruction, although he wears a neatly tailored loincloth and some nifty booties. But Dr. Brockton insists that "Trog," as she sweetly calls him, can be studied and even humanized.

At first, the creature seems on his way to moving up from his missing-link level of half ape, half man. He plays a game of catch-the-ball with the good doctor; he grunts menacingly or purrs contentedly; he learns to identify colors; and during this tutelage, Dr. Brockton encouragingly says things like, "Come on, Trog—you can do it—that's my good boy!" and gently strokes his face. At this point, the creature resembles the disheveled Esther Costello on speed. Of course, a human villain emerges, urging the townsfolk to kill the beast, a favor obligingly performed by the police.

Exteriors were filmed in Berkshire and interiors at Bray, but all during production Joan suffered a heavy cold that developed into bronchitis, which may be detected in her voice for most of the movie. As the *New York Times* acknowledged, *Trog* "proves that Joan Crawford is grimly working at her craft." Indeed, this picture was a regrettable coda to a distinguished motion picture career of forty-five years.

Obviously unwell for most of that summer, Joan was nevertheless alert to the problems of others. Favored with a Rolls-Royce and a chauffeur for transport to and from the studio and location shooting, she learned that a crew member had a dental emergency. Joan sent her car and driver to collect the man and deliver him to a clinic, and then she instructed the chauffeur to proceed to a restaurant famous for its chicken soup, which she had delivered to the patient's home. This was revealed only when the crew member reported it to producer Herman Cohen.

"She was always doing this kind of thing during *Berserk* and *Trog*," Cohen recalled. "She was very close to the crew and knew them all by their first names." Cohen also recalled that Joan gave Christina a check for five thousand dollars and told her to spend it on a holiday. "I was right there at the time it happened," he added. "She was giving her daughter a big dinner party at Les Ambassadeurs [a restaurant club in Mayfair]. None of this is covered in *Mommie Dearest,* because Christina doesn't mention the nice things Joan always did."

One chilly day on location, Cohen's assistant brought the news that Joan's respiratory infection had worsened. He hurried to her caravan and found her pale and short of breath. "Oh, Herm—please get me a doctor—I can't work." He turned to leave the large trailer, smashed his head against the low door frame and reeled dizzily. With that, Joan leaped to her feet—"Oh, Herman, Herman, darling—are you all right? Come here, lie down." As he recalled, "she found a cold compress for my head, and then said, 'You rest—I'll work!'" Within an hour, she was back on the set, "forgetting her own sickness now that she was taking care of me." Those were memorable incidents, but there were problems. "On *Trog,* her drinking was worse than during *Berserk.* She had a huge frosted glass marked Pepsi-Cola, but inside was hundred-proof vodka. I had to reprimand her a few times."

———

JOAN RETURNED TO NEW YORK during the autumn of 1969 and almost immediately traveled to Universal Studios in Los Angeles, to appear in a premiere segment of a Rod Serling television series called *Night Gallery.* With Barry Sullivan (her costar in *Queen Bee*) and a twenty-two-year-old novice director named Steven Spielberg, she worked for a few days on a half-hour episode called "Eyes." Joan played a wealthy and blind New Yorker who bribes a doctor to find someone desperate enough to give up his healthy eyes to her— even though her sight will be restored for only a day at the most. The operation is performed and the bandages removed. Alas, no sooner does she look up at her splendid chandelier than everything goes black—it is the evening of the great Northeast power failure of 1965, and though her sight is now restored, she can see nothing for the duration of the blackout. When the sun rises next morning, she sees it—and then loses her sight forever. Reaching out blindly, she falls through a terrace door to her death.

"Eyes" was the first of Steven Spielberg's noteworthy professional achievements and the last of Joan Crawford's.[3] Ironically, her large, pellucid and radi-

---

3. From January 1970 to September 1972, Joan acted in at least three television dramas; her last performance in any medium was a beleguered asthmatic terrorized by ESP fanatics, on an episode of *The Sixth Sense* broadcast in September 1972.

antly expressive aqua-blue eyes had never been photographed to full effect until that year—not in *Ice Follies of 1939* nor in *Torch Song, Johnny Guitar, The Best of Everything* or *Berserk*. Because of advances in film stock and careful color correction in the lab, it was only in *Trog* and *Night Gallery* that audiences saw at last an aspect of her beauty that had so long impressed those who knew her in person.

Her schedule for 1970 included a twenty-four-city tour in America and a ten-day sojourn in Brazil, all for Pepsi (whose corporate name had been changed to PepsiCo in 1965, when the soft drink company merged with Frito-Lay), and quick trips to Los Angeles for appearances in two television dramas. That year alone, she logged 345,000 miles of travel, "and at every pause, I fell flat on my face."

On February 2, at the Golden Globes award ceremony in Los Angeles, Joan received the Hollywood Foreign Press Association's Cecil B. DeMille Award "for her outstanding contributions to the motion picture industry." And in April, she accepted an invitation to Stephens College, where she had lived for a short time in the fall of 1922. The citation recognized Joan's achievements "as an actress, businesswoman, homemaker, mother and philanthropist." Her brief remarks concluded with a tearful smile: "My kids will never believe this," she told the audience at the convocation, "because I never graduated from this fine school—I was a dropout!"

In addition to her travel schedule, Joan made time to dictate random thoughts that were augmented, edited and reshaped by Audrey Davenport Inman into a book called *My Way of Life,* published by Simon & Schuster in 1971 and intended for her audience of fans. "Charm is a touch of magic. Try to make it a part of *your* way of life." So concludes the book, described by the publicity notice as a compendium of advice from Joan on "how to get more out of your life, your work, your play, your clothes, your looks, your home, your marriage." She offered diet tips ("nibble on raw vegetables and dill pickles"), advice on wardrobe (wear bright colors) and fragrances (try Lauder's Youth Dew and Lanvin's Spanish Geranium), recipes (meat loaf, cole slaw) and hints on "how to create an exciting and comfortable home."

My Way of Life was not a controversial book, but American women snapped it up in great numbers—especially when Joan was present. "Every time she appears at a department store," said Dan Green, the publisher's director of promotion, "she gets 3,000 to 7,000 people, and we sell a minimum of 500 books right there."

As she publicized the book, her relations with Christina became ever more strained, often because of Joan's drinking. By this time, Christina's two-year marriage to Harvey Medlinsky had ended in divorce, and Joan learned that her daughter was jotting notes and going through old correspondence with a view to one day writing an autobiography. When she asked about it, her daughter said nothing, and there, for the present, the topic ended. Except for exchanges of infrequent letters and greeting cards, Christina's last communication with her mother was a telephone conversation at Christmas 1971. Soon after that, she moved from New York to Los Angeles, where she planned on pursuing a movie career. Like her aspirations to act onstage, that goal was abandoned, after a total of three small television roles.

CHAPTER FOURTEEN

Fade-Out

| 1971–1977 |

J AMES BACON, WHO interviewed Christina on the day she performed in the *Dr. Kildare* television series, had known Joan and her children since 1950. For many years, he had covered the movie business for the Associated Press, the *Hollywood Reporter* and the *Los Angeles Herald-Examiner,* and he wrote three books about his experiences in Hollywood. Bacon was known never to minimize or dilute a good story, even at the risk of alienating friends. A frequent visitor to the Crawford household in Brentwood, he saw the "strict discipline [Joan] imposed on her children at home. Joan didn't spoil her children, like most Hollywood mothers did, but she was a loving and kind mother. I know that for a fact." A few people disputed that assessment, but one person's idea of discipline is another's notion of indulgence.[1]

Christina's book, *Mommie Dearest,* was published nineteen months after

---

1. In a memoir published shortly before her death at ninety-two, Helen Hayes discussed Joan as a mother in uncomplimentary terms. But the book, written by Katherine Hatch, shows the author's awareness of *Mommie Dearest* and thus bears a sharp sense of *post hoc ergo propter hoc.*

Joan's death, and at once, many who had known mommie and her little girl took sides. Myrna Loy had toured in Neil Simon's play *Barefoot in the Park,* which reached Chicago in 1965. "We didn't have any problems until Christina Crawford [joined the cast]," Myrna wrote in her autobiography. At first, she was delighted to welcome her old friend's daughter. But then things went bad. "I've never known anyone like her—ever," she added. "Her stubbornness was really unbelievable. She would not do a single thing anyone asked her to do . . . and she completely disregarded her blocking [i.e., her assigned positions onstage]. She was going to do it all her way, and it was self-defeating and sad, because the girl had potential." Eventually, the playwright arrived to see the production, and after a conference with the director, Christina was dismissed.

Except for confidences entrusted to a few friends, Joan's public statements were both protective and complimentary: "My daughter Christina is a very fine actress," she typically replied in answer to questions about her daughter's career.

"Christina wanted to be Joan Crawford," according to Myrna. "I think that's the basis of the book she wrote afterward, and of everything else. I saw what her mind created, the fantasy world she lived in. She envied her mother, grew to hate her, and finally wanted to destroy her."

Costume designer Nolan Miller, who also knew the Crawfords, added that Christina "had her own axe to grind. She did get punished a lot, but she was a very strong-willed child. I used to see Joan tell her to do something, and she flatly refused. As a result, they locked horns early. All that frustration came out in the book [*Mommie Dearest*]. At the end of Joan's life, she and Christina weren't speaking."

"*Mommie Dearest* was not an accurate portrait of who Joan Crawford was as a person," said the film historian Jeanine Basinger, who also knew Crawford. "How many people do you know about whom you can say, 'This is a person I can count on one hundred percent'? If she was your friend, she was there."

Apart from the tale of the wire dress hangers in Christina's book—the incident that perhaps determined Joan Crawford's image for countless people forever after—*Mommie Dearest* often evoked shock without due cause.

At Christmas, for example, fans, friends, colleagues and total strangers flooded the Crawford house with literally hundreds of presents for the children. Joan gave them some of the packages, kept back others for their birthday parties and other appropriate occasions and—explaining to her own children exactly what she was doing—donated many of the parcels to children in orphanages and hospitals.

Christina described this annual holiday tradition *à la Crawford* as a fair example of her mother's monstrous cruelty. But this method of distributing the presents seems, after all, a thoughtful response to outrageous excess and a way of preventing her children from becoming spoiled. "I haven't got a clue whether any of [Christina's horror stories] are true or not," said Howard Cady, one of several editors who prepared *Mommie Dearest* for publication. "But as long as we've got those two scenes"—Joan's destruction of a rose garden during a nighttime drinking spree, and the rage over wire hangers—"we'll sell a million copies." That number turned out to be conservative, and sales advanced exponentially on release of the film version, a horror movie heavy with factual errors past counting, which is typical of biographical motion pictures (or "biopics," as they are called in the business).

———

IN EARLY APRIL 1972, Joan rang the Manhattan offices of Columbia Pictures, which had distributed several of her recent pictures and arranged her publicity tours for them. She was rearranging her personal library; she wanted to give away some books; and, as usual, she wanted to have her extensive bookshelves in perfect order. "Who knows about books and is polite?" she asked Leo Jaffe, Columbia's president. A thirty-one-year-old assistant story editor named Carl Johnes was recommended, and soon he arrived at Joan's apartment to begin the temporary job of librarian.

Thus began a friendship deep and true, uncomplicated by romantic love. Neither a fawning devotee nor a scheming opportunist, Carl remained, during the last years of Joan's life, one of the few she could count on for help, companionship and even advice. As usual for Joan in her friendships with gay men, she rejoiced that Carl was living happily with a man, and he frequently returned home with a present she had given him. Later, he recalled this as "one of the most rewarding friendships" of his life.

That spring day, Carl found an entire twenty-foot-long wall with floor-to-ceiling bookshelves that looked dangerously close to collapsing under the weight of about a thousand volumes.

"Well, you see the problem," Joan said. "I just have to get rid of some of these, and I really don't know where to start. We have to decide which ones go to the children, which to the grandchildren, and then there are various charities, and of course Brandeis," the university where her friends Nate and Frances Spingold had established an arts center and, in Joan's honor, a dance program. That first day, Carl found signed books dedicated to Joan with affectionate sentiments from Noël Coward, James M. Cain, Paul Gallico, Allen Drury and many others.

———

JOAN'S CHECKBOOK STUBS AND receipts for that year reveal a dazzling number and range of charities to which she sent donations: the Muscular Dystrophy Association, the March of Dimes, the National Conference of Christians and Jews, New York Hospital, the Layman's National Bible Committee, the Sloan-Kettering Cancer Center (later renamed Memorial-Sloan Kettering), the New York Infirmary, the Republic School for Boys, Project Hope, the Veterans of Foreign Wars, the Southwest Indian Foundation, the Institute for Rehabilitation Medicine, the Heart Fund and the Korean Relief Fund.

Also: the United Services Organization (USO), the Catholic Actors Guild, the Wiltwyck School for Boys, the Winston Churchill Memorial Library, the Salvation Army, the New York Shakespeare Festival, Guiding Eyes for the Blind, the National Jewish Hospital and Research Center, the Synagogue Council of America, the American Jewish Committee, the United Negro College Fund, the Epilepsy Foundation, the Boys Athletic League, the City of Hope, the Girl Scout Council of Greater New York, the Actors Studio and New York Universal Medical Center. In the last years of her life, the long list of charities to which she wrote checks expanded annually, as did the amounts of money she sent.

Joan's correspondence with friends continued uninterrupted, as her archives attest. By 1972, she had known William Haines for forty-seven years. He always addressed her as he had decades earlier—she was his devoted "Cranberry," the nickname he devised when she first said she hated "Crawford" in 1925. Billy and his lifelong partner, Jimmy Shields, always stayed in contact with Joan by phone and letter—not only when there was important news, but also to exchange recipes, tidbits of gossip or items of industry business. That year, he was trying to recover from a cancer surgery: "More than anything," Billy wrote to Joan at Christmas 1972, "I am grateful for the long years of a deep and holy friendship." She replied, adding her hopes for his speedy recovery and assuring him of prayers that the new year would be one of good health for him and Jimmy.

"In private life, Joan was a lovable, sentimental creature," according to George Cukor. "A loyal and generous friend, very thoughtful—dear Joan, she forgot nothing: names, dates, obligations. These included the people at Hollywood institutions who had helped to make and keep her a star. When it was fashionable to rail against the studio system and the tycoons who had built it, she was always warm in their defense. She spoke of Metro-Goldwyn-Mayer as a family in which she was directed and protected, provided with fine stories and just about every great male star to play opposite; later, she built up a similar relationship with Warners."

Cukor was on the mark: Joan's friendships were many, deep and enduring—a short list would have to include George himself; Haines and Shields; Anita Loos, who had written a quartet of important Crawford movies; Nate and Frances Spingold; John Springer; Dore Freeman, a young man for whom Joan had found a job at Metro and who became a lifelong confidant; Genie Chester, whom she had met in New York decades earlier . . . their names were legion.

"She never took any friendship for granted," according to Carl Johnes. "In fact, I think that one of her many talents was the one for friendship—perhaps it was her greatest. Once she made the decision to enter into a real friendship with another person, she became devoted to that person forever. She worked at it, and she understood the importance of it."

———

ON APRIL 8, 1973, Joan was interviewed onstage at New York's Town Hall. John Springer was producing a series of events at which major Hollywood stars spoke about their careers and answered questions from the audience. Another actress withdrew on short notice, and Joan sprang to John's rescue. "It was a real act of friendship," recalled Springer, "because she really didn't like getting up before a live audience, and she was so frightened that we almost had to push her onstage. But when she stepped out to a rousing standing ovation, she began to relax, and she was wonderful, just wonderful—and those in the audience who weren't in love with her when they arrived, certainly were when they left."

Six days later, Joan picked up the morning newspaper and read that she had been dismissed from Pepsi's board of directors; no one had had the courtesy to inform her personally about this, and at first she thought it was a wild rumor. Later, the company estimated that her interviews on their behalf on television and radio, and her publicized association with them in newspapers, magazines and books, had reached more than 350 million people worldwide: her name was indelibly linked to Pepsi wherever the soft drink was sold.

Her dismissal from the company meant a reduction of sixty thousand dollars in Joan's annual income. At once she asked the management of Imperial House if a smaller apartment might be available, and in September, with the help of Carl Johnes and a few other able friends, she moved from the nine rooms of unit 22-G into 22-H, which had five rooms. When the superintendent and his crew made the routine final inspection of the empty 22-G, they were amazed to find the apartment cleaner and in better condition than on any previous occasion when a tenant had vacated a residence in the building. "Well," Joan said with a wink when they complimented her on the care she had taken, "I didn't play Harriet Craig for nothing." They may not have caught the reference, which was recalled by a friend who was present.

The new, smaller apartment was her home for the last four years of her life. Sparsely but brightly decorated in yellow, lime green and white, the parquet floors waxed to a high sheen, the place featured no new pieces, and she gave away a great deal of furniture she had deposited in storage from Brentwood, East Seventieth Street and 22-G.

Joan had to laugh at herself when, before she welcomed a team from *Architectural Digest,* she recalled the gamut of styles she had tried and discarded over five decades. In her first rented house, in Beverly Hills, she had hung paintings of dancing girls with blond hair, rhinestones and pearls, done on black velvet. When Paul Bern first saw this display, "he gulped—and I got rid of them fast." After that, she had Billy Haines's advice, which caused more than a few arguments—"but he always won because of his excellent taste and knowledge, and my lack of both." Her next home was decorated in what Billy called "Ming Toy Cocktail Chinese." Then came her Early American phase—"I was hooking my own rugs, and there were little rocking chairs all over the place." That was followed by her baroque period, and then came eighteenth-century English. But by the end of 1973, everything had become much simpler indeed, and not only for economic reasons. At sixty-seven, she longed for simplicity, in life as in furnishings.

The day after Christmas, Joan had a call from Jimmy Shields: Billy Haines had succumbed to cancer at the age of seventy-three. She was confined with bronchitis that week and could not attend the funeral in California, but she telephoned Jimmy every day for almost a month, which comforted him enormously; they reminisced, laughed and wept together. Three months later, Jimmy wrote a note—"It's no good without Billy"—and took an overdose of sleeping pills. With those two deaths, as Joan said, she lost "the happiest married couple I ever knew."

Joan now began to refer to herself as an "ex-movie star." This self-designation began, as she said, when she "was waiting for an elevator, and I actually heard a woman beside me say to another, 'See her? She used to be Joan Crawford.' I couldn't burst into tears because I was about to speak [at a charity board meeting], but at that moment, I suddenly felt old, and I've felt old ever since." She did not like the movies Hollywood was grinding out, and she especially loathed *The Exorcist,* the biggest commercial success of 1973. As for the film and television projects her agents sent, "Most of them are trash," as she told an interviewer. Eventually, she told the men at the William Morris Agency to stop sending her scripts.

Joan was now, as her friends saw, achingly alone. "I have too much loneliness," she said to a visitor one evening. "But I guess people figure, what the hell have I got to say that's interesting? I'm not an actress any more; I'm not a so-called executive [with Pepsi] any more. I'm not involved in politics. God knows I'm not an intellectual. I'm a private person, and I don't speak well off the top of my head. My vocabulary is limited, and it shrinks up completely when someone asks a question. So I guess people don't think I'm very interesting." That was a pity, as former directors like Vincent Sherman and Charles Walters insisted. "She was very lonely in the last years," said Walters, "and a lot of people deprived themselves of her vibrant company. They were the losers. She could certainly be difficult and demanding, but the rewards of her friendship were incalculable."

Much of the first half of 1974 was taken up with painful operations due to periodontal disease and bacterial infections in her jaw. In July, she was resting at home but could not invite friends: "I'm so sorry I can't see you," she told the writer Adele Whitely Fletcher, whom she had known for fifty years. "I'm having this painful dental work, which I'd rather you not mention—I don't want everybody clucking that I'm really having a face-lift. When I do, I'll say so myself." After the quick procedure she had at the time of *Torch Song,* Joan never had additional cosmetic surgery; as she explained to a friend: "After all, I don't want to look as if I haven't lived."

When her old friend Rosalind Russell was honored at a reception at the Rainbow Room that September, Joan gladly attended; they had never lost contact since their first meeting and collaboration in 1934. The party was a noisy, crowded affair, but the two old friends managed to steal a few moments together. Russell, cheerful and valiant, was very ill with rheumatoid arthritis, and she was suffering the side effects of frequent cortisone injections. She did not tell anyone that she had also recently received a diagnosis of cancer. The press took pictures all evening, and over the next several days Joan was not the only one horrified at the newspaper photos: it seemed as if editors had gleefully selected the most unflattering shots of the two stars. "If that's the way I look," said Joan, "they've seen the last of me." With extremely rare exceptions, she kept her word: for the next three years, Joan was virtually a recluse.

In her solitude, she drank more than ever, and one evening in December 1974, she took a terrible fall. Suffering a deep cut on her forehead, two black eyes and a badly bruised arm, she had to have nursing care for a week. But the accident had a remarkable outcome: Joan never took so much as a sip of alcohol for the rest of her life. It would be impossible to make this assertion with any certainty were it not for the witness of all her close friends and her twin daughters, who had begun to visit with their own children, making the trip from their homes outside New York.

Douglas Fairbanks Jr. visited Joan several times in her last years, and he recalled her drinking tea or Pepsi while he had Scotch. Their friendship had been interrupted only during the war, and their occasional meetings were always amiable; to others, they spoke about one another only in the most affectionate and respectful terms.

"It was a remarkable achievement that she stopped drinking," according to Johnes, who had previously seen Joan down three double vodkas in a short time. Henceforth, she served alcoholic drinks to him and one or two other guests, but she did not join them. Why had she given it up? "I really don't think I knew who I was any more," she told Carl, "and I wanted to find out." She spent the rest of her life finding out, and the discovery bore dividends. Instead of perpetually assuming other identities through her work, the real Joan Crawford emerged from the shadows—generous to friends in every way possible, lavish to charities and never a burden to anyone, even when she was mortally ill. When she learned, for example, that her former Los Angeles assistant, Betty Barker, was bringing a few relatives and friends to Manhattan for their first visit, Joan paid their airfare, bought them theater tickets and paid for all their meals for sixteen days. There were many such displays of generosity.

Instead of making painstaking preparations to show herself in public looking like Joan Crawford the star, she preferred to remain at home, where she welcomed the few she could trust—and she was not coiffed, made up and dressed like the star, but rather like the woman (if not the girl) next door. At last she was working with a clean slate: the flapper had faded like a watercolor exposed to the sun; romantic triangles had become warm friendships; terrified and terrifying characters onscreen were dismissed. Now there was only a calm, self-possessed lady of a certain age, content with a few confidants, a telephone and a television set.

Her life had been a battle between the fantasy of movie stardom and the intrusion of reality—mostly in the form of failed marriages, disappointing love affairs and the constant terror of losing her professional status. Her life's work had been the maintenance of the image she herself had created—of Joan Crawford the star. This had allowed her virtually no time to discover who she was; as a result, many who knew her (and more who did not) insisted that there was no authentic person behind the artificial creation. That was not merely smug and presumptuous—it was also dead wrong.

———

NO OTHER STAR IN the so-called golden age of Hollywood projected Joan's brand of glamour: it was not seductively soft or otherworldly—it was defiant, challenging. In her photographs and in her movie roles, she demanded that we rethink what it means to be female. Dancer, actress, corporate executive—she was not to be stopped, and she was rarely out of the news. For over fifty years, her image offered much of what she herself was: an ambitious person who appealed to women who were ignored, exploited, cajoled or seduced, from the flapper era to the dawn of women's liberation. Nurturing a lifelong desire to rise above her childhood background and to prove herself, she was often possessed by her roles as much as she grafted them onto her own character; but in an attempt to control her fame, she had often been its servant. Similarly, in her romantic life, she was a woman who desperately wanted to belong to another. But this hope she never realized, perhaps because in that regard, too, she tried excessively to direct the relationship and to play Joan Crawford the star.

But with all her drive and all her desires fading in her last years, she realized—not too late—that she had not developed a real private life and a sense of self. "I worked too hard, and a lot of my relationships failed because of that. I was a commodity, a piece of property, and so I felt an overwhelming obligation to my career. That's why I was an actress first, a wife second, and a mother third. I worked almost constantly, and even when I wasn't working, there was that image thing—having to look like a star. I just went ahead like a bulldozer, and I'm afraid I was a very selfish woman." It is, at the last, this forthright honesty that justifies admiration, not star worship. Those who saw "no one at home" behind the mask were in fact uncomfortable with her complexity.

Although she had long been possessed by image and driven by the need for fame, she finally saw reality through the prism of a quiet and sober life. She welcomed a few friends to her home without makeup, jewelry or extravagant dress; often, she opened the door in a simple, pretty housecoat, her graying hair tied with a band or casually swept back over her ears. She telephoned Sydney Guilaroff, the Hollywood stylist who had so often designed for her movies, and asked if she might send a lock of her hair for him to design a new style. "Gray?" he asked, incredulous. "Oh, Joan, you shouldn't have done that!" He recalled that she sounded hurt by his remark, which he at once regretted; she never sent the lock of hair.

Joan's expressive blue eyes took on new warmth and her manner a fresh patience and softness in her last years, and these changes beguiled old friends and attracted new ones. All were impressed by her good humor and her refusal to complain about the increasing debilities that taxed her energies and finally destroyed her health.

———

REGARDING HER RELATIONSHIPS WITH her adopted children, Joan was astonishingly honest. "I'm aware that there were times when I didn't pay enough attention to them, and times when I was too strict," she told journalist Roy Newquist late in her life, during a book-length series of interviews conducted over several years. "I expected them to appreciate their advantages, the things they had as children that I hadn't had—but in Hollywood that's hard to do. If we as adults couldn't find any reality, how could they?" As for the final assessment of her role as mother: "I wish you'd ask my children. I loved them, and I think they loved me—but you'll have to ask them."

During Joan's last years, Cathy, who was then married to Jerome LaLonde, lived in Pennsylvania with her two children, Carla and Casey. Cindy had married John Jordan and resided for a time in Iowa with her two, Joel and Jan. Both twins were eventually divorced, and both raised their children alone, devotedly and attentively. After Joan died and *Mommie Dearest* was published, the twins and their families broke off all communication with Christina—and also with Christopher, who issued shrill and bitter statements about Joan and endorsed anything Christina had to say. Cindy Crawford Jordan died at the age of sixty in 2007, a year after the death of Christopher.

Asked in 2008 to describe her life with Joan, Cathy said her mother was "just a wonderful Mom—generous, loving and nurturing, strict but kind and caring . . . *Mommie Dearest* was fake and fictional." Her son, Casey LaLonde, was only five when his grandmother died, but he remembers Joan (whom the children called JoJo) preparing roast chicken luncheons for them and always giving them a little present when they departed. He remembered her as "very thin, very frail . . . but very pretty. She greeted us in her housecoat, and she was very relaxed. My parents went out for dinner, and she baby-sat us. It was just like anybody's grandmother." His sister Carla agreed: "All I can say is that she was a very loving grandmother."

Casey and Carla had been told in advance that JoJo's apartment was very tidy and always very clean, and they were to be very careful not to slide on her immaculate parquet floors. On one visit, when the children were still under seven years old, Cathy and Joan were chatting when they heard a slipping noise in the living room. "I'm so sorry, Mommie," Cathy said as she rose to stop the children from sliding on the floor.

But Joan grasped her daughter's hand. "No, it's all right, Cathy. They're enjoying themselves—let them slide." And then she smiled. "I've mellowed."

But there was no rapprochement with Christina. "Tina and I have nothing to say to each other," Joan told Carl Johnes in 1976. "But I hear she's found another man, and I hope she's happy."[2]

On October 28, 1976, Joan signed her Last Will and Testament. She bequeathed $77,500 to each of her twin daughters, Cathy and Cindy, and $5,000 to be held in trust for each of the twins' children, until they turned twenty-one. Bequests of $5,000 each were made to five friends; her New York secretary, Florence Walsh, received $10,000; and Betty Barker was left $35,000. In addition, shares of her estate were bequeathed to the Muscular Dystrophy Association, the American Cancer Society, the American Heart Association, the Wiltwyck School for Boys, the USO of New York and the Motion Picture Country Home and Hospital, in California, which cared for elderly and ailing former employees of the film industry. "I've been on the receiving end of so many good things," she told her secretary when she dictated these bequests. "I just have to give something in return."

But the most quoted clause of the document turned out to be Joan's penultimate statement: "It is my intention to make no provision herein for my son Christopher or my daughter Christina, for reasons which are well known to them." Unfortunately, her attorneys did not advise her to leave token bequests to these two; had she done so, they might not have contested the will, claiming (against all evidence) that Joan was mentally incompetent when she drafted the document; eventually, the court awarded Christina and Christopher $27,500 each.

For all the hostilities between them, Christina's final statement about her mother was astonishing: "I always knew that Mother loved me—that she really loved me. She may not have agreed with me, she may not have even

---

2. On February 14, 1976, Christina was married a second time, to David Koontz; they were divorced in 1982. She subsequently married Michael Brazell, and this union too was dissolved.

liked me sometimes, but she respected me and she loved me as I loved her." With those words, Christina herself seemed once and for all to contradict her own published portrait of Joan Crawford.

———

IN EARLY 1976, JOAN had purchased a hospital bed—"just because it's more comfortable," she said. Most evenings, she watched television shows like *The Waltons* and *Little House on the Prairie*. But that year, her weight dropped alarmingly, she was able to eat very little, and even walking to the door to greet a friend was a slow, laborious and painful process. All during that year, she rarely left her apartment, but when she could, she welcomed into it Cathy and her husband, Jerome; Mary Jane Raphael, who had been her assistant at Pepsi; Peter Rogers, who had helped to create the Blackglama Mink advertising campaign for which Joan had been photographed; Leo Jaffe, from Columbia Pictures; Stan Kamen, her agent at William Morris; and a few other friends and neighbors. Eventually, they all learned or correctly deduced that Joan was suffering from terminal cancer. When Sydney Guilaroff called back to inquire about the lock of hair, Joan's voice sounded thin and her breathing labored. "It doesn't matter, dear," she said quietly. "It doesn't matter at all. I'll wear my hair the best way I can."

No one can recall a whisper of complaint, even when (as they sometimes noted) her features were involuntarily contorted with pain, for which Joan took no other remedy than plain aspirin. Attempting to abide by the tenets of Christian Science, she refused to see physicians.

"Gradually, I filled my life with faith," Joan had written a few years earlier. "It took me a very long while to stop fighting frantically and let God help, but I learned. No one goes the long road alone. God is my inexhaustible source. This I know, but sometimes I get in His way."

The last period of Joan's life was in fact a time of quiet interior contrition. "I wish I had been easier on people around me, especially my husbands and my kids," she told an interviewer not long before she died. "It's as though I was having such a god-awful time learning my part and place in life that I never really had the time to project myself onto other people's positions, to find out what they were feeling. I'm afraid that through most of my life, if you took a simpatico rating on the scale of one to ten, I'd have come out zero." But that was a severe judgment that perhaps no one could endorse.

By the end of April 1977, a month after her seventy-first birthday, she was mostly confined to bed. Carl Johnes recalled their last telephone conversation. "She sounded timorous, wavering and very weak but assured me that she was fine, even though her back troubles were still painful. Conversation was difficult. She said that she hadn't watched any television for months, preferring to go to bed early and read her Bible." He sent her a bouquet of spring flowers, mostly yellow rosebuds.

"There's nothing presented to us that we cannot cope with," Joan had written to a friend in crisis years earlier. "There is a Power much greater than any one of us, Who created us and Who continues to give us strength and courage—not only daily but hourly. Learn to depend on that. It's the only thing one can depend on when one is in great need."

On the morning of May 10, 1977, the housekeeper arrived and went to ask if she should prepare breakfast as usual. The bedroom was quiet, and Joan did not respond. On a small table at the bedside were her Bible and the vase of yellow roses, now in full bloom.

ACKNOWLEDGMENTS

Over many months, the staff of the New York Public Library for the Performing Arts at Lincoln Center provided expert and cheerful assistance as I made my way through the voluminous Joan Crawford Papers, Scrapbooks, Letters and Ephemera. Similarly, I am grateful to Stacey Behlmer and her colleagues for indicating important relevant collections at the Margaret Herrick Library of the Academy of Motion Picture Arts and Sciences, Beverly Hills. Closer to my home turf, I have relied on the scholarship and generosity of Claus Kjær, at the Danish Film Institute, Copenhagen.

An especially important part of my research was provided by friends who granted extended interviews over several years: Diane Baker, Olivia de Havilland, the late Douglas Fairbanks Jr., Judy Feiffer, Judy Geeson, the late Karl Malden, the late Joseph L. Mankiewicz, Marian Seldes and the late John Springer.

A trio of remarkable Joan Crawford admirers has organized Internet Web sites indispensable for researchers—Stephanie Jones (http://www.joancrawfordbest.com), Neil Maciejewski (http://www.legendaryjoancrawford.com) and Donna Nowak (http://www.filmsofcrawford.com). I salute their careful and thorough presentations of rich materials and their kind interest in this book. My research would not have been complete without their contributions.

I am also grateful to those who, over many years, spoke on the record about Joan Crawford—among them, Jeanine Basinger, Ann Blyth, Ben Cooper, Christina Crawford, Christopher Crawford, George Cukor, Melvyn Douglas, Sydney Guilaroff,

Cynthia (Cindy) Crawford Jordan, Carla LaLonde, Casey LaLonde, Cathy Crawford LaLonde, Dick Moore, Anita Page, Betsy Palmer, Otto Preminger, Cliff Robertson and Vincent Sherman.

I owe very much indeed to precious friends: Thomas Cahill, John Canemaker, Mart Crowley, John Darretta, Olivia de Havilland, Paul Elliott, Mary Evans, Lewis Falb, Mike Farrell, Chuck Griffis, Tippi Hedren, Sue Jett, Joseph Kennedy, Irene Mahoney OSU, Patricia Milbourn, Gerald Pinciss and Greg Schreiner.

My wise agent, dear friend and invaluable confidante, Elaine Markson, has looked after my literary interests for four decades. Her associate, Gary Johnson, is equally a treasure and has an enormous claim on my thanks for (literally) daily assistance and counsel. Also at the Markson Thoma Agency, Julia Kenny smoothes the tangled paths of international and subsidiary rights.

David Highfill, at the William Morrow imprint of HarperCollins, New York, was enthusiastic from day one—a gifted editor and an unfailing champion of the book. In David's office, Gabe Robinson efficiently dispatched the daily routine of important tasks.

Once again, I dedicate a book to my husband, Ole Flemming Larsen. A respected school administrator and a highly talented artist, he is at the very center of my life. Ole's wisdom and his graceful intelligence enrich me; his humor and patience leaven every day; his unwavering support makes all my efforts possible; and the depth of his commitment to me, and to our life together in Denmark (my adopted country), brings me a wealth of blessings past counting.

DS

Sjælland, Denmark

April 2010

NOTES

Unless otherwise indicated, all direct quotations attributed to Joan Crawford derive from these sources:

1. The Joan Crawford Papers (1932–1976), the Joan Crawford Scrapbooks (1925–1960) and Letters to Joan Crawford (1972–1976), all on deposit at the New York Public Library for the Performing Arts at Lincoln Center.

2. *Conversations with Joan Crawford,* the book-length series of interviews JC gave to Roy Newquist; see Bibliography..

3. *A Portrait of Joan,* a memoir by JC, written with Jane Kesner Ardmore; see Bibliography.

4. *My Way of Life,* a second memoir by JC, written with Audrey Davenport Inman (who is uncredited); see Bibliography.

   For brevity's sake, other sources of interviews and quotations from periodical literature are supplied only at their first citation; subsequent remarks attributed to the same source derive from the identical interview or article first noted. Sources referenced here only by the author's last name can be found in the Bibliography.

CHAPTER ONE

2 *It was January 1925* On the so-called flapper era, see Allen, 94–95; G. Stanley Hall, "Flapper Americana Novissima," *Atlantic Monthly,* June 1922; Bruce Bliven, "Flapper Jane," *New Republic,* September 9, 1925.

8 *"She was just the little girl"* For Don Blanding's poem, see http://www.don-blanding.com, under "First Lines."

9 *"scrubbing floors for money"* Patricia Bosworth, " 'I'm Still an Actress! I Want to Act!' " *New York Times,* September 24, 1972.

11 *"She made arrangements"* Christina Crawford, 61.

12 *"Moving pictures have given me"* JC, interview by John Springer, Town Hall, April 8, 1973.

14 *"In that little talk"* JC, interview by Philip Jenkinson, BBC-TV, 1968; similarly, see Roderick Mann, "Crawford: 'Listen,' She Says, 'I Like to Work,' " *New York Times,* August 24, 1969; and Bosworth, "I'm Still an Actress!"

16 *transferred her to the Oriol Terrace* On the history of the Oriole Terrace nightclub, see, e.g., Björn and Gallert, 17.

19 *"When Miss Le Sueur came"* Joan Cross, "Name Her and Win $1,000," *Movie Weekly,* March 27, 1925.

CHAPTER TWO

20 *"as a member of"* MGM memo from R. B. McIntyre dated January 5, 1925, to Mayer, Thalberg, Rapf, et al. The purpose of the memo was to alert the payroll department to begin drafting checks to JC that month.

21 *"From the day Lucille arrived"* Adele Whitely Fletcher, "I Remember Joan," *Modern Screen,* August 1977.

24 *"The imaginary life"* Morin, 81.

27 *"It's very clear"* JC always took great delight in countering any assertion that she had been foolish enough as to appear in pornographic films: she was, from day one, too serious about her career and too conscious of the dangers of a bad reputation to make a potentially fatal mistake. She spoke openly about these early threats—e.g., to Patricia Bosworth, " 'I'm Still an Actress! I Want to Act!' " *New York Times,* September 24, 1972.

"I know she will be" For Rapf's comment on her name and other details of the contest to rename Lucille Le Sueur, see, e.g., *Movie Weekly,* March 27, 1925.

28 *"Lots of newcomers"* JC's comment from 1925 was used with studio publicity photos over the next decade—in this particular form, it accompanied a still image taken on the set of *I Live My Life* in 1935.

29 *"Joan always worried terribly"* See also Kotsilibas-Davis and Loy, 41.

"When they did not appear" Fletcher, "I Remember Joan."

30 *"I hated that name"* Bosworth, "I'm Still an Actress!"

Metro drafted a check A copy of the check duly sent to Mrs. Artisdale was preserved in the MGM archives: the payment was company check number 8382, drawn from the Culver City branch of the Pacific Southwest Trust & Savings Bank.

33 *"Don't exhaust the audience"* Tapert, 44.

34 *"I forgot how to say no"* Chandler, 69.

Constance Bennett One of the finest summaries of Constance Bennett's life and career can be found in Tapert, 151–65.

35 *glamour* My observations on glamour owe much to the thinking and writing of Virginia Postrel; see, e.g., her essay "Starlight and Shadow," *Atlantic,* July–August 2007.

36 *"Everything in Hollywood"* Ingrid Bergman to author, May 8, 1975.

37 *"He gave me great advice"* Chandler, 67.

38 *"She wanted to be profound"* Tapert, 220.

CHAPTER THREE

41 *"He was a fine man"* Chandler, 93–94.

"Professionally, she was good" Ibid., 94.

42 *"I was just an MGM contract player"* Quirk and Schoell, 17.

"ever go through a ceremony" "Young Cudahy's Mother Warns of Annulment," *Los Angeles Times,* May 6, 1926.

43 *"Michael and I agreed"* "Love Knot Untied by Fair Joan: Miss Crawford and Scion of Famous Cudahy Family Break Off Engagement," *Los Angeles Times,* June 8, 1926.

"a chronic liver complaint" Obituary for Michael Cudahy, *New York Times,* February 16, 1947.

44 *"I'm so sorry I made"* Vogel, 34.

"a piece of junk" Review of *The Boob, Baltimore Sun,* June 15, 1926.

"He was a horny wise-guy" Quirk and Schoell, 17.

"She had a reputation" Ibid., 18.

45 *"Joan Crawford rides high"* James R. Quirk, *Photoplay,* cited in Quirk, 43.

"so befuddled" Review of *The Understanding Heart, Time,* May 23, 1927.

"I have decided" Gloria Swanson, "Hollywood Remembers," in *Hollywood Biographies* (Passport Prods., 2001); also, Tapert, 16.

47 *"Joan Crawford is one"* Langdon W. Post, review of *The Unknown, New York Evening World,* June 5, 1927.

49 *"Joan Crawford is quite charming"* Mordaunt Hall, review of *West Point, New York Times,* January 2, 1928.

50 *It's a common misconception* There is a considerable literature on the early days of talking pictures. A good introduction may be found on the Internet, in the ancillary material provided for *The Jazz Singer* at http://www.imdb.com.

51 *"began the awakening"* Katherine Albert, "Why They Said Joan Was 'High Hat,'" *Photoplay,* August 1931, 65.
"passionate possessiveness" Fairbanks, 24.
"there was no great warmth" Ibid., 151.
"My parents divorced" Douglas Fairbanks Jr. to the author, March 29, 1990.

52 *"She was a few years older"* Fairbanks, 122.

53 *"a vital, energetic"* Ibid., 123–24, 133.
"To be honest" Ibid., 134.

54 *"a warm reception"* Ibid., 132.
"The most important contribution" Ibid., 135–36.

56 *"Miss Crawford does"* Edgar Waite, review of *Rose-Marie, Los Angeles Examiner,* February 12, 1928.
"as one of the most admired" St. Paul Pioneer Press, cited in *Quirk,* 57.
"she simply walks off" George Gerhard, review of *Four Walls, New York Evening World,* August 13, 1928.

57 *"does the finest work"* Bland Johnson, review of *Our Dancing Daughters, New York Mirror,* September 3, 1928.
"Hundreds of young women" *Time,* October 22, 1928.

58 *"the right script material"* Review of *Dream of Love, New York Sun,* December 3, 1928.

59 *"Adrian had a profound effect"* Tapert, 53.
"That's been quite a burden" JC, letter to fan and friend Dan Mahoney of New York, November 22, 1928; also see Vogel, 40.

60 *"Mostly he seemed"* Christina Crawford, 63.

CHAPTER FOUR

62 *"Miss Crawford is as gorgeous"* Harry Mines, review of *The Duke Steps Out, Los Angeles Daily News,* March 19, 1929.

63 *"It was Louis B. Mayer's rule"* Pamela Blake, quoted in her obituary, *Daily Telegraph* (London), October 26, 2009.

64 *"Billie cried with relief"* Douglas Fairbanks Jr. to the author, March 29, 1999.
"I had no particular desire" Ron Alexander, "Douglas Fairbanks Jr. Tells His Story (Some of It, That Is)," *New York Times,* April 20, 1988.

65 *"Neither Billie nor I"* Fairbanks, 148, 153.

"I didn't know enough" JC, interview by John Springer, Town Hall, April 8, 1973.

When she told him JC recalled her meeting with Marafioti in JC with Ardmore, 49—where the name is incorrectly spelled as "Marafiotta."

67 *"The house, which they call"* 426 North Bristol Avenue was described in "The Homes of the Stars," *New Movie* magazine, December 1931. William Haines's subsequent contributions to redecoration were nicely summarized by Lockwood.

69 *"It would all be quite lamentable"* Lucius Beebe, review of *Our Blushing Brides, New York Times,* July 20, 1930.

70 *"Joan Crawford displays"* Elizabeth Yeaman, *Hollywood Daily Citizen,* September 12, 1930.

71 *"Douglas had been reared"* From an article written for JC, approved by her and subsequently published under her name: "What Men Have Done to Me," *Modern Screen,* November 1951.

"I was out to" Tapert, 46.

72 *"she wanted to develop"* Sherman, 196.

75 *"If I have to do one more"* W. E. Oliver, *"Blushing Brides* Is Talisman," *Los Angeles Evening Herald,* August 2, 1930.

"Joan Crawford can hold her own" Review of *Paid, Time,* January 12, 1931.

CHAPTER FIVE

82 *"He seems slightly puzzled"* Review of *Laughing Sinners, Time,* July 13, 1931.

"Miss Crawford has seldom looked" Andre Sennwald, review of *Laughing Sinners, New York Times,* June 3, 1931.

"Regardless of the script" Quirk and Schoell, 55.

84 *"There were many times"* JC, interview by Philip Jenkinson, BBC-TV, 1968.

85 *"It was a wild, wild place"* Charles Champlin, "Olivier Better Than Ever," *Los Angeles Times,* January 19, 1976.

86 *"I fought to keep my marriage going"* JC, "What Men Have Done to Me," *Modern Screen,* November 1951.

89 *"They gave me everything"* JC, e.g., during television interviews with Mike Douglas, Merv Griffin, Johnny Carson, David Frost and others.

"Miss Crawford adds" Mordaunt Hall, review of *Possessed, New York Times,* November 28, 1931.

90 *"It's the best work"* Review of *Possessed, Photoplay,* December 1931.

90 *Remarkably often, it has been claimed* On JC's wide range of roles in the 1930s, see Basinger, *The Star Machine.*

91 *"Our relationship was private"* Chandler, 188.

92 *"We have members in all sections"* Marin L. Dommer's Joan Crawford Fan Club letter is reproduced in Thorp, 100–101.

93 *"dull to the point"* George Jean Nathan, review of *Grand Hotel, New York Herald,* December 28, 1932.
"one of the drollest" Ibid.

94 *"unstable"* JC, interview by Philip Jenkinson.
"felt sorry for her" Robert Montgomery, *The Hollywood Greats,* TV documentary on Joan Crawford, August 3, 1978.
Sydney Guilaroff Sydney Guilaroff to the author, February 26, 1991. See his obituary in the *Independent* (London), May 31, 1997, and an unpublished interview by Jimmy Bangley for Classic Images, available online at http://www.classicimages .com/past_issues/view/?x=/1997/january/sguilaroff-interview.html.

95 *"accessory characters"* Marie Belloc Lowndes, foreword to *Letty Lynton,* n.p.

96 Letty Lynton *gown* Gledhill, 74–89.

CHAPTER SIX

102 *"She liked to pose"* Hurrell's recollections of JC were documented in Kobal; in a 1941 issue of *International Photographer;* and in *Interview* magazine, vol. 2, no. 3 (March 1981). For an important article on Hurrell, see Virginia Postrel, "Starlight and Shadow," *Atlantic,* July–August 2007.

105 *"There will be no divorce"* Katherine Albert, "The Inclusive [*sic*] Inside Story of the Separation of Joan and Doug," *Modern Screen,* May 1933.
"Doug had married" Donald Marshman, "The Second Rise of Joan Crawford," *Life,* June 23, 1947.

106 Dancing Lady On the production of *Dancing Lady,* see esp. Haver, 136–48.

110 *"I admire my sister-in-law"* Alma Whitaker, "Joan Crawford Wants Sister-in-Law's Baby," *Los Angeles Times,* December 31, 1933.

111 *"No actress living"* Cameron Shipp, "The Last of the Movie Queens," *Cosmopolitan,* April 1951.
"cares more than anyone" Helen Louise Walker, "Joan Crawford: The Most Remarkable Girl in Hollywood," *Silver Screen,* January 1934.

116 *"This is one of Miss Crawford's"* Variety, December 20, 1934.

117 *"He contributed greatly"* JC, "What Men Have Done to Me," *Modern Screen,* November 1951.

118 *Hollywood Presbyterian Hospital* On the matter of Joan's bequest to Hollywood Presbyterian Hospital, see, e.g., Quirk and Schoell, 269.

"In the two years after 1937" Robert White, "The Joan Crawford No One Knows," *Los Angeles Times,* May 21, 1939.

120 *"not a distinguished performance"* Howard Barnes, review of *No More Ladies, New York Herald-Tribune,* June 15, 1935.

"the appeal of cold turkey" Review of *No More Ladies, Time,* June 24, 1935.

"There was a time" Joan's remarks were pasted on the back of a publicity still taken during *No More Ladies* and sent out to the press.

122 *"I became a pretty good"* Patricia Bosworth, "'I'm Still an Actress! I Want to Act!'" *New York Times,* September 24, 1972.

"Joan Crawford welcomed me" Olivia de Havilland, interview with the author, January 27, 2010.

CHAPTER SEVEN

127 *"She must get her homework done"* Basinger, "A Woman's View," 132–33.

130 *"A light fell on top of him"* See Moore, 147.

131 *"a vapid Cinderella pipe dream"* Howard Barnes, review of *The Bride Wore Red, New York Herald-Tribune,* October 16, 1937.

"underlying shabbiness" Frank S. Nugent, review of *The Bride Wore Red, New York Times,* October 17, 1937.

132 *"she remained in her suite"* "Joan Crawford's Father Is Dead," *Fort Worth Star-Telegram,* January 1, 1938.

133 *"The part of me"* Vogel, 55; the letter was sent to her friend Genie Chester.

"Practically all the major studios" *Independent Film Journal,* May 1938; see also *Time,* May 16, 1938.

"It used to be" *Time,* May 16, 1938.

135 *"I hope we will always"* "Divorce Granted to Joan Crawford," *New York Times,* April 12, 1939.

138 *"I'd play Wally Beery's grandmother"* JC said this often; see, e.g., JC with Ardmore, 90.

139 *"With George in command"* Vogel, 59.

"She was serious about improving" George Cukor, "She Was Consistently Joan Crawford, Star," *New York Times,* May 22, 1977; this was the text of Cukor's eulogy at the Los Angeles memorial service for JC.

141 *"I don't think Clark"* Chandler, 281–82.

143 *"a formula turned into"* *Time,* April 8, 1940.

143 *"A rich experience"* Donna Marie Nowak, manager of the important and valuable Internet Web site http://www.filmsofcrawford.com.

145 *"thrilling and fun"* Crothers, 19.

146 *"I don't think God"* Ibid., 165.

147 *"it has more to say"* Time, July 1, 1940.

"She found all the comedy" Cukor, "She Was Consistently Joan."

CHAPTER EIGHT

149 *"I don't think he"* Chandler, 277.

"I was amazed" Swanson, 381.

151 *"I left California with the baby"* Chandler, 278.

152 *Joan documented many episodes:* JC's grandson, Casey LaLonde (the son of Cathy LaLonde, whom Joan adopted as a baby in 1947), found the home movies among his mother's possessions and edited the contents for the sake of economy and interest. For a detailed summary of the contents, see http://www .filmsofcrawford.com/id163.html.

"very sentimental about him" Christina Crawford, 74.

Joan's silence about the baby girl The adoption was first mentioned in the *Los Angeles Times,* May 24, 1940, and in *Time,* June 3, 1940.

"Her transcontinental journeys" Jimmie Fiddler, "Joan Crawford Adopts Baby: Star Explains Mystery of Trips to New York," *Los Angeles Times,* May 25, 1940.

153 *"Mother and I were"* Christina Crawford, 23–24.

157 *"She played a disfigured"* George Cukor, "She Was Consistently Joan Crawford, Star," *New York Times,* May 22, 1977.

159 *"fine, palatial residence"* Deatherage, 82–95.

"She adored you" Ibid., 91.

160 *Rachel Crothers was the most famous* See her obituary in the *New York Times,* July 6, 1958; reviews in the same newspaper by Brooks Atkinson of *When Ladies Meet,* October 7, 1932, and *Susan and God,* October 8, 1937; and Jean Ashton, "The Neil Simon of Her Day—And an Ardent Feminist," *New York Times,* May 25, 1980.

163 *"walking into the sunset"* Walker, 137.

164 *"Making it was hell"* Roger Clarke, "Jules Dassin: You'll Never Work in This Town Again," *Independent* (London), August 9, 2002.

165 *"I think Joan"* Quirk and Schoell, 118–19.

"Reunion in France is glibly untruthful" Review of *Reunion in France, New York Times,* March 5, 1943.

165 *"Whatever it is"* Review of *Reunion in France, Time,* January 4, 1943.

166 *"The hour and a half"* Review of *Above Suspicion, New York Times,* August 6, 1943.

CHAPTER NINE

168 *"I imagine you've heard"* Vogel, 71.

"*I was so pleased*" Chandler, 296.

169 *"There were spells"* Tapert, 59.

170 *"a miniature Disneyland"* Christina Crawford, 33.

"Joan Crawford's daughter Christina" Hayward, 90.

"Mr. Mayer was" JC, interview by John Springer, Town Hall, April 8, 1973.

"It was difficult to leave Metro" JC, letter to Lotte Palfi Andor, September 1, 1943.

171 *"It was as if"* Walker, 142.

172 *"I'll tell you something, Joan"* The anecdote about JC's meeting with producer Henry Blanke is reported by the director of *The Damned Don't Cry* in the commentary track on the DVD: *The Damned Don't Cry,* DVD, directed by Vincent Sherman (1950; Burbank, CA: Warner Home Video, 2005).

173 *The only drama in Joan's life* "Woman Held After Row," *Los Angeles Times,* January 17, 1945, and *Los Angeles Examiner,* same date.

175 *"These damn pads"* The incident has been widely reported: see, e.g., Walker, 147.

176 *"The Joan Crawford I knew"* Ann Blyth's comments are drawn from her introduction to the TV broadcast of *Mildred Pierce* on the Turner Classic Movies network, and from her remarks at a screening of the same film at the Castro Theater, San Francisco, July 21, 2006.

"The hours are" JC, letter to Genie Chester, in Vogel, 79.

177 *"Romance wasn't quite the word"* Cain, 279.

"It always came back" Ibid., 303.

178 *"to Joan Crawford"* According to a memorandum in the Warner Bros. Archives at the University of Southern California, this message was inscribed in a copy of *Mildred Pierce* for JC on March 7, 1946.

180 *"One day he just"* Christina Crawford, 37.

"I was unutterably lonely" Tapert, 59; see also Newquist, 154; JC and Ardmore, 97–100; and Johnes, Crawford, 62.

182 *For the first time in five years* On the Academy Awards for 1945, see Osborne, 86–89.

185 *"adored making that film"* JC Archives/NYPL: letter to Joseph Parades (the Pepsi-Cola Company), August 12, 1974.

185 *"Moviegoers will note"* Review of *Humoresque, Time,* January 13, 1947.

186 *"Joan Crawford was slightly confused"* Hedda Hopper, "Looking at Hollywood," *Los Angeles Times,* March 12, 1947.

"sharp words and nagging" For remarks about the Crawford-Bautzer affair, see Chandler, 365–67, and an interview with Bautzer at http://www.filmsof crawford.com/id150.html.

"the most photographed" Edwin Schallert, *Los Angeles Times,* October 1, 1946.

187 *"Joan Crawford turned in"* Hedda Hopper, "Looking at Hollywood," *Los Angeles Times,* February 5, 1948.

"Joan Crawford's flare-up" Dorothy Kilgallen, "Voice of Broadway," *New York Journal American,* July 14, 1948.

"that scared the daylights" Christina Crawford, 66.

189 *"performing with the passion"* James Agee, review of *Possessed, Time,* June 16, 1947.

CHAPTER TEN

190 *"I seem to be the follow-up"* Hedda Hopper, "Looking at Hollywood," *Los Angeles Times,* February 10, 1947.

191 *Eager to give more children* On the natural parents of Cathy and Cindy Crawford, see Shirley Downing, "Quest Led Joan Crawford Twins, Others, to Tennessee," *Memphis Commercial Appeal,* September 11, 1995.

"the kindest, sweetest man" Chandler, 346.

193 *"When Joan didn't include"* Tapert, 64.

"That evil goddamned" Christina Crawford, 213, 215.

195 *"Unexpected moments"* Ibid., 237.

"Mommie was with me" Morton J. Goulding, "The Revolt of Joan Crawford's Daughter," *Redbook,* October 1960; this is also the source of Christina's subsequent quotations unless otherwise specified.

196 *"She was not a maternal"* Tapert, 65.

198 *"Joan never complained"* Chandler, 78.

"loved those children" *Joan Crawford: Always the Star,* television special, first broadcast 18 October 1996 by A&E, written and directed by Gene Feldman and Suzette Winter; this is also the source of the comments by Herbert Kenwith and Cindy Crawford.

"I think Christina was jealous" Cindy Crawford Jordan, "Was She Devil or Doting Mom?" *People,* October 19, 1981; see also Downing, "Quest Led Joan."

199 *"My mother was a very warm"* Cathy Crawford LaLonde, *Good Morning Ameri-*

ca, ABC-TV, May 28, 1981; see also Jordan, "Was She Devil" and Chandler, 551–59.

199 *"Christina had, in a way"* Judy Feiffer, interview with author, September 10, 2009.

"never out of control" Chandler, 362–63.

"Everything about the book" Christopher Lehmann-Haupt, review of *Mommie Dearest* by Christina Crawford, *New York Times,* December 6, 1978.

200 *"utterly nonsensical"* Howard Barnes, review of *Flamingo Road, New York Herald Tribune,* May 9, 1949.

201 *"an amazingly deft"* Review of *It's a Great Feeling, New York Herald Tribune,* August 2, 1949.

202 *"I had heard so many stories"* Feldman and Winter.

"She phoned me" Sherman spoke and wrote widely about his relationship with JC. See Sherman, 204 and 195–217; Chandler, 368–424; and Sherman's remarks in his commentary on *The Damned Don't Cry,* released on DVD in 2005, and in *Joan Crawford, The Ultimate Movie Star,* directed by Peter Fitzgerald (Turner Classic Movies, 2002).

206 *"The part of me"* Vogel, 55.

208 *"In many ways"* Sherman, 209.

"The big house" Cameron Shipp, "The Last of the Movie Queens," *Cosmopolitan,* April 1951.

"Somehow, I couldn't follow" Ibid. See also Crawford, "What Men Have Done to Me," *Modern Screen,* November 1951.

211 "Goodbye, My Fancy *could have been"* Vogel, 116.

212 *"For some reason"* Sherman, 212.

214 *"This picture is trash"* Thompson, 195.

CHAPTER ELEVEN

215 *"Warners was putting me"* Vogel, 115.

220 *"By reducing a performer"* Review of *Torch Song, Time,* October 12, 1953.

222 *"It was a miserable time"* Morton J. Goulding, "The Revolt of Joan Crawford's Daughter," *Redbook,* October 1960.

"My brother and I" Christina Crawford, 152.

226 *"Unfortunately . . . McCambridge's alcoholism"* Joan Crawford, The Ultimate Movie Star, directed by Peter Fitzgerald (Turner Classic Movies, 2002).

"As a human being" Tapert, 55.

228 *"repeated dinners"* "John Ireland Remembers Joan Crawford," an excerpt from John Ireland's unpublished autobiography, appeared in *Scarlet Street* magazine, no. 50 (2004).

229 *"with such silky villainy"* *"When she is killed"* Reviews of *Queen Bee* published on November 8, 1955—by William K. Zinsser in the *New York Herald-Tribune* and by Bosley Crowther in the *New York Times,* respectively.

231 *"I was unutterably lonely"* Thomas, 190.

"The first meeting was strange" Goulding, "The Revolt."

CHAPTER TWELVE

233 *"It was sheer hell"* Richard Gehman, "Joan Crawford: Her Fourth Marriage—The Beginning, the End, the New Future," *McCall's,* December 1959.

"We were very much in love" Patricia Bosworth, " 'I'm Still an Actress! I Want to Act!' " *New York Times,* September 24, 1972.

237 *"a mature study of loneliness"* William K. Zinsser, review of *Autumn Leaves, New York Herald-Tribune,* August 2, 1956.

"I admired her" Miller and Arnold, 13.

238 *"I think she felt fraudulent"* Feldman and Winter.

239 *"She will be able to study"* Barbara L. Goldsmith, "Joan Crawford Introduces Her Daughter to Show Business," *Woman's Home Companion,* August 1956. Photographer Eve Arnold documented Christina's week with Joan in New York and later wrote an essay laced with factual errors and noteworthy for her intense and dyspeptic hatred of JC.

"If you ever decide" Morton J. Goulding, "The Revolt of Joan Crawford's Daughter," *Redbook,* October 1960.

"and yet after each day" Ibid.

"I began to have" Christina Crawford, 241.

240 *"Christina dear"* Ibid., 243.

"I continued to get" Ibid., 244.

241 *"Joan Crawford is a star"* Review of *The Story of Esther Costello, Time,* November 4, 1957.

244 *"for the utter waste"* Quirk and Schoell, 200.

"I know how lucky I was" Dora Albert, "Joan Crawford: 'The Hollywood I Knew,' " *Screenland,* January 1964.

245 *"not merely a sentimental gesture"* Widely reported in the press—e.g., *Los Angeles Times,* May 7, 1959.

"I plan to be a working member" *Time,* May 18, 1959.

245 *"I thought that coming out"* Laura Jacobs, "The Lipstick Jungle," *Vanity Fair,* March 2004.

246 *"No matter what others"* John Springer, interview with author, May 4, 1991.

"What I would have done" Roberta Ormiston, "Life Is for Living," *Lady's Circle,* May 1972.

247 *"I have turned to work"* Albert, "Joan Crawford."

248 *"That was my first experience"* Diane Baker, interview with author, November 2008 and May 2009. See also Susan King, "For Diane Baker, One Scene Leads to 50 Years," *Los Angeles Times,* August 26, 2009.

For one awkward scene Hope Lange's contretemps with JC and JC's redraft of a scene in the Sommer screenplay were reported in Gehman, "Joan Crawford."

249 *"I don't kid myself"* *Life,* October 5, 1959.

"It's difficult to get" Gehman, "Joan Crawford."

252 *"I sent the novel"* Robert Aldrich, "Care and Feeding of '*Baby Jane,*'" *New York Times,* November 4, 1962. On the production of *What Ever Happened to Baby Jane?* see Newquist and Crawford with Ardmore; also JC's interview by Philip Jenkinson, BBC, 1968, and her interview by John Springer, Town Hall, April 8, 1973.

253 *"they were sisters"* Sherman, 201.

255 *"Bette Davis is a joy"* JC, letter to Ann Gundersen, August 25, 1962.

256 *"Will it be disappointing"* Hedda Hopper, "Bette and Joan: No Collision Course for Hollywood Stars," *Los Angeles Times,* September 16, 1962.

"Months before the awards" Albert, "Joan Crawford."

"Bob Aldrich loves" JC, interview by John Springer.

CHAPTER THIRTEEN

257 *"I want to make it"* James Bacon, "Child of a Living Legend," *Chicago Tribune,* September 23, 1962.

"My mother was genuinely" Christina, 246–49.

261 *"Among the new players"* Dora Albert, "Joan Crawford: 'The Hollywood I Knew,'" *Screenland,* January 1964.

"She was the boss" Susan King, "For Diane Baker, One Scene Leads to 50 Years," *Los Angeles Times,* August 26, 2009.

262 *"We'll end on me"* Diane Baker recalled the circumstances of making three films with JC during interviews with the author in November and December 2008 and in May 2009.

269 *"Okay, bring 'em on"* John Ireland, "John Ireland Remembers Joan Crawford," *Scarlet Street* magazine, 2004.

270 *"I was the cosmetician"* Simon Doonan, "A Condom for Your Couch? Carleton Varney on Mrs. Clean," *New York Observer,* February 25, 2002. See also *Architectural Digest,* March–April 1976 and the "Celebrity Homes" special edition of 1977.

"I'm up early" Roderick Mann, "Crawford: 'Listen,' She Says, 'I Like to Work,'" *New York Times,* August 24, 1969.

271 *"When Joan arrived"* Weaver, 79; the chapter on Cohen and Crawford is also reproduced at http://www.hermancohen.com/interview-attack6.html.

"Joan Crawford said" Judy Geeson, interview with author, 1998 and 2002; see also *Joan Crawford, The Ultimate Movie Star,* directed by Peter Fitzgerald for Turner Classic Movies, 2002.

"She wears her loneliness" Mann, "Crawford: 'Listen.'"

273 *"I didn't want them"* Robert Windeler, "Joan Crawford Takes Daughter's Soap Opera Role," *New York Times,* October 23, 1968.

"was beginning to relive" Christina Crawford, 255.

"I refuse to apologize" Patricia Bosworth, "'I'm Still an Actress! I Want to Act!'" *New York Times,* September 24, 1972; Mann, "Crawford, 'Listen.'"

274 *"proves that Joan"* New York Times, October 19, 1970.

"She was always doing" Weaver, 79; http://www.hermancohen.com/interview-attack6.html.

276 *"and at every pause"* JC, *My Way of Life,* 124.

"Charm is a touch of magic" Ibid., 212.

277 *"Every time she appears"* McCandlish Phillips, "Book Promotion," *New York Times,* December 31, 1971.

CHAPTER FOURTEEN

278 *"strict discipline . . . imposed"* Bacon, 23.

279 *"We didn't have any problems"* Kotsilibas-Davis and Loy, 324.

"had her own axe to grind" Tapert, 64.

"Mommie Dearest *was not an accurate"* Ibid., 64–65.

280 *"I haven't got a clue"* Carl Johnes, "Why Joan Crawford Won't Go Away," *Hollywood Then & Now,* August and September 1992.

"My daughter Christina" JC, interview by John Springer, Town Hall, April 8, 1973.

"Who knows about books" Alvin Klein, "Meet Carl Johnes—Actor, Agent, Editor, Author," *New York Times,* January 13, 1985.

281 *"one of the most rewarding friendships"* Johnes, 16.

281 *Joan's checkbook stubs* JC's checkbook stubs and receipts are on deposit with her papers at the New York Public Library for the Performing Arts at Lincoln Center.

282 *"More than anything"* William Haines, letter to JC, December 25, 1972, JC Archives/NYPL.

"In private life " George Cukor, "She Was Consistently Joan Crawford, Star," *New York Times,* May 22, 1977.

"She never took" Johnes, 96–97.

283 *"Well . . . I didn't play Harriet Craig"* Ibid., 28.

285 *"Most of them are trash"* Patricia Bosworth, " 'I'm Still an Actress! I Want to Act!' " *New York Times,* September 24, 1972.

"She was very lonely" Charles Walters, interviewed in *The Hollywood Greats,* television series, first broadcast 3 August 1978 by BBC-TV, written by Barry Norman and directed by Judy Lindsay.

"I'm so sorry I can't see you" Adele Whitely Fletcher, "I Remember Joan," *Modern Screen,* August 1977.

289 *"just a wonderful Mom"* Cathy Crawford LaLonde, interviewed by Lois Cahall on *Good Morning America,* ABC-TV, March 16, 2008.

"Mommie Dearest *was fake"* Al Weisel, "Mommie Weirdest," *US* magazine, November 1998.

"very thin, very frail" Casey LaLonde is noteworthy for his consistent and ardent defense of his grandmother. See especially http://www.legendaryjoan crawford.com/askcasey.html and http://www.midnightpalace.com/interview caseylalonde.htm.

"All I can say is that" Cathy LaLonde, Cahall interview.

"I'm so sorry, Mommie" Chandler, 558–59.

290 *"I've been on the receiving end"* Fletcher, "I Remember Joan."

"I always knew that Mother" Christina, 275–76.

291 *"just because it's more comfortable"* Bosworth, "I'm Still an Actress!"

"Gradually, I filled my life" JC, *A Portrait of Joan,* 122–23.

292 *"She sounded timorous"* Johnes, 158–59.

"There's nothing presented to us" JC, letter to Pearl Pezoldt, December 14, 1943.

BIBLIOGRAPHY

Allen, Frederick Lewis. *Only Yesterday: An Informal History of the Nineteen-Twenties*. New York: Harper & Bros., 1931.

Arnold, Eve. *In Retrospect*. New York: Knopf, 1995.

Bacon, James. *Made in Hollywood*. New York: Warner, 1978.

Basinger, Jeanine. *A Woman's View: How Hollywood Spoke to Women, 1930–1960*. New York: Knopf, 1993.

———. *The Star Machine*. New York: Knopf, 2007.

Bellah, James Warner. *Dancing Lady*. New York: Farrar and Reinhart, 1932.

Belloc Lowndes, Marie. *Letty Lynton*. London: Hutchinson, 1931.

Björn, Lars, and Jim Gallert. *Before Motown: A History of Jazz in Detroit, 1920–1960*. Ann Arbor: University of Michigan Press, 2001.

Cain, James M. *The Postman Always Rings Twice, Double Indemnity, Mildred Pierce and Selected Stories*. New York: Knopf/Everyman's Library, 2003.

Castle, William. *Step Right Up! I'm Gonna Scare the Pants Off America*. New York: G. P. Putnam's Sons, 1976.

Chandler, Charlotte. *Not the Girl Next Door*. New York: Doubleday Home Library Edition, 2008.

Cowie, Peter. *Joan Crawford the Enduring Star*. New York: Rizzoli, 2009.

Crawford, Christina. *Mommie Dearest*. New York: William Morrow, 1978.

Crawford, Joan, with Audrey Davenport Inman. *My Way of Life*. New York: Pocket, 1972.

————, with Jane Kesner Ardmore. *A Portrait of Joan*. New York: Paperback Library, 1964.

Crothers, Rachel. *Susan and God*. New York: Random House, 1938.

Deatherage, D. Gary. *The Other Side of My Life*. Nashville, TN: Winston-Derek Publishers, 1991.

Engstead, John. *Star Shots*. New York: E. P. Dutton, 1978.

Esquevin, Christian. *Adrian—Silver Screen to Custom Label*. New York: Monacelli Press, 2008.

Fairbanks, Douglas, Jr. *The Salad Days*. New York: Doubleday, 1988.

Gledhill, Christine, ed. *Stardom—Industry of Desire*. London and New York: Routledge, 1991.

Haver, Ronald. *David O. Selznick's Hollywood*. New York: Knopf, 1980.

Hayes, Helen, with Katherine Hatch. *My Life in Three Acts*. New York: Harcourt Brace Jovanovich, 1990.

Hayward, Brooke. *Haywire*. New York: Knopf, 1977.

Hopper, Hedda. *From Under My Hat*. Garden City, NY: Doubleday, 1952.

Johnes, Carl. *Crawford: The Last Years*. New York: Dell, 1979.

Kanin, Fay. *Goodbye, My Fancy*. New York: Samuel French, 1976.

Kobal, John. *People Will Talk*. New York: Knopf, 1986.

Kotsilibas-Davis, James, and Myrna Loy. *Myrna Loy: Being and Becoming*. New York: Donald I. Fine, 1988.

LaValley, Albert J., ed. *Mildred Pierce*. Madison: University of Wisconsin Press, 1980.

Lockwood, Charles. *Dream Palaces: Hollywood at Home*. New York: Viking, 1981.

Miller, Eugene L., and Edwin T. Arnold. *Robert Aldrich: Interviews*. Jackson, MS: University Press of Mississippi, 2004.

Moore, Dick. *Twinkle, Twinkle, Little Star*. New York: Harper & Row, 1984.

Morin, Edgar. *The Stars*. Translated from the French by Richard Howard. Minneapolis: University of Minnesota Press, 2005.

Newquist, Roy. *Conversations with Joan Crawford*. New York: Berkley Books, 1981.

Osborne, Robert. *70 Years of the Oscar—The Official History of the Academy Awards*. New York: Abbeville, 1999.

Postrel, Virginia. *The Substance of Style: How the Rise of Aesthetic Value Is Remaking Commerce, Culture, and Consciousness*. New York: Harper Perennial, 2004.

Quirk, Lawrence J. *The Films of Joan Crawford*. New York: Citadel Press, 1968.

Quirk, Lawrence J., and William Schoell. *Joan Crawford—The Essential Biography*. Lexington: University Press of Kentucky, 2002.

Rivkin, Alan, and Laura Kerr. *Hello, Hollywood!—The Story of the Movies by the People Who Make Them*. Garden City: Doubleday, 1962.

Sherman, Vincent. *Studio Affairs—My Life as a Film Director*. Lexington: University Press of Kentucky, 1996.

Spoto, Donald. *Blue Angel: The Life of Marlene Dietrich*. New York: Doubleday, 1992.

———. *Laurence Olivier: A Biography*. New York: HarperCollins, 1992.

———. *Notorious: The Life of Ingrid Bergman*. New York and London: HarperCollins, 1997.

Swanson, Gloria. *Swanson on Swanson*. New York: Random House, 1980.

Tapert, Annette. *The Power of Glamour*. New York: Crown, 1998.

Thomas, Bob. *Joan Crawford—A Biography*. New York: Bantam, 1979.

Thompson, Howard. *The New York Times Guide to Movies on TV*. Chicago: Quadrangle Books, 1970.

Thorp, Margaret Farrand. *America at the Movies*. New Haven: Yale University Press, 1939.

Vogel, Michelle. *Joan Crawford—Her Life in Letters*. Louisville, KY: Wasteland Press, 2005.

Walker, Alexander. *Joan Crawford—The Ultimate Star*. New York: Harper & Row, 1983.

Weaver, Tom. *Attack of the Monster Movie Makers*. Jefferson, NC: McFarland, 1994.